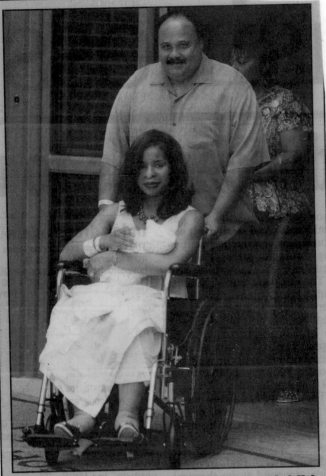

Martin Luther King Jr.'s first grandchild

Martin Luther King III pushes his wife, **Arndrea Waters King,** and his newborn daughter, **Yolanda Renee,** out of Northside Hospital for a brief news conference Tuesday in Atlanta. Yolanda, born Sunday, May 25, 2008, is the first grandchild of civil rights leader Martin Luther King Jr. (AP Photo)

May 28, 2008

GROWING
UP
KING

GROWING
UP
KING

An Intimate Memoir

DEXTER SCOTT KING

WITH
RALPH WILEY

IPM
INTELLECTUAL PROPERTIES MANAGEMENT, INC.

IN ASSOCIATION WITH

WARNER BOOKS

An AOL Time Warner Company

Warner Books, Inc., 1271 Avenue of the Americas, New York, NY 10020
Visit our Web site at www.twbookmark.com.

 An AOL Time Warner Company

Printed in the United States of America

First Printing: January 2003
10 9 8 7 6 5 4 3 2 1

The Library of Congress Cataloging-in-Publication Data

King, Dexter Scott.
    Growing up king : an intimate memoir / Dexter Scott King with Ralph
Wiley.
        p. cm.
    Includes index.
    ISBN 0-446-52942-7
    1. King, Dexter Scott, 1961– 2. King, Martin Luther, Jr., 1929–1968—
Family. 3. African Americans—Biography. I. Wiley, Ralph. II. Title.

E185.97.K5 K52 2003
323'.092—dc21
[B]   2002027211

CONTENTS

GROWING
UP
KING

PROLOGUE

Memory is not always to be trusted, yet memory is all we have, where we all live. I've learned memory is all that can be trusted, in the end.

For any five witnesses to an event, there are five versions of what happened. Which is closest to truth? In this book I trust my memories, and those of my siblings, my mother, friends, and family members. I looked at documents, notes, newspaper clippings, magazine articles, books, film documentaries, and other references, the better to refresh and confirm this collective memory. I searched myself as well. But I also know no book that has been written has captured how much I loved my father in Atlanta when I was six, or how I felt at seven, when he was killed in Memphis.

There is no polite way to bust out of prison. Jailbreak! is how it felt after the verdict came in at the civil trial of Loyd Jowers in Memphis in December of 1999. I didn't care about Jowers's role in my father's murder on April 4, 1968. I didn't care about conspiracies, or anybody going to prison. I cared about getting out of prison. I'd faced up to what had happened to us. Pope John Paul once said that the quest for freedom is one of the great dynamics of human history. Such a quest can take many forms. I went back to Atlanta. I thought back as I drove past the National Historic Site, past 501 Auburn Avenue, the house where my father was born, past Freedom Hall complex where his remains lie in a crypt in the plaza of the Martin Luther King, Jr. Center for Non-Violent Social Change.

The plaza stands next to old Ebenezer Baptist Church, at the corner of Jackson Street and Auburn Avenue, Northeast. "Kodak products available here," reads a sign. I had pictures in my memory. My grandfather's leathery hands lifted in supplication. My grandmother at the organ. Daddy's ascending voice. Gunshots in the pulpit. The old church is a relic, for tourists who can't see or hear what I see and hear in my memory. The new Ebenezer Baptist Church is on the opposite side of Auburn Avenue. A sculpture of a black man holding a baby up toward the heavens stands in an amphitheater on the grounds of the National Park Service's King Visitor Center. The sculpture was inspired by the scene from *Roots*: "Behold, the only thing greater than yourself," Omoro Kinte said to baby Kunta; Kunta, as an adult, repeated it to his daughter, Kizzy, in Alex Haley's epic tale. It reminded me of Daddy and me. His marble crypt stands in the middle of a reflecting pool on the grounds of the King Center. The inscription is simple:

Rev. Martin Luther King, Jr.
1929–1968.
"Free at last, free at last, thank God Almighty, I'm free at last."

Amen, Daddy, I thought. Inside the King Center hangs a framed newspaper article:

King Children Reflect on the Values Their Father Taught

Hours later I was at the Four Seasons at Troon North in Scottsdale, Arizona, preparing to bring in the new millennium,

Y2K. A photo was taken. For years I'd looked in the mirror and seen my father's face trapped in mine. Now my face relaxed. Free at last. Was I? Were we? I go back now, in memory, to try and find the answers.

CHAPTER 1

SLEEPING BEAUTIES

I felt inadequate to the task at hand, the scene before me, though my role seemed simple enough. Yoki had already shown me a picture of Prince Charming in a book of fairy tales, so I knew what he was supposed to look like. I'd seen myself in a mirror. Didn't see the correlation, didn't think I could ever look like that or act like that. But my older sister kept on insisting I was the Chosen One, who must bend down and kiss my baby sister Bernice, lying on one end of our seesaw, acting dead, like Sleeping Beauty. Yoki was saying, "Let's do this." I was steadily refusing.

"Nope," I said. "Nope, nope, nope."

The corners of Yoki's mouth curled. "Yes—that's what you mean to say. Right?"

She was about to unleash a verbal volley accompanied by a twisting pinch of arm flesh if I wasn't quick enough, which, by the warm, so-called Indian summer of 1967, I usually was.

I was six and a half years old when I asked Yoki, "Why me?" while fixing a pleading eye toward my older brother, Martin III, who stood behind me in the backyard of 234 Sunset, Vine City, Atlanta, Georgia, behind the house where we grew up.

Marty wasn't about to buck Yoki's authority; he grew deaf, looked the other way, whistled.

I'm in my forty-first year now, but thinking of what it was like back in 1967, when I was a boy but six years old, makes me smile. A wry and cautious smile. Yoki was eleven. An eleven-year-old girl isn't to be trifled with by her younger brothers. "You ask too many questions," she said, her calm that comes before a storm; we knew this, and she knew that we knew. Yoki was my terrible older sister Yolanda. Now I know she isn't so terrible. Now I feel I must call her Yolanda. It has more formality—something expected of Yolanda, Martin, me, and Bernice. Ever since I was seven, I've felt I must be formal. But I didn't feel it in '67. Then she was my crazy terrible sister; Yoki-poky, as Daddy called her when we were children and didn't have the responsibilities or memories we have now. Formality, seriousness, certitude—all these are difficult poses to maintain, even if you're a person with perfect equilibrium, with all the drama life throws at you.

Speaking of what life throws at you, just then a green walnut came whizzing over the fence, crashing into our swing, cracking open its unripe cover, its powerful astringent scent filling the air. Could just as well have been a peach, apple, fig, or pecan—each of those species bloomed in the backyards of the small houses in Vine City. Walnuts made more of an announcement when arriving via this kind of air mail. Marty and I looked at each other. We were being paged.

"C'mon!"

One of the neighborhood boys was summoning us without risking an audience with Yoki. Smart move. We'd relocated to Vine City from the Old Fourth Ward in 1965. I spent my first four years in the Old Fourth Ward, up from Auburn Avenue, on Johnson Avenue, in a house the color of the yellow brick road in *The Wizard of* Oz. A liquor store now stands where the backyard of the house used to be. What's now Freedom Parkway was once our front yard.

Granddaddy's house in Old Fourth Ward, where the package store now stands, was on a hill, three blocks away from Ebenezer

Baptist Church, where he was pastor, two blocks down from 501 Auburn Avenue. Granddaddy's name was Martin Luther King, Sr. He had two sons. The younger was Alfred Daniel King, Sr., Uncle A.D., named for my great-grandfather A. D. Williams, who'd also been pastor at Ebenezer, and who was the father of Alberta Williams King, my paternal grandmother, whom we called Big Mama. My father was the elder son, Martin Luther King, Sr.'s co-pastor at Ebenezer, among other things.

His name was Dr. Martin Luther King, Jr.

When my mother became pregnant with me, the family was moving to Atlanta from Montgomery, Alabama, where my father had been pastor of Dexter Avenue Baptist Church. He'd become famous or infamous there, depending on one's slant, as one of the architects of the Montgomery bus boycott. That action was spawned by Mrs. Rosa Parks's refusal to give up her seat on a city transit bus, a watershed event of the Civil Rights Movement. We moved to Atlanta after that.

The move helped my grandfather. His eight-hundred-seat church and his clout in Baptist circles were enhanced having my father rejoin him as co-pastor. But as far as joining him in the more affluent western suburb of Collier Heights, my father wasn't hearing it, in spite of my grandfather's insistence. We'd live in Vine City, with the plain folk.

A freeway was coming, as was Bunny. We moved because we needed more space and the freeway construction would displace us. The freeway became known as Freedom Parkway, which now takes you by the Carter Presidential Center. Back when the freeway was being planned, it was to be called Stone Mountain Freeway, taking you to Stone Mountain, where images of Confederate generals were blasted into the granite. But both the name and the route were changed. We needed a place, so we moved to the modest, roomy brick house on an undulating street, Sunset, at the foot of the Atlanta University Center, the consortium of five historically black colleges and universities.

It was a split-level house with a full basement; you entered the main floor by walking up exterior stairs aided by wrought-iron banisters painted white. The house is larger than it appears from in front. From that position you can't get the depth of it. Your idea of a thing is often based on the angle from which you view it. The house isn't narrow, yet it's much deeper than it is wide.

As you enter, on your right side facing in is the dining room; on your left is the living room, filled with memorabilia, family pictures, a sofa. The kitchen is beyond the dining room. There my mother or the ladies who helped her, Mrs. Dorothy Lockhart or Mrs. Newman or sometimes Mrs. Rachel Ward, caused a racket of pots and pans. Mrs. Ward and Mrs. Patricia Cook Latimore sometimes looked after us when Mom and Dad had to do important business. The family room is beyond the kitchen. The four of us made a hubbub of children and toys in there. The hallway splits the house in half, running perpendicular from the front door straight from front to back, connecting four bedrooms and a study, my parents' bedroom at the end of the hallway to the left, the study to the right. The first room to the left was the boys' room, the second to the left was the girls' room, and in later years, vice versa; to the right was the guest room. Connecting our rooms was a play room; a door was between us. It was the doorway to fun, conflict, happiness. We bolted and flitted around these dimensions at incredible speeds, as children do. From here we plotted childhood.

There was sibling rivalry among us. We jockeyed for the attention of our mother and father, the way sisters and brothers sometimes do. There was a little jealousy on the part of the others whenever the next one was born.

Bernice, whom we called Bunny, was the baby, four going on fifty-two in '67, precocious, but quietly so. She never experienced jealousy pangs, but she had her own cross to bear. It wasn't so much that she was tomboyish—that was fine by Marty and me. We'd throw her in there if we needed to round out a side, or boost her up into trees, and she'd try her best to keep up. Occasionally she might bark a shin, earn a bruise some other way. Marty was the world's foremost tattletale, the one who'd say, "I'm gon' tell Mama," if a boy happened not to be quick enough to break his baby sister's fall. After spankings delivered by Mother, or, worse, Granddaddy's leather belt or ham hands, we still had a backyard in which to retire and ruminate.

Martin seemed to always know the trouble would blow over. He and Yolanda were such amiable children. Bernice was more pragmatic, or so it seemed at the time. She'd look at me and in her quiet baby talk take up for Martin. So even when we had falling outs, soon we all were as thick as thieves again, welcoming the neighborhood children into our domain.

Our home at 234 Sunset was kind of home central, the neighborhood headquarters. All the kids came by to play. My mom treated them like hers, which wasn't always reassuring for them. Coretta Scott King was a disciplinarian, took no guff from hers or any others. Froze you with a look. "Time out" was a call we made in football, not what fell from her lips in our direction. Under her eye or not, we'd play "hide-and-go-seek," as we called it, football, softball, kickball, tag, marbles in the red clay; we'd spin tops, ride homemade skateboards, "pull" friends along by pedaling bikes standing up as the friend rode on the passenger seat. We had a swing set, seesaw, and slide. I loved the slide. I loved playing on the gym set. I loved it all, really. We had a hoop too. Ours was, in these regards, a typical family home—or so I thought back then.

This area in northwest Atlanta known as Vine City got its name from the heavy kudzu vines that grew all over the place; Vine City was a "Negro" enclave, in the era of segregation into which we were born. The Magnolia Ballroom was on the corner. James Brown and popular "Negro" entertainers would come to perform there. Often we'd pretend to be James or the Famous Flames, his backup singers, doing choreography, hitting spins and splits, feigning fainting spells with an old bedspread thrown over our shoulders.

That apartment building over there? Former Atlanta mayor Maynard Jackson's family had lived there. Next door were Reverend and Mrs. Hall and their children. Across the street from our house were the Davis children. We played with them all the time. Miss Toomer lived over there. Next to her were the Martins. Julian Bond's family lived next to the Martins. We grew up with his kids, Phyllis, Michael, Cookie, Jeffrey, and Horace Mann Bond III, otherwise known as Manny, who got his name from his grandfather. A block over was the new John F. Kennedy Middle School, where we played, and where I later went to summer school.

The whole area was known as lower Vine City—cheek by jowl with the AU Center of Morehouse College, Spelman College, Morris Brown College (it stood closest; we could almost read the football-field scoreboard from our driveway), Clark College, and Atlanta University. Vine City became the " 'hood" later, after Daddy was killed and integration patterns became widespread and "Negroes," black people, could move, if not to where our hearts desired, then to where our purses allowed. Many did move, leaving memories, the luckless, the Aftermath . . . leaving only a few committed to their memories, or bound by lowering prospects in Vine City. The pendulum swings both ways, though, if you can last, if you can hold on, hang in—if you can remember.

My brother, my sisters, and I would walk down to Sunset and Simpson to a parlor we called Flavor Palace. Flavor Palace had the best ice cream anywhere—outside of the deep country, a place with which we were familiar, where ice cream was rarer but homemade, hand-cranked, tastiest with a little vanilla extract and lemon juice added. At Flavor Palace it was almost as good as homemade. They also made Polish sausage sandwiches with onions and jalapeño peppers. I salivate now just thinking about them. We stopped there often. The proprietor, Mr. Patterson, a brown-skinned man with the thin, sculpted mustache favored in those days, often gave us a free taste. I never made a correlation between his generosity and my father's being in jail, but there may have been one. Jalapeños and onions on top of a Polish. He fixed one up and handed it to me. I fished for my meager coins and he said, "No, no, you do good for your fahdah, now . . ."

Egan Homes was around the corner. If you heard somebody

lived in the Egan Homes, you felt he was trouble. "Don't mess with them niggas what live over there in them Egan Homes," was often said or implied by the very same Negroes who lived in Egan Homes! They were talking about themselves, to be agreeable; those were accepted words in the better homes in our gardens.

But I knew people who lived in Egan Homes. After people said don't mess with them, I asked why. I knew you had to go by there to get to Washington Park unless you took the long way. You had to learn to suppress your fear. If you did, you found that while some Egan Homes people might be trouble, some might not be. Some might help you out.

Egan Homes is long gone now. Razed, and replaced by a new mixed-income development, part of urban renewal.

My father would take us down to the Ollie Street YMCA all the time. Everything in Atlanta is renamed by people who live near it. "Booker T." was Booker T. Washington High School, where Dad went. It's right over there. Everything in Atlanta was "right over there." We stayed in our communities. The Ollie Street Y was where my father took us for recreation. I learned to swim there. He taught me. He was good at it and enjoyed it. And the YMCA is still there today.

At Washington Park, we had cookouts. As children, we didn't know we were "Negroes," or if we did, we didn't know exactly what that meant. We didn't realize we lived in "segregation," didn't know there were better pools than the one we crowded into at the Y, or that we and our friends would be considered "have-nots" if our father wasn't the co-pastor of Ebenezer Baptist Church. We weren't aware that we could and would be turned away from public accommodations, educational institutions, or turned away from desirable living spaces by the real estate restrictive covenants. We weren't aware that we were shunned by society, murdered over mere glances, made to feel less than human. We were children, and children are more than human; we were blessed, but sooner or later we'd grow up and have to face this prison of segregation, unless Daddy won his struggle. There was this great social upheaval, this "great getting-up morning" going on that would redefine our lives and existences, and those of the people around us.

Like I said. We were rehearsing Yoki's play as the alley and our friends beckoned to us. In a nearby house, Lou Rawls's "St. James Infirmary" wafted up from a "record player." Yoki also had a "record player," on which spun large-mouthed 45s filled by yellow prong adapters; "Ain't Too Proud to Beg" by the Temptations, Otis Redding's "Try a Little Tenderness." My father preferred Mahalia Jackson singing "Amazing Grace," or Aretha Franklin singing "O Mary Don't You Weep." He often tapped his foot and bobbed his head to secular music, and he didn't deny it to us—he couldn't, not in Vine City. Music was everywhere. Like Yoki.

Yoki was five years older than me and forever putting on plays and musicals. We were her troupe. It was not often that anyone else got a starring role with Yoki around. At my shoulder was Martin III, Marty then; he was restless, sighing heavily, looking away, mumbling. Yoki was telling me what I must do to make things right before we could leave.

"You're supposed to lean over and kiss her. On the lips."

My face continued to betray me, and my lack of enthusiasm.

Bernice was lying with lips chapped, eyelids closed, then fluttering. She was pleased to be Sleeping Beauty. Usually her role was Yoki's handmaiden, subject to taunting. Yoki was a stern taskmaster, particularly for Bunny. We often teased Bernice, saying she'd been left on our doorstep by mistake, or was adopted. Now I was in Yoki's sights, subject to her derision—but it wasn't enough to make me kiss a girl, particularly my little sister, for no good reason at all.

"Why do you want me?" I whined.

"Why?" Yoki repeated. "Why do you always ask why? Because I said so, that's why. Because that's the way the play goes. You're supposed to kiss Sleeping Beauty; that will break the spell cast by an evil witch and everyone will live happily ever after. Don't you want to live happily ever afterward, you stupid boy? Don't you know anything?"

"But she isn't Sleeping Beauty. She's Bunny."

"Not right now. She's Sleeping Beauty right now," Yoki countered.

"Well . . . why can't Martin kiss her? Why does it have to be me?"

Yoki's voice dripped with venom. "Because I said so."

". . . But it don't make no sense," I whispered.

"Don't make any sense," Martin said. He was trying to get back to playing. If we were lucky, once Dad got home he might take us over to the Ollie Street Y. If we were really lucky, Uncle Ralph and Aunt Jean's children would go with us too. But we had to get past Yoki first.

"Go on, get it over with," Martin whispered, smiling at Yoki when she looked daggers at him. So I leaned over and kissed Bernice. On the cheek. I still feel her tiny cheekbone rise beneath my lips. "Don't smile too quick, Bunny," Yoki chided. "Let the kiss take effect."

Martin and I made our escape into the alley and whatever devilment we were up to. As we ran, the scent of honeysuckle mixed with the occasional open garbage can to sweeten and make pungent the late summer air; gravel secured our feet to the red clay; we raced by kudzu-choked fences in varying states of repair.

Yoki didn't bother calling after us. The play was given the following evening at home for our parents and a few of our aunts and uncles; so it was, and always has been. But even long after we grew up, we kept doing plays under her direction, the last time when she turned forty. She wanted to do what she loved, what was in her blood, and to make Daddy proud of her. We all wanted that.

I was born worried. I was born anxious. I was born on January 30, 1961, in the Hughes-Spaulding Hospital, a private hospital for "Negroes" in Atlanta. My father was in Chicago at the time, but rushed home as soon as he got the word. "Negroes" was then the term for Americans of discernible African descent. What to call us, what to do with us—these questions were not for children but rather for their parents who wanted the best for them one day. "Negro" households in Atlanta not on public assistance utilized that one hospital, Hughes-Spaulding.

Atlanta has always held a special spot. At one time it was called Terminus; railways began and ended here and ran throughout the South, so it's always had a pivotal position. But it was basically a big old landlocked town, and still is. It's also a cliquish, insular town, and it can be hard for outsiders coming in. It can be difficult for insiders who don't conform.

Atlanta remains a difficult town to crack the code on.

In terms of the black/white so-called race relations, Atlanta has always been just smart enough to be smarter than most. I don't know if it's because of what happened during the Civil War, General Sherman burning it down. Since then Atlanta had the sense to recognize it needs to be peaceful, though there have been lynchings of blacks and bombings of Jewish synagogues here and there; there have also been efforts to stem the tide of hatred by being civil in that southern, intimate way, by being "down home." The raw, murderous violence of Alabama and Mississippi didn't seem to cloak Atlanta. But in my youth, it was rigidly, bitterly segregated.

Before the '60s, before the Civil Rights Movement and social reformation, "Negroes" in Atlanta—never "blacks," not then; calling somebody "black" back then would get you a look, maybe even a punch in the nose—weren't as affected by the segregation dooming the poor in other places; in Atlanta, "Negroes" had infrastructure. It was by comparison small and circumscribed, but it was there, not rich compared to the Augusta Country Club and the riches that spawned it. But "Negroes" did have social clubs, financial institutions, schools, churches, some land, so in that respect there was hesitation with change; there was a risk of losing what little you had. You felt like you finally had acquired something you didn't want to lose.

Blacks in Atlanta weren't as downtrodden as in the Mississippi

Delta, or in Lawndale on the West Side of Chicago, or in the rice paddies of the Sea Islands off the Carolina coast, or in the black belt of south-central Alabama, where my mother's parents lived, or other places South and North. "Negroes" in Atlanta were not as anxious as they were in other places, where people were trying to gain access, rights, a crust of life, because they didn't have anything to lose, they were trying to get a little something. In Atlanta, "Negroes" already had a little something; in some cases they had nice somethings. This made it more impressive to me, later, to realize that my father, in spite of his privileged position, would take up the civil rights struggle, battle against the system of segregation. Because he really would have had it made, relatively, in old Atlanta. Could've gone with the flow, succeeded Granddaddy as pastor at Ebenezer, conducted weddings, funerals, encouraged generosity from the Ebenezer flock, attended National Baptist conventions, risen to be an H.N.I.C.—Head Negro In Charge of what little we had, and we had a nice if not an idyllic life.

I don't know how it was in Daddy's mind. I've been asked many times, as have many if not most other black people, "What do you want?" I can't answer for him. He was, if nothing else, a man of his own conscience. The '60s were idyllic to me. How they were for him, I don't know. He could've limited his battles to Ebenezer, local politics, as my grandfather did. But he didn't; wasn't that kind of a man. Greatness was thrust upon him, and for some internal reason or external destiny, he did not turn away. Because he was the man that he was, I was born six weeks premature.

My mother was traumatized during her pregnancy with me. All of us were born and raised in struggle. In January of 1956, Yoki was ten weeks old and they were living in Montgomery when a bomb was set off at their house. My father spoke of having an epiphany at the kitchen table in this same house a few days before that. The bombings—the one at my parents' house was not the only one—were owed to the violence of vigilante whites, poor whites, after the bus boycott led by the Montgomery Improvement Association, for which my father served as president. He held some of the smaller meetings at his Dexter Avenue Baptist Church; Uncle Ralph's—Rev. Ralph Abernathy's—First Baptist Church held larger mass meetings. My father had talked about being "paralyzed with fear" during this time.

But at the kitchen table in the house in Montgomery, he had an epiphany; he said all the fear left him, and he gave himself and his Cause over to the hand and grace of God.

It wasn't until this bombing in Montgomery on January 30, 1956, that it dawned on him: it wasn't just him but also his family who were involved in this Cause. Yet only he had the epiphany.

In April of 1960, after having dinner, my parents were returning the southern writer Lillian Smith to Emory University Hospital, in DeKalb County, where she was getting cancer treatments. After dropping her at the dorm they were stopped by police. My father was a black man; a white woman had been in the car. My father was recognized by the DeKalb County police and arrested because he had not changed his driver's license from an Alabama license to a Georgia license in the three months since they left Montgomery. Daddy answered the summons, was fined $25 for "driving without a proper permit," given a suspended twelve-month sentence by Judge Oscar Mitchell, and released on probation. This occurred at the time of the Greensboro, North Carolina, lunch-counter student sit-ins to protest segregated public facilities, on the heels of the Montgomery, Alabama, bus boycott sparked by the arrest of Mrs. Rosa Parks. Shortly after this event, sometime in June, my mother discovered she was pregnant with me.

These were heady, dangerous days. But my father, pleased my mother was pregnant for the third time, was undeterred by his arrest. My mother did her usual thing and exploded in size; she was one of those women whose entire body, not just the belly, became larger when she got pregnant. By October, she was five months gone, and showing like nine.

This was when my father agreed to be a part of a lunch-counter demonstration at Rich's department store, protesting segregated eating facilities—the only time he joined any such local demonstration in his hometown of Atlanta. He did it against his father's wishes, to support idealistic student leaders like Lonnie C. King, Marian Wright, now Marian Wright Edelman, and John Porter. They'd ask for service at a snack bar at the downtown Rich's, which, like most department stores in southern cities, "welcomed" black patrons through a back entrance to come spend their money as long as they didn't use rest rooms, drink from water fountains marked "Whites," try on hats, or get refreshments.

My father was first to be arrested, then the students; tactically, they didn't accept a $500 bond from Judge James Webb. Dad was carted off to Fulton County Jail along with seventy-five "lawbreakers," mostly student leaders from the Atlanta University Center. They would agree to be released only if the charges against them, based on unjust Jim Crow laws, were dropped. After reaching a settlement with the affected parties the students were released on their own recognizance.

People say that's when Senator John F. Kennedy got involved, but actually that's when my father's friends and admirers got moving. One of them worked for the Kennedy-for-president campaign. His name was Harris Wofford. He started calling around—Atlanta mayor Bill Hartsfield, a local lawyer named Morris Abram, anybody he could call that might be able to help. Mr. Wofford had great admiration for my father and Mohandas Gandhi. He was a learned, sensitive man who had gone to Howard University Law School after graduating from Yale.

Mayor Hartsfield was about to broker a deal to let the students and our father go anyway. But Daddy was kept in jail. Monday morning, a DeKalb County deputy sheriff came, put him in manacles and leg irons, and took him from jail in Fulton County to DeKalb County—which in those days was going from the dragon's back into its mouth. Murders of civil rights workers by rogue law enforcement officers and other vigilantes were routine occurrences; such deaths had been common for the hundred years since the Civil War. DeKalb County was a Klan stronghold. My distressed mother, with me floating in her belly, went to the hearing at the DeKalb County courthouse with Granddaddy and my Aunt Christine. Members of the faculty at Morehouse College and AU Center students went as well.

Judge Oscar Mitchell found my father guilty of violating his probation over the misdemeanor involving the "invalid driver's license," then sentenced him to four months' hard labor at Reidsville State Prison, which was isolated far downstate. There was pandemonium in the courtroom. Immersed in this was Mother, me in her amniotic sac, feeling each twitch and strain, feeding off her moods.

Yoki was four, Marty was about three, but they weren't there. Mother was shocked when Judge Mitchell announced the sentence; my father's sister, Aunt Christine, broke into tears. So did Mother, and she wasn't given to crying. Staid male professors fell prostrate and wept.

Mother said she felt helpless and out of control and desperate despite the fact my father's family was with her. They were not inside her. I was. She was emotional, weepy; Daddy had not seen her like this, and said so. "You have to be strong now, Corrie," he said. Mayor Hartsfield, in Atlanta and Fulton County, backed off from Judge Mitchell's sentence, saying it "didn't happen in Atlanta." Hartsfield was mayor when the chamber of commerce came up with the slogan that billed Atlanta as "The City Too Busy to Hate." At the time, Georgia wasn't too busy.

Governor Ernest Vandiver crowed about Daddy's dilemma.

Phone lines buzzed. My father's friends—like Stanley Levison, Harry Belafonte, Mahalia Jackson, Jackie Robinson, and a horde of less famous but equally concerned folk whose common denominator was being American and feeling for my father—they all made calls or had aides-de-camp making calls to see what could be done for Dad. Of these, Harris Wofford was best positioned to effect change, being connected to the 1960 Kennedy presidential campaign. He spoke to Sargent Shriver of JFK's staff. Shriver balked— the first law of political campaigns is to say anything but do nothing. In the end, Wofford convinced Shriver at least to run it by

Senator Kennedy, presidential candidate, that maybe he should call the wife of Martin Luther King and offer her comfort. The woman was pregnant, alone. There was all sorts of palavering first. But, cutting through all the political intrigue, JFK wound up calling Mother on impulse, against advice and all political logic, not because it might get him votes. In that climate, it might easily have cost him votes; his advisers were not shy about pointing it out. But JFK called my mother anyway, because Harris Wofford had the right phone number to give Sargent Shriver; it flashed in JFK's mind that calling Mother was the decent thing to do. I believe that was his motivation, and also why things turned out well for him in the election. You get back what you put out. My mother was at home, preparing to go see Morris Abram, a Jewish lawyer who was a family friend. At this point, Robert F. Kennedy, head of JFK's presidential campaign, probably wouldn't have had JFK call Mother for all the tea in China.

The phone rang anyway. My mother spoke with Senator Kennedy; he said he knew it must be hard, he knew she was expecting; if there was anything he could do feel free to call. Mother said she'd appreciate anything he could do to get my father out of prison. Meanwhile, Bobby, JFK's campaign manager and soon to be attorney general, called Judge Mitchell to see why my father couldn't get bail on a misdemeanor. What the hell was going on? Bobby wanted to know.

Who knows what went through Judge Mitchell's mind, but Daddy was released, and the Southern Christian Leadership Conference (SCLC) chartered a plane to bring him home from Reidsville. My Grandaddy King said at a mass meeting after my father was released that if he had a suitcase full of votes, he'd take them and put them at Senator Kennedy's feet in the election just a week away. We can thank a cop harassing my father and Judge Mitchell as much as the Kennedys: the long and short of it was that JFK's political intervention on my father's behalf during the final days of his campaign was a decisive factor in his election as president of the United States in 1960. Senator Kennedy won by the equivalent of

one vote per precinct nationwide, and his campaign wisely made
what hay it could in "Negro" precincts.

After the election, the Kings were seen as an influential family,
even a royal family, in the well-lit backdrop of the Civil Rights
Movement, except our imperial conditioning was different. Where
the Kennedys or the British royals were given latitude and a very
long leash, the Kings were seen as these pious moral exemplars—
a difficult posture for human beings to maintain.

I was born six weeks premature in January of 1961. Only my
mother can know what she went through, mother of two at the
time, pregnant with a third, dependent on Daddy, worried about
his safety, whether something would happen to him because they
had whisked him off in the middle of the night to Reidsville. They
could as well have been taking him to Hell. He could have easily
not even made it to that prison—could have wound up bloated in
an earthen dam. It was known to happen. It seems incredible, but
those were the harsh realities of the times. So, my mother was in
a nervous state for the entire time she was pregnant with me.
Everything I've read or heard of since implies that the emotional
state of the parents, particularly the mother, is transmitted to the
fetus. I felt what she went through. My mother thinks it had a
bearing in shaping me, may have forced me out sooner, the urgency
of the times.

My paternal grandfather also made his mark on me. He made
his mark on all of us, on the whole city of Atlanta, long after he, as
Mike King, at age sixteen, had hopped a freight from Stockbridge,
Georgia, Henry County, south by southeast of Atlanta, back in the
day. Later he argued with his father in order to stay in Atlanta at
Bryant Preparatory School, where he was learning how to read and
write. Neither of his parents could read or write. When his father,
James, went to Atlanta and demanded Mike come back to the
farm, because they couldn't make it without his labor, Mike de-
clined. He'd stay on at the school and go about ministering the
Baptist way in nearby East Point. Mike King had been born in 1899,

to Delia Lindsay and James Albert King, whose father was a white Irishman. He courted and married Alberta Williams, the daughter of the well-known and respected Rev. A. D. Williams; was determined and felt the call to be a Baptist preacher.

Martin seemed a more appropriate name for such a calling, so he adopted it; such given-name changing was a fairly common practice among this generation of young black men making or trying to make a transition from fields to halls of learning. In his twenties, Granddaddy went to Morehouse, graduated, eventually inheriting the wind at Ebenezer from his father-in-law. He remained country strong. Two words best describe him: no-nonsense. Eventually he was overshadowed by the legacy of his son.

Daddy was not just charismatic away from home. His personal magnetism had nothing to do with the Civil Rights Movement on the level I'm talking about. I'd watch him when he wasn't looking, in different states of activity or repose. He insisted we have family time to discuss what was going on, and why he had to be away.

Him sitting at the dining room table with us was a good time for conversation. Sometimes his mind wandered and he seemed lost in thought, absently eating green onions. My father liked stalks of green onions with sweet, white, bulbous roots. They sat in a plate in water, like celery; before a meal he'd pick and eat them like fruit, especially before meals containing turnip or collard greens. He would say he was laying down a bed of straw before the cows and pigs—the rest of the meal—came home. This was ancestral. His father's family was from rural Georgia, my mother's family from rural Alabama. You can see a plate of green onions in photos of tarpaper shacks in the black belt of Mississippi, Alabama, and Georgia; they were staples of the sharecropper's diet.

I can still see him walking down the hallway at home in his slippers. He had a burgundy-colored satin-like robe he always wore to breakfast. Whenever he wore his robe, I was happy, because it meant he wasn't going anywhere for a while. That meant I could watch him or, if not that, simply be reassured he was there if needed. Every time I was in his presence, I felt deep compassion from him. Many times he felt like a playmate, like somebody who was Dad in terms of compassion and sensitivity, but was not so removed, because he enjoyed playing too, and could relate to a child's problems. We had fun playing softball. He'd pitch. If I swung and missed he'd be disappointed. "Aw, Dexter," he'd say, lobbing in another underhand toss.

When he'd come back from a trip, we'd hide from him, trembling with excitement; he'd find us, have us jump off the refrigerator top into his arms. He called it the Kissing Game. We'd take turns, starting with the eldest. Yoki would be first; she'd jump off into his arms, completely trusting that he'd catch her, and we would follow, and then he'd say, "Where's your kissing spot?" Hers was a corner of her mouth. Martin would have his spot—the forehead. Then I had my spot—the temple. Bernice had her spot— a corner of her mouth. We'd jump into his arms, take our turns; there were four of us, he divided his time equally—what little time he had left. He tried his best. The only one who may have felt he didn't was Yoki. Yoki and my father had a special bond, but he gave us all our specialness. More than just having a spot on his face to kiss, he had an intimate spot in his heart for everybody; we felt it, it made us feel special. He knew how to relate on our level. The memorable thing is that he knew how to relate to us. He was a universal communicator, even to his children, and he knew how to embrace you in a way where you felt a part of some greater plan.

The one thing Daddy didn't like was to be disturbed when he was in his study, writing down his thoughts, scheduling, composing sermons, reading and making notes in the margins of his books. There was a contemplative thought process at work in him. He compartmentalized it. If he was working, then he worked. If he was playing, then he played. He didn't mix the two.

"Now, Dexter, when Daddy's working, don't disturb him. Daddy will play with you soon."

Most people might think, because of the way he was projected as such a serious person, that he was always so, but sometimes he was the opposite of that, or the balance of that; he needed an outlet, a way to break the tension. He sought refuge in his children, his family. He became us.

It seemed we were always going to an event, a church for a meeting, a picnic—there'd always be a banner or a sign or something with the letters SCLC on it. I used to think the letters meant "King Family Outing." Whether it was a Voter Registration Project or a strategy session, they were all outings to us.

I never knew a man with so many brothers and sisters as my father—and resulting aunts and uncles for me and my brother and sisters. Not only was there Uncle A.D. and Aunt Naomi, or Aunt Christine and Uncle Isaac, our own blood relatives and his in-laws, there was also Uncle Andy, Uncle Ralph, Uncle Harry, Uncle Bob, Uncle Junius. Uncle Ralph was Ralph Abernathy. Uncle Andy was Andrew Young. Uncle Harry was Harry Belafonte. Uncle Junius was Junius Griffen. Uncle Bob was either Robert Green or Robert Johnson. Everybody was related, even if not by blood. And if anybody got in trouble, my family showed up to support him or her, because that was our habit.

Some would question, Why are you there, why would you get involved with, say, a Ralph Abernathy, Jr., after his brush with the law as an elected official? Why would you show up at his trial? Well, we were like family. We don't leave our people behind. Ralph III and I grew up together. We lived in each other's homes. We were roommates in college. We'd go to outings, cookouts, retreats. Our parents took us to work-related events. Even though we were kids just running around, a lot did rub off on us, just through osmosis, being in the environment, the SCLC conventions where Aretha Franklin sang. We had no idea of the momentous nature of Daddy's work. He and his colleagues were about ending the system of segregation in American life, no small or simple matter.

When the Hyatt opened, the brand-new Hyatt, with the blue dome, I was riding in the futuristic glass-walled elevator feeling like

I was on a spaceship above Atlanta. Architect John Portman was a pioneer in developing new-age spaceship elevators, and duplicated them in buildings he designed elsewhere. Child that I was, I felt like this had been put in place just for my father, to whisk him up on high. I knew he was famous. Going to those ceremonies and conventions and remembering the entertainment there always had the sense of electricity, music in the air—this always stood out to me. I always remember best the entertainment and the music.

I had no conception of segregation, of how unprecedented such mixed gatherings were, the meaning of a Nobel Peace Prize, which my father had received in 1964, the same year the system of formal segregation was abolished by law if not by practice in Atlanta. Daddy's point had won. He'd persevered. His cause was just and its righteousness prevailed, at least in Atlanta. I was almost four years old and just knew that all of a sudden we were at the Dinkler Plaza Hotel one winter's night. The way I remember it, there were thousands of people there—fifteen hundred, as it turns out: black, white, in between, all to honor my father. The new mayor, Ivan Allen; Dr. Mays; other dignitaries, businesspeople, but no entertainment. No Aretha Franklin. Not my kind of room.

We were introduced to the crowd as the children of the winner of the 1964 Nobel Peace Prize. Yoki got up and waved, though I didn't understand why; she hadn't put on a play. Marty got up and bowed from the waist. The way Mother remembers it, when my name was called, when it was my turn to face the crowd, I slid under the chair instead of standing up on it. The crowd laughed. Slid under the chair? Is that what I did? No wonder everyone laughed.

Police were always around. I admired them. I admired their uniforms, their sidearms, their garrison caps and badges and official gold braid. I would stare. I couldn't tell if they stared back, because they wore dark glasses. Their expressions never changed. Besides admiring police from afar, I admired entertainers up close, whether it was Harry Belafonte or Bill Cosby, or any number of others who contributed to what the grown-ups referred to as "the Cause," or "the Movement." At times our parents would be called into active duty. Whether the campaign was in Selma, Birmingham, Montgomery, Albany (Georgia), Chicago, Memphis, didn't matter, because we were told they were going to fight for their country to be greater, for people to be treated fairly and equally under the law. This was for all of our futures, we were told. We understood our parents were doing good work. Sometimes we'd be teased, which affected Yoki more because she was older and more aware and was so connected to my father. When teased about our father going to jail, Yoki would tilt her head upward and say, "Yes, he did, but to help poor people."

There are photographs of us sitting at the table, playing ball in the yard, at the piano as Mother plays and sings. Daddy had invited a man to our house—Camera Man. He took pictures of us. I was fascinated by his equipment, his cameras, lights, flashbulbs popping. I thought, "I can do that." Camera Man took a photo of me sitting on Daddy's lap, Daddy calmly looking at the camera. I'm looking off to one side, mouth sprung, seemingly in awe of something, comforted and protected in Daddy's lap. Secure. I won't fall even if I fail. He'll lift me up. I know this. I can look over the abyss of whatever it is I'm in awe of in the photo—maybe it was only Yoki making a face at me—I know my father will not let me go. I can take the risk because he's there. I trusted him like I have trusted no man before or since. I had the security to be insecure. And then . . .

The photographs remain. He knew they would.

Camera Man had a name. Flip Schulke, a photographer for *Life* magazine, as Gordon Parks had been. Though my father was protective of us at home, didn't let reporters or photographers in, Schulke came by many times to document. I gave him a nickname. My father gave us names of affection: "Yoki-poky," "Dexter-wexter," "Marty-bopy," "Bunny-bopy." Bunny was Bernice, Yoki was Yolanda, Marty was Martin III, but Dexter was just Dexter. I felt special; I was named after a church, an old, historic church too, which had been pastored by a man named Vernon Johns before our father arrived. I was glad to be named Dexter, after the church. It set me apart. Everybody else was named for a person.

Yolanda Denise. My mother had liked that name. Martin was named for my father and my grandfather. Bernice Albertine—Bernice for my mother's mother, Albertine for my father's mother, Alberta. Martin and Yolanda were born in Montgomery. People came up to me all the time and said, "Yes, Dexter, I remember when you were a baby in Montgomery; you were named after the church there." I would never correct them and say, "Yes, I was named for the church, but I was born here in Atlanta. I'm a homeboy." I would let them get it out and then say, "Well, I think you're talking about my brother." Martin III and I were always kind of seen as a unit, interchangeable. Even today. People come up and swear it was me who came and spoke at their school or church, when it was my brother. People say things like, "You should've been named Martin—you look just like your father." I learned not to bristle when I heard this. I learned to say, "My brother and I agree that the Lord often works in mysterious ways."

We were all close as children. Yoki was five years my senior, seven years Bernice's. I don't remember her being as much a part of our circle as Bernice, Martin, me—especially Afterward . . .

Martin and I would tussle. He thought he was my father. Mom generally took us to restaurants, shopping, church, on outings. We drew attention, but that didn't stop our parents from giving us a semblance of normalcy. It was only a semblance, though. We couldn't do things together as frequently as normal families, because both parents weren't as available. At times we'd go with friends of the family; we might go with the Abernathy kids, Ralph III, Juandalyn, and Donzaleigh; or with Uncle A.D's and Aunt Naomi's children, Alveda, Al, Derek, Darlene, and Vernon; or with my father's sister, Christine King Farris, and her children, Angela and Isaac. Martin III was three years older than me. Isaac and I were a year apart. Isaac lived in Collier Heights, where professionals, particularly teachers and preachers, lived. My grandparents lived in a spacious house with a yard so big Mr. Horton had to use a Snapper riding mower to cut the grass. Aunt Christine, Uncle Isaac, Angela, and Isaac lived near our grandparents in Collier Heights. Granddaddy still wanted my father to move. Daddy said we were okay in Vine City.

My cousin Isaac and me, our relationship started out rocky. Fought like cats and dogs. Out of it came an ironclad friendship. Wasn't love at first sight, though. Maybe the problem was me attempting to be Isaac's parent, according to Isaac—trying to be to Isaac what Martin tried to be to me. Most in our family are headstrong. Wonder where we get it from. I think it mostly comes from my grandfather, Martin Luther King, Sr., who cast a long shadow. He was a strong-willed, bullheaded man, and he passed it down; the only one who was able to escape it and establish his own identity was his youngest son and namesake, Martin Luther King, Jr.

CHAPTER 2

Peace Be Still

Isaac and I were in the balcony of Ebenezer Baptist Church, listening to our grandfather deliver the Sunday Word.

Being accustomed to the surroundings, Isaac and I were playing around up in the balcony. I could listen to the gospel choir roll out rollicking Baptist hymns all day. We weren't the only ones Granddaddy had in the palm of his hand. He was a strong Baptist preacher.

Going to church was a chore for us at the time. Granddaddy, affectionately known as Daddy King, was already eyeballing his young grandsons for possible pulpit heirs, and was finding no takers. Who could live up to it? He was a big man, outsized in frame, voice, gaze, everything. We weren't rebellious—too much fear of him for that—but we sensed we were being studied for suitability.

I had a hard time focusing on church activities, being still and concentrating; consequently Isaac and I were most of the time running around at church, in church, around church, outside church—church being of course my grandfather's tidy, eight-hundred-seat red-brick Ebenezer, at the corner of Jackson Street and Auburn Avenue, where my father was co-pastor.

We were not only sons of a preacher man: we were the grand-sons of a preacher man, and the great-grandsons of a preacher man. My grandmother Big Mama's late father, A. D. Williams, only vaguely intimidated us via sepia-toned photographs. Isaac and I were terrors anyway, and though Martin wasn't my running buddy anymore, he too found his ways to escape the collared noose, though Martin was always too shrewd to be caught doing the things Isaac and I got caught doing routinely. People probably thought we had fallen a bit far from the tree. We had fun, though.

My father was not always in the pulpit on Sundays; the Cause had taken over his life. Granddaddy took more of a disciplinarian role, and my mother too, in the absence of my father.

So on that day when we were in the balcony Isaac said something to make me giggle. One giggle. It was inappropriate, but as a kid you don't think like that; we were kind of talking through the service and my grandfather didn't play that. Did we think we had already obtained salvation? If we did, he had an update for us. He called us down after his sermon. My grandfather called us down on the wine-colored carpet. He asked—that's funny, "asked," right, he "asked" me and Isaac to come down—"Come down here!" That was a long walk. Church members nodding solemnly. Peers looking on, dropping heads to hide grins. Marty surreptitiously drawing a finger across his throat.

"Now, my grandboys will tell the congregation what the message was about."

Maybe it was genetically encoded. I didn't recall the sermon then, and don't now, but for whatever reason, I was able to wing it; people were "Amen"-ing, and our young peers were disappointed that we were not in for more public humiliation. I shocked my own self.

"Well . . ." I began (several church members echoed me: "Waal, waal"), ". . . you talked about the importance of the Lord, not just on Sunday, but every day. You said there were too many Simons and not enough Peters, too many Sunday Christians and not enough everyday Christians."

People kept "Amen"-ing, and "Waal"-ing, so I figured I was getting by. Finished her off by saying Abraham had a son after age one hundred, so you never know what God has in the storehouse for you. Isaac whispered to me to remember that Leviti cussed and Deuter ronomied.

My grandfather's massive, waxy-looking hands worked as if our young necks were in them and he might strangle them. Veins in his temples throbbed. He looked at Isaac, and said, "And what's that you say, Isaac Newton Farris? What's your interpretation of the message today?"

Isaac, being typical Isaac, said, "Well . . . I . . . actually think Dexter summed it up well."

A few people nearly rolled in the aisles laughing. We'd winged it. Later people said, "You know, you boys ain't all that dumb. Your day's coming." A slow—and I mean a very slow—smile crept across Granddaddy's face.

Martin Luther King, Sr., didn't play. He'd leave the pulpit to collar us; or he'd send a deacon to retrieve us, inside the sanctuary or out. Often we were out, across the street, at Carter's Sundry. He believed sparing the rod meant spoiling a child. If he was preaching and you got up to leave he would challenge you.

"Where you going, Brother So-and-so? Do you not need to hear the rest of God's word?"

Evidently what my grandfather saw in me and Isaac at that age brought him little comfort in the way of succession. I don't think we did anything any different from any other youths. Nobody else's youths were expected to sit through these stifling Baptist services; because of who we were different standards were applied. We resented it. We'd see other kids on walkabout, not coming at all, coming down with Sunday morning flu, and we'd say, "How come we have to do it when they don't?" Martin's public face was more in keeping with tradition, as were cousin Al's and Derek's, Uncle A.D.'s sons. Martin was shrewd; he'd put up a good front, usually avoided Granddaddy's belt. I envied him. I knew deep down he didn't have any plans to be a preacher any more than we did, but he didn't bridle against it so openly. When time came to pray, he'd pray hard. Pray to be spared becoming a preacher. He'd say something like that out of the side of his mouth to get us going, we'd laugh, get called out, feel the sting of a strap later. Martin would shake his head like one of the octogenarian deacons: "Um-um-um, them boys ought to be shamed of themselves."

We had a program called children's chapel, a kind of Sunday school, actually one of my Uncle A.D.'s ideas, a prerequisite to grown-up church that gave children a chance to worship with children, and taught you how to prepare to graduate to full service. That was nice. I enjoyed it more so because you were around your peers. We'd still do our running around, but when my father was scheduled to preach, somehow we'd end up in the front row of the balcony, forearms resting on the railing, listening intently. Daddy had a style; he'd mastered it, and it mastered the listener. Even a child was charmed not only by what he said but also by the way he said it. It wasn't haphazard, came from work, study, talent. And he never once asked if we would preach.

My mother would tell us—usually it would be Isaac and me, or Martin and me—"Don't do thus-and-so because this could happen." "Don't play in the street," or something very simple, and Martin would automatically respond, "All right, Mother." Isaac would say, "We better not. Aunt Coretta said not to." If Mother said, "Martin, Dexter, and Isaac, don't you all go around that corner, because there's a saber-toothed tiger on the other side," Martin would say, "Uh-oh. Mama says a tiger's over there." Isaac would say, "I ain't scared, but Aunt Coretta won't like it if we go." But I'd say, "Let me see it then! I want to see what that tiger looks like!"

My mother would get frustrated because I seemed to have a great need to know why. Some parents say you're not supposed to ask "why?" as a child.

"Because I said so, that's why."

That was my mother's unfailing reaction—and Yoki's too, as

the younger version of her. I was the type that came across like I was questioning authority, but I had a need to explore and see how things worked. That was just me; some people may have taken it wrong. I think Mother even took it as me being defiant. But I didn't feel defiant. She didn't have much tolerance for foolishness either way. She'd spank us—"whip" us, as they call it in the country. My father wouldn't. He didn't spank us. She would. Daddy might sit down and explain things. "This is why you shouldn't do that, son." He would deal more on a mental level, try to get us to understand why things were.

One day my brother, Martin, Isaac, and I came across a treasure trove. Plastic toy guns! Immediately we were having a ball, playing army, playing war, playing gangsters, cops and robbers, the Untouchables, cowboys and Indians. There are a lot of different ways boys can play with toy guns. We were going "bang! bang!" feigning death throes, the things boys do when they play with guns, me, Martin, and Isaac. Daddy must have been watching from a window, must have stood watching us for the longest time; I wish I knew what all was going on in his mind. He came out, sat down heavily, gathered us at his knee.

The indoctrination of children who are being exposed to violent instruments of war—he didn't want to see it happen to his sons, his nephews, or anybody, but it was hard if not impossible to stop it, even within the borders of his own home in the society in which we came up. He knew this; it weighed on him. That's why when he came outside he sat so heavily and sighed so deep.

It was me who most enjoyed playing with toy guns. Any kind. Water guns, cap pistols shaped like six-shooters, shaped like .45 automatics, you name it, I was fascinated. Whenever we were around policemen I stared at their holstered sidearms. I don't think Marty was that keen on it at all, not as keen as me. I'd stick a toy gun in my pants pocket in a minute and practice my quick-draw, like cowboys on TV, James Arness as Matt Dillon on *Gunsmoke*, or Chuck Connors as the Rifleman. I'd make a mock badge out of tinfoil off chewing-gum wrappers and pretend to be a sheriff. I'm sure Marty got sick of me bang-banging away, insisting he was dead. I didn't often get chances to play with toy guns because we weren't given any to play with; you had to come upon them in our forays into the neighborhood, but this one time, someone had given us these plastic toy guns all our very own and we were getting good wear out of them.

My father extended his palm and asked us for the guns. Martin gave up his right away. I hung on to mine, frowning as my father's hand closed around the barrel and he gently tugged. "Dexter, let it go, son," he said. I wanted to ask why I had to give up the gun when I was having such fun playing with it. My father looked at me levelly. When my father looked at you like that, you had better be right in your position. Slowly my fingers relaxed and I released the gun.

Daddy laid them down in front of us, then said, "Boys, sit here with me for a little while."

He was always kindly in speaking to us, unlike Granddaddy, who often roared.

"Why do you suppose we, as young men, are fascinated by firearms?"

"Fascinated, Daddy?"

"Why do we enjoy them? Holding them, pointing them at each other, pulling them out, waving them around, twirling them around our fingers, making the noises that a gun makes?"

"Bang! Bang! Like that, Daddy?"

"Duh-duh-duh-duh-duh-duh, that's the way the machine gun sounds, Daddy!"

"Yes, Dexter-wexter. Why do you think we enjoy it, Marty-bopy?"

"To kill bad people?"

"And how do you tell who the bad people are?"

"They're the people who get shot!"

"Not always. Not always."

"By how they look?"

". . . No."

"Then . . . then . . . I don't know."

"Me neither."

"Then we're together," my father said. "I don't know either. But I do know this: You should only use your imagination. Never use real guns. Never even use toy guns."

My disappointment must have been obvious.

"I don't want you playing with these. All right?"

Silence.

"Is that all right?"

"If you say so, Daddy," said Marty. My father nodded at him. Then . . . "Dexter?"

"I won't play wif 'em, then," I said, sounding unconvinced, I'm sure. "But everybody else will anyway, Daddy. They all will."

Then Daddy sighed again and sat there, silent for a while, before saying, "The guns these toys represent have one use. They're not like Granddaddy Scott's .22 hunting rifle. These represent handguns; they're only used to kill or maim people. If you saw what they did to people, you'd be sad. Suppose somebody shot somebody you loved?"

I looked at him as if to say, No, that could never be, thinking as a child, that "bang-bang" meant you were "dead," but you could get up and argue about whether you were "dead" or not.

"You don't want another human being's death on your conscience," my father said. "You want to have life. I'd rather see you boys play sports like football than play with guns. I'd rather you play a musical instrument, debate, or even fight . . . but not with these . . ."

He talked with us for a while longer. The way he spoke was so effective that at the end of it he actually had us destroy those plastic guns. We put them in a metal trash can and burned them, melted them down. I didn't fully understand it then. I liked the toy guns, and the real guns police and security officers wore. But I was moved by what my father had said. He had such a cool way of explaining things that it was almost like we were happy to do what he had asked us to do, even though I still didn't quite know why.

This and other lessons stuck with me. He was very much a talker, he would talk about subjects with us, was intimate in his feelings, in terms of our being able to understand the subject and his feelings. You felt like his equal, almost, like he was bringing you up in the world to his level, not like he was coming down to you. He was soothing to listen to, authoritative you knew, because he was Daddy, but also deliberate, precise; when he spoke, you listened.

I don't remember exactly where, it was probably a passerby in later years who didn't want to believe that my father had mortal qualities, vices, fallibilities, and shortcomings; these would come out when he was under duress. "Your father never smoked a cigarette in his life," I heard from people who claimed to be authorities, "believers" of my father's life and work. They were talking about what they'd read. I'm talking about what I'd lived, seen, and felt.

I thought to myself, "Not only are there photos of him holding a cigarette, my sister and brother and I once took his cigarettes and hid them." Maybe it was something he wanted to keep private. He struggled with it. He knew it was not good for him, but it happened.

There was an unbelievable amount of stress on him at the time. He didn't start smoking until the last few years of his life.

Early in 1968, he seemed more quiet than usual; he was being pulled into causes around the country. Yet he was just a man. He'd just returned from a trip. Now there were calls from Rev. James Lawson, for him to go to Memphis.

We just wanted him to take us to Pascal's Restaurant, or to an amusement park, or to the next SCLC outing that spring, or up to the Ollie Street Y, but he didn't have any more time.

He planned to take me and Marty on a quick trip around Georgia in March. We just knew it was a trip with Daddy. He was drumming up support for his Poor People's campaign. It was then that Yoki, Marty, and I hid his cigarettes. Maybe this was to get his attention, I don't know what our motivation was, really, but we

hatched an elaborate scheme first to find where he kept his cigarettes, then take them out and squirrel them away, and surprise
him when he couldn't find them, and tease him. A whole carton
too. We hid his carton of cigarettes in the closet of the guest room.
He didn't smoke regularly that we saw; he only smoked when he
was going through tense times. By the time I turned seven years
old, in January of 1968, all his times were tense. We were children
and didn't know specifics. He'd been to California right after New
Year's, he'd spoken there at a college. Now he was getting requests
to go to Memphis. Memphis I knew nothing about; my mother said
some garbage men—"sanitation workers"—wanted my father to
help them. I plotted with Yoki to steal Daddy's cigarettes. Don't
know why. Yoki's motives were nobler. Maybe she didn't want to
see him smoke. I know she ended up smoking when she was older
(and has since stopped). She may have started as a way of com-
muning with him. We hid them, and he came looking for them. He
hit the ceiling when they were not where he had left them. This
was the only time I ever saw him angry.

"Where are my cigarettes!"

Silence. Three young faces looking at each other, confirming
each other's impending doom.

"Yolanda! Martin! DEXTER!" No nicknames or "bopys" put at
the end of our given names meant serious business was at hand.
Our answering "Sir?" was weak, as I recall. I think that was the first
time, probably, all of us saw him truly upset, where he was obviously angry. Oh, he knew.

Imagine now—you're going to get your vice, not finding it
where you left it, somebody has messed around with it. I'm not
sure if he was addicted to nicotine; to a degree he was, wasn't a
pack-a-day smoker, but he was accustomed to smoking feeling like
a diversion to him, a diversion that in his mind may have been relaxing. I know how I am when somebody moves basic stuff in my
domain and I can't find it. Imagine if he's in a fix, needs nicotine,
can't find it, going through a hard time. I'm sure I would be angry
too. At this moment I wasn't curious to see how much angrier my

father could get. I can still see his contorted expression as he stormed out his bedroom and came down the hall looking for us. "Where are my cigarettes!? Who took my carton of cigarettes?"

It was obvious what had happened. We started running—down the hall, out of the back of the house; we were so guilty. My mother always said that Daddy didn't believe in spanking, but she also said if he had spent more time around us, he might have changed his mind.

This was an example of him spending more time around us. We were thinking we could do whatever we wanted and he'd understand. That's the only time I saw real anger when I was there with him. I've seen footage after the fact, and I've heard things from scholars, where something made him upset, or angry. But that's the only time I actually saw it. I never wanted to see it again, either. It was some time before Martin and I got back into his good graces, but by bedtime, Yoki was sitting with him, sniffling apologetically, holding his fingers in her hands.

My maternal grandparents were Obadiah Scott (everyone called him Obie) and Bernice McMurry Scott. My maternal grandfather's parents were Jeff and Cora Scott. Jeff Scott ended up owning 450 acres of black dirt, rich, black-belt Alabama farmland outside Marion, Alabama, seat of Perry County, some eighty miles south by southwest of Birmingham, eighty miles due west of Montgomery, cheek by jowl with Dallas County, where the county seat was Selma. Jeff Scott was a preacher's steward in the African Methodist Episcopal Church. He had thirteen children with great-grandmother Cora, and after she died, at age forty, great-grandfather Jeff married Fannie Burroughs and had twelve more children before he died at sixty-eight in a car wreck. My maternal great-grandfather, Martin McMurry, was a mixture of black, white, and Native American. He was two years of age when slavery ended.

My grandfather Obie and my grandmother Bernice awaited us when we made our summer car trips down to the family farm near Marion, four hours from Atlanta. Going to Marion was like an outing. We'd always drive. It took several hours, so we got a chance to all be together in the car, a Plymouth station wagon later, but before that, during my father's lifetime, a Chevy, a blue Chevy, which we still have. A '65 Impala. The green Pontiac Bonneville was the car he got before—before Memphis. But we still have that blue Impala. I remember riding to the farm in it.

My granddaddy Scott was a nice man. He'd let us do anything we wanted, mostly, including driving his old three-gear pickup truck. We liked him for this. I hate to say it because it sounds so trivial, but he ran a store, like the old combination gasoline "filling" station–small grocery store. Candy and everything was in the store, and he told us to "help yourself," against my grandmother's wishes. Her thing was, "Child, you need to eat healthy. You're going to work here."

Her cooking was great, southern country cooking, the fresh taste. I mean even till this day, once you've sampled it, you can never forget it. Fresh turnips, collards, okra, squash, onions simmering over roasts, and hams stuffed with cloves and a raisin glaze; cornbread, eggs, bacon, tomatoes, fresh everything, made deliciously. Now you and I know time gilds—often dietary habits you had as a child are remembered so fondly until other people from other families in other parts of the country find it all too appalling. You ate grits!? Indeed we did, ate them and loved them as they were prepared in the country, slathered in fresh butter or in a puddle of brown gravy off the rendering fat of chicken or ham with a touch of celery or bell pepper. Those grits back then were not just plain grits you get from a box or some Denny's. In my memory, they were right—creamy, smooth, delicious, all so good and remembered well.

Granddaddy Scott was a hardworking, frugal man, who learned from watching his father. It must have been hard to maintain a simple abundance in a system where a black man's life was virtually worthless and he could be "disappeared" for working hard, accumulating something, a little more than some few of his white neighbors down the road. An authentic line from *Mississippi Burn-*

ing, delivered by Gene Hackman, talking about how his poor white southern character's father felt about a "Negro": "If you ain't better than a nigger, who are you better than?" We could talk about the psychology behind that line, or dryly recite events of the day. But no need. Great-granddaddy Scott and Granddaddy Scott lived when it was an unforgivable crime for a "Negro" to get ahead.

Granddaddy Scott's home was a wood-frame house on a large tract of land. Animals in the backyard; cow pasture, barn behind the house, adjacent to the hog shed and chicken shack; vegetable garden and produce trees on the side of the house; then cropland, several hundred acres elsewhere; the farm itself, and main house, on about fourteen acres. My grandfather was well regarded in the community—you got that sense. Marty and I would come in the store and work. He'd let us tag along, teach us how to work a cash register, let us help wait on people who came to get gas.

You could tell that everybody looked up to Mr. Obie. Mr. Obie was for all intents and purposes the local bank and the local barber. He did some of everything. Cut hair on his porch. When people couldn't afford to buy groceries, he'd extend them credit. There were so many people who owed him money that if they paid him off, seemed like he would've been a millionaire. He gave away so much at the end of his life and didn't have a lot to show for it. Some people see that as mismanagement, other people see it as I do—he worked at what he loved, he helped people out, wasn't in it for the money. He saw it as justice. He'd been fleeced himself. He was always courteous and giving to people. Some people took advantage, cheated him right to his face, let's say on his gas pump. "Three dollars on regular," a bad one might say, when he'd actually put in five. Granddaddy didn't spend his life chasing the bad ones, or trying to keep them more honest. He was honest himself, never let other people's transgressions affect him or the way he lived. And I saw this, and at the time it confused me, but in later years I began to understand it better. It took a while, though.

"Granddaddy, did you see what that man did?" . . . "Yeah, boy, I sure did. Think I'm blind? Make sure you don't go around doing things like that." . . . "You gonna let him get away with it, Grand-daddy?" . . . "Ain't for me to let him get away or not. The Lord will make an accountin'."

Now, does that make sense to you? It didn't to me back then. The Lord was up in the sky, and Granddaddy was cheated on earth. I didn't understand. Yet he seemed to want for nothing.

It was busier than you might imagine for the country, or for what I had always thought the country would be like—everybody lolling about being indolent with a piece of hay stuck in their teeth. Oh no. He worked at a sawmill, bought a truck, hauled logs and timber, cut hair on the weekends. He later bought a sawmill that was burned down two weeks later by racist whites. My grand-mother had borne her children—my mother, Coretta, her sister, Edythe, and their brother, Obie. They tended crops when they grew up, hired out to pick cotton at harvest. My grandfather used to say he wouldn't tolerate laziness in his house. When we visited, we worked. We didn't go on vacation. We all had chores. When I say it was mixed work and play, what I really mean is on one hand, we thought we were going on vacation, because we were going away from home, but the truth is, we were working harder there than anywhere else. Granddaddy Scott could soften his approach; my grandmother was always strict. But they were both all about work. My grandfather would come in at 6 A.M. "Y'all get up! Work to do!" . . . "We did it yesterday." . . . "Do it every day. You need to be up. Open that shade. Let the Lord's light in here!"

Obie Scott was old school, with the ethic of: You work your life through, and if you're not up doing something, you are wasting time, your life has no purpose. So we didn't really mind. We wanted to sleep later, don't get me wrong. And we kind of knew if we wanted to go back to bed, we could just turn the light off and he wasn't coming back to check. That was Martin's move, to jump up and say, "Yessir!" and then plop back down after my grandfather left the room.

My grandmother, Nana, as we called her, wanted us to partici-pate in the process: help her prepare the food, help her do chores, which we didn't mind, typically. We learned a lot. Like milking cows. Not something on my list to learn how to do, but I did learn. Granddaddy would take Martin to the slaughterhouse. I don't remember going; Martin never had much to say about it. Granddaddy owned cows and hogs and chickens and everything; they somehow became cut-up slices and slabs of meat; he'd send us back to Atlanta with what seemed like a whole cow or pig, cut up. We'd have six months' supply of sirloin, T-bone, ham, and bacon. We never wanted for meat, not as long as he kept livestock. He also ran a hauling business; Martin and I learned to drive a standard shift with him. "Drive, boy," is all he would say, and I ground gears and killed the engine misapplying the clutch before I got the feel. That was fun. I didn't have my driver's license, but on those country dirt roads, I could play around with his pickup or tractor.

It was a diversion from city life, going to the country to do things not available in the city. Even my mom, even though she was a parent and concerned, would relax the standards. I don't remember my dad being in that setting as much. When he did go, he almost always disappeared.

Sometimes my mother's sister, Edythe Scott Bagley, her husband, Arthur, and their son, Arturo, would visit the farm with us. Uncle Obie, Mother's brother, was always around to help and support us as well. In later years, his wife, Alberta, became an invaluable member of our family. Arturo is actually probably two years younger than Bernice, and that is the only cousin we had on that side of the family—the only first cousin. Now, we had all kinds of more distant cousins. That was the other special thing about "the country." My great-grandfather had twenty-five children. We were literally related to most of the county. We would meet new people on a regular basis who would just come up and say, "I'm your third cousin, So and so." Oh, is that so? My mother or grandmother would say, "Yes, that's So-and-so's child." A lot of times they would embarrass you, and take a little pleasure in it too. You might have met them before, just a quick meeting, and they might say, "You 'member me, don't you? What's my name?" How can you remember all these people? So it's funny on one hand; in the country they all know each other so it doesn't matter that they are that many times removed. Inevitably they all know each other. There's some comfort in that.

It was always like a homecoming, or a reunion; people would find out we were there and they would drive over from their farms, just to come and say hello to the Kings, or the "Kangs," as some of them pronounced it, and ask, "Is the Rev'un here? Can we shake hands with the Rev'un?" His name preceded him. They appreciated my father. Mother knew them all by name, but I honestly can't say I could keep track of them all.

My parents were always very loving. I think the best word for their marriage is partnership. It wasn't like one parent was dominant over the other. You felt shared responsibility. When we would sit around the table, they both would have input in the drift of the conversation. My mom gave my father respect, as man of the house.

I never heard them argue. Maybe they were good at keeping it from us, since the married couple doesn't exist that hasn't had arguments. My mother was always a concerned parent who would say her piece; if he was going somewhere and wanted to take my brother and me with him and if this was a trip that she thought might be in some way inappropriate, or maybe dangerous, she'd say, "Well, Martin, I don't know if you should take the boys on this one."

And we would say, "But we want to go, we want to go!"

And he'd say, "Well, I think it would be okay." And she wouldn't press it, not in front of us. She would just look at him and lower her head, but not her eyes. Usually, later on, he'd wind up explaining to us why we couldn't go. We'd gone on just a few trips, like the James Meredith march in Mississippi, and were surprised when in late March of 1968, she allowed us to go with him on a tour around Georgia. Just us fellas. She wasn't the type that challenged him in front of us, but later, when it was just them, one-on-

one, she got her point across. If she had a concern, she would express it, but after being heard she wouldn't press it. So she respected him as a man, as the father, as the head of the household.

Christmas and other holidays and birthdays were celebrated in our house regardless of any current situation, campaign, or cause. Gift giving, gift exchange, and reflection on spirituality were what holidays meant. My mom is a big believer in traditional celebrations and ceremonies.

The last Christmas we all shared was in 1967. At the time, we didn't know it was the last Christmas we'd all share. It was just another great Christmas. Mother bought my father and me identical bicycles. Mine was just a junior version of his. Same brand, same color, same style. Purple. A new three-speed with the shift knob in the middle on the column. A purple metallic, sparkly color that transfixed me; a new model. The "in" thing. Really the coolest thing going.

Mine had training wheels. His did not. His was also bigger. I remember my father and me riding them together Christmas of 1967, down Sunset; we always felt kindred, there was always a shared sense of closeness between us because we both had January birthdays and our birthdays were close to Christmas, so when it came down to gifts, we knew we had a double hit coming.

"Dad-day! Wonder what else we're going to get, Daddy?"

"Isn't this enough, Dexter?"

"It sure is. Until our birthday."

He laughed with me. And there we remain forever. It was our last Christmas together.

I don't remember our birthdays that followed in January of 1968 very well, for some reason; Dad's birthday was typically celebrated with staff more than family. The whole Movement family, the Cause—all would do things for him and my mom would kind of incorporate family into that, but our mother would do celebrations for all of us individually at home on our birthdays.

My father and I did get to ride our bicycles together once or maybe twice more. We rode them up and around the gently undulating red clay hills in Vine City in January of '68, with the smell of honeysuckle and the sound of music and children playing replaced by winter's chill and desiccated leaves blowing in the wind between us. I remember chinging my bell, hearing him encouraging me to try and keep up, gently saying, "Careful, Dexter, until you get a feel for it."

We rode our bikes on the streets of Vine City, past shotgun houses, Egan Homes, Magnolia Ballroom, Flavor Palace, Pascal's, the Bonds', the Davises', the Halls', Mrs. Toomer's, the Ollie Street Y, Washington Park . . . our world. My father had insisted that we be in an environment where we would be with the people, not be on a mountain talking down to the valley, but in the valley, and perhaps go up the mountain together one day, in a perfect world. I remember biking beside my father, him not going so fast as to leave me behind. Remember how I said some were afraid to go by Egan Homes? When we rode by Egan Homes and my father waved to a few of the people, they waved back and said, "There goes the Reverend King and one of his boys. Spit that boy out. Look just like him." I ended up making a couple of good friends from Egan Homes . . . Afterward.

The couple of months after Daddy's and my birthdays in January of 1968 felt ominous. Martin, Yolanda, and myself asked Daddy not to go to Memphis. We might have been worried. Not that Daddy would die . . . just that he might be put in jail again. He went to Memphis two or three times that spring. The first time he went, we didn't say anything; it was after he came back, and planned to go again, that I recall this nagging feeling that something was wrong, something was off. The three of us felt it, Yolanda, Martin, and me. Something bad was going to happen. He knew it better than we did. How we picked up on it, I don't know. It was a frustrating period for all of us because we felt we had no control. And when it happened, Afterward, you felt death had been hovering over you all along, death seen from a child's view, and it would always be there, after that. We knew things were changing, and not for the better.

CHAPTER 3

Shattered

Suddenly, he was just—gone. Just like that, his short life like an exploding flashbulb that blinds you momentarily, fixes you in time, reveals you to yourself—then expires forever.

We were watching television. That's how I learned. TV told me. Special Bulletin. Yolanda says that until this day every time she sees one, it's a shock to her system. Now this is part of her imperial conditioning too. If she sees a Special Bulletin—"we interrupt this program for a Special Bulletin from CBS News"—her pulse races, she feels faint, her throat closes, she senses death.

I, on the other hand, feel nothing but numb.

Martin and I were sitting on the floor in front of the TV. Yoki was there somewhere, but I'm not seeing her or Bunny in this picture, in the same room with us. Yoki was twelve. We were sitting on the floor watching TV, I don't remember what—maybe some game show. If it had been on Saturday, earlier in the day, it would've been *American Bandstand*. The Special Bulletin came on, and an unforgettable voice said, "Dr. Martin Luther King, Jr., has been shot in Memphis, at 6:01 P.M."

Martin and I looked at each other. We said nothing.

We both jumped up and ran back into our parents' bedroom.

Mother sat on their bed, ankles crossed, fingers of her free hand and the phone receiver at her mouth. "Mother? Mommy? Mama? You hear that? What do they mean?"

Mother held up a finger, telling us to be patient, quiet, to wait; she was being briefed, on the phone to Memphis, with Jesse Jackson, who was the first to call her. She was obviously just getting the news from him. We waited for her to get off the phone—and dreaded her getting off.

She kept saying, "I understand." I'll never forget those words, how I couldn't understand why she would keep repeating them. I wanted her to get off the phone and make me understand. She replaced the beige receiver back in its cradle and turned to us. Yolanda came in; Mother's mouth opened, but before she spoke the phone rang again. It was Uncle Andy from Memphis this time. Mother listened again. "I understand." She hung up. Yolanda pressed her hands over her ears. "Don't tell me! Don't tell me!" she screamed. She fled the bedroom. Pain filled Mother's face. She encircled us boys in her arms and drew in a deep breath, as if about to dive underwater.

"Your father—there's been an accident." From then on our mother was stoic. She made you feel she was in control. No hysterics.

The phone rang again. Mayor Ivan Allen, offering to escort Mother to the airport. Yolanda composed herself, came back to the bedroom to help Mother pack. As they worked, I asked, "Mommy, when are you coming back? When's Daddy coming back?" She didn't seem to hear.

Soon she'd leave the house with Aunt Christine and Uncle Isaac, in a car with Mayor Allen and his wife to go to the airport. Aunt Christine had been in her kitchen in her Collier Heights home when the Special Bulletin had come. She'd left the house after getting a baby-sitter for Isaac and Angela. While Mother waited for her and Uncle Isaac and the Allens to arrive, Martin said nothing, only sniffled. I turned back to Mother.

"Mommy, when is Daddy coming home?" I kept repeating.

"I'm going to Memphis to see Daddy, Dexter. When I get there I'll call and let you know."

"Okay."

Then they left for the airport. Sooner than expected, she would come back. She arrived at the airport and was informed there was no reason to rush. Dora McDonald, my father's secretary, met my mother at the airport to accompany her to Memphis; she was the first person to share the bad news. She saw Mother and walked toward her in the terminal. She asked Mother to sit down. She did. Then Mayor Allen received the news on the phone. When he returned, Mother knew without his saying it. But he had to say it anyway. "Mrs. King, I've been asked to tell you that Dr. King is dead." Her husband, our father, was dead.

Hope went out of many lives. We were not alone in that, and never would be alone in it from then on. Wherever America went, particularly black America, we'd go careening with it.

Mother came back to 234 Sunset. People were here by then. Mrs. Rachel Ward had come quickly. We had no time to sit and talk or break down or anything else on our own because people had started coming to the house right away. The phone rang. Mrs. Ward answered it. People in Memphis were communicating with our house, not knowing Mother was gone. Mrs. Ward was on the phone one minute, the next minute she screamed and fell straight back, collapsing onto her back as if she had been shot or snatched onto her back by a giant hand. That's when I knew—when the thought first struck me, never again to leave: "Daddy is dead."

Mrs. Ward was catatonic. Then came emotional people gathering at our house, coming to our aid, with best intentions; then their hysterics upon seeing us, the grief uncontrollable.

I knew what had happened. Then, of course, it was official on the news. But I knew when Mrs. Ward fell back. As a seven-year-old I didn't have an understanding of death, but I knew it was worse than the first report: he had been shot; he had lived. Now the worst had happened. By the time Mother returned, I was in bed. Bernice was asleep. Every time someone had mentioned my father, she had mimicked Yoki and left the room with her hands over her ears. Sleep came as a blessing to her. Martin and I went to bed; he got up. I couldn't sleep either.

Mother had dreaded coming back to the house, dreaded having to tell us the news, not knowing quite how. How do you tell a child, let alone four children, that their father is not only dead but has been murdered? You don't, in our case. The world let us know. Yolanda and Martin were still up. Yolanda asked my mother, "Mama, should I hate the man who killed Daddy?"

"No. You shouldn't."

I could see both of their faces, golden in the lamp-shaded light. I stood watching. "Then I'm not going to cry," Yoki said. "I'm not going to cry because maybe my daddy is dead physically but his spirit is alive and one day I'm going to see him again in Heaven. Oh Mommy, you're such a brave and strong lady. I don't know what I'd do if I was in your shoes."

With a wrenching exclamation, Mother pulled my sister to her and they hugged tightly. Mother said, "Your father would be so proud of you." Mother wiped her face and they sat holding each other's hands. Finally Yolanda got up, strong and ladylike, and left the room.

Soon, Mother came back to our room.

"Dexter . . . do you know your father was shot?"

"Yes."

"He was hurt badly."

"But why?"

"Dexter, why don't you go to sleep now and I will tell you all about it in the morning. Sleep."

"All right, Mother . . . Mother! Are you going to sleep here? Where will you be?"

The next morning, there was this great droning hubbub around our house—and unbeknownst to us, chaos was now reigning in a horribly destructive way all across America in neighborhoods like

Vine City. Vine City itself was quiet, morose, calm, but our house wasn't.

My mother was taking calls; family, friends, and people who worked with our father were descending on the house. Mother didn't know how she was going to get to Memphis. Then a call came in. It was a Kennedy—the second time a Kennedy had called 234 Sunset. This time, it was Bobby. He offered to send a chartered plane for her, to take her to Memphis to get the body. He offered to put phone lines in the house, telling my mother she would need extra phones now; by daybreak it was done. Uncle Ralph and Uncle Andy were there. They were quiet around Mother but whispered of ramifications on RFK's campaign for the presidency, in its primary season. Uncle Andy was back from Memphis and had come to the house—when, exactly, I don't know. Could've been the morning of that Friday. It could have been Saturday. There was no sense of time. Uncle Andy talked to us, kept calm. I could see hurt in him. It was Uncle Andy who actually told us my father was dead. He told us, and said we'd talk more about it later, but that we would have to look after our mother now, because that's what our father would've wanted. I don't know how much time had passed. I don't know if I slept, or how. At some point we had a conversation, Uncle Andy, my brother, Martin, and me, in our bedroom. He told us our father did not die in pain, and that he would not want us to mourn in vain, or stand still in bereavement, but to move on, live, prosper, take advantage of the world he dreamed of, remember what he said at the Lincoln Memorial, that he wanted his four children to one day be judged by the content of their character, not the color of their skin—it was us he was talking about. Please don't let him die in vain.

I said to Uncle Andy, "The man who shot my father with a gun must not have known him, because everybody knew my father, and everybody knew he was a good man."

"Yes," Uncle Andy said. "Yes, he was."

We went to the airport to meet the body. I had Bernice with me; even though I wasn't that much bigger than her, I kept picking her up then putting her down because I wasn't big enough to carry her. Then Uncle Andy picked her up and we headed toward the airplane. I questioned why. I went to my safe asking-why place with it. The question I played over in my head is, Why did this person kill my father? I wouldn't have thought it was because the killer was a "racist" and wanted to see "segregation" stay in place. I thought of my father's voice, how it sounded different when he preached at Ebenezer, and when he asked us not to play with toy guns. Why would anybody shoot him? I didn't understand. Uncle Andy had addressed it more from a suffering standpoint—Daddy was never in pain; if he'd lived he would've been paralyzed. Uncle Andy was trying to help us understand that God had taken one of his disciples home, so we could come to grips with it.

We got to the airport; we boarded the airplane, an American Airlines Electra that Bobby Kennedy had chartered. I remember American Airlines because of the metallic finish. We walked up the portable stairs. Bernice kept asking, "Mommy, where's my daddy?"

Mother sat her down right in the front of the plane. And then suddenly we were at Hanley's Bell Street Funeral Home, which handled all of our family's burial needs. My memory goes back and forth between the inside of the plane and the dully lit back parlor of Hanley's. I'd looked around at the plane's interior, anywhere but at the coffin. I didn't want to think about my father in there, unable to get out. They had taken out some seats. I kept asking Mother unrelated questions, like, "What's this?" pointing to parts of the plane. She knew I was avoiding the fact of our father's corpse being on the plane. I didn't understand the inanimate part of death, never had seen anybody dead or even been to a funeral. I was curious about him being in the casket, but I didn't want to face it. Mother spoke about being worried about how my father would look when they opened the casket. She was concerned the funeral home in Tennessee had "fixed his face," as she called it.

"Bunny, your daddy is . . . asleep. He's lying in a casket and won't be able to get up and speak to you, but he'll know what you're feeling, he'll know what you're thinking. Your daddy's gone to live with God." Bernice stood looking at him at the funeral home.

I felt in a dream state. Wasn't sure what was going on, where we were. Our father's body lay in state at Sister's Chapel on the Spelman College campus from Saturday until Monday afternoon.

On Monday, we were taken to Memphis by Harry Belafonte— the three oldest children and Mother. There was a march. Numbly we marched too. The people were kind, yet Memphis seemed like a forbidding place, a different evil kingdom where my father was killed. People were dressed in black mourning clothes and wearing placards bearing his name as they walked along silently, crying; they looked in great pain, and so many of them were black, and so many of them were sad, and also sad for us, but mostly just sad. My mother marched with us in Memphis. It was so quiet. Only the scuffing of shoes on the asphalt could be heard. She gave a speech at City Hall. I wasn't used to hearing her give speeches. I'd seen Uncle Andy giving her papers at the airport and saying, "Here's your speech, but I think you should just talk from your heart." My mother said, "I think so too." She spoke for fifteen minutes to a crowd downtown near City Hall. Martin, Yolanda, and I sat and looked out at the crowd, where men who looked beaten wore signs that read I AM A MAN and DR. KING: NOT IN VAIN. Once we got back to Atlanta, people were everywhere. Bill Cosby and Robert Culp even came to Atlanta and played with us, trying to distract us. On the day of the funeral, Jackie Kennedy came to our home, looking stricken. People came from all over to offer condolences. The phone was always ringing.

The funeral was at Ebenezer that Tuesday morning. The sanctuary was packed with nearly eight hundred people—there would have been many more, but that's all the church could hold. Tens of thousands more were outside, millions more were there in spirit and via TV. You could feel the weight of everyone's mourning. The day before, Uncle A.D. gave a sermon Daddy had planned to give that Sunday at Ebenezer. It was called, "Why America May Go to Hell." I heard Daddy speak at the funeral—a tape-recorded sermon he had given in February. Bernice roused when she heard his voice and looked around, but slumped back into Mother's chest when she did not see him, only his remains in the casket at the front of the church. Then there was the lonely clip-clop of the mule-drawn wagon, and the tired, trudging feet of tens of thousands, an ocean of moving bodies that accompanied his body and his spirit across town from Auburn to Vine City, onto the campus of Morehouse, where a memorial service was held at Harkness Hall. There the Morehouse Glee Club sang "O God Our Help in Ages Past" and Miss Mahalia Jackson sang, "Precious Lord, Take My Hand." I tried not to feel. I watched Bernice instead.

Afterward . . . we went back to our normal routine, though we knew it was a somber and serious time. I didn't take in the seriousness of the moment in terms of understanding what it all meant to everyone else. I was sad because my father was dead. I didn't realize many people felt almost the same way I did even though they weren't related to him. My own reaction was held inside me, like Mother's, like Yolanda's. I never cried over my father's death. I watched Mother and took cues from her. I never saw her seem agitated or disturbed. She knew how closely the four of us watched her. If she'd gone to pieces . . . But she didn't. I thought that was the way you were supposed to act. That was the first death really close I'd been exposed to. I do remember her and Yolanda in the living room, sitting there, Yolanda wringing her hands in her lap and telling my mother she was so wonderful, she was so magnificent— what else was there to say? That was my clearest vision of my father's leaving—my mother and older sister sitting alone, consoling each other over the death of a husband, a father, working it out, being strong, as African-American women have been for generations, whenever their men's lives were summarily cut short.

It is the way of our people.

I must have heard clearly and taken as subconscious command Mother's instruction to sleep. For the longest time after Daddy's death, my sleep patterns changed. No more deep, dreamless sleep. Now I had dreams. In these dreams, he was still alive. We did a lot of the things we'd once done together, riding bicycles, playing softball, sitting in his study, me on his lap; I'd have pleasant dreams; it was exciting to see him alive, I had no feeling of him not being alive in the dreams; they were in color. Then I would wake up and find myself in the bedroom with Martin, who was asleep, his breathing buzzing, rustling under the covers. I knew then it was a dream and our father was dead. In the dreams I was happy. Then something would awaken me, I'd realize he was not here, and feel betrayed. Why is he here one minute and gone the next? For years I had the dreams. When I was dreaming, it felt real. It was my way of holding on. Don't know how crazy or weird it sounds, but I know if you love someone you'll go to great lengths to keep him or her with you.

None of it had happened. It was all some big April Fool's joke. The top came off the casket and he pushed it aside and sat up and smiled at me, and laughed that slow, sincere laughter of his. It was like we were interacting again, almost like a replay of things he had said and how he had laughed before. I might dream about the toy gun incident, or riding our bikes, or him teaching me to swim or just having fun, and there was no seriousness about it, no lesson to be learned. It was just the act of engaging together. I was just starting to learn how to be from watching him.

The dreams for me were not strange but rather vital; I saw him on one level as a playmate and on another as a role model, neither the deified figure people saw, nor a father in the traditional sense. He could weave in and out of that role; here he was again, we were going . . . we were going to . . . My eyes would open and I was staring at our bedroom wall and didn't need to check to know he wasn't there and never would be again. Another day would pass, another night would come, and then I'd dream of him again. I was still having this relationship with him through my dreams, so the ceremony, the funerals, the people congregated at the house all the time, the famous visitors, all that was peripheral. Like a dream itself. Dreaming was my preferred reality. During daylight hours, I was there, but not there. I hadn't made a connection yet in terms of what it meant, not until later. The permanence of it. I was in my own world, I was creating a make-believe dream world because I wasn't relating to my father being in a casket. I asked questions: How did he feel? Cool? Warm?

Back in 1968, I was often under the assumption he was around here somewhere. Sometimes I'd look under my bed thinking he was hiding there to surprise me. Except for my own family, what was in my heart for him was on a different level from what everyone else felt, including those who wept and cried, or those across America who burned, who gave up, who became bitter or beaten down. I had a different demeanor when I was among everybody else. I saw them grieving; it didn't impact me the same way. I had a secret. I still had him, in my dreams.

Once I dreamed we were living in Chicago, in a poor section called Lawndale, but I didn't care that it was in Chicago or that it was poor, because my father was with us again. Why we were there, I don't know; my father had his Cause; I assumed it had to do with that. The calendars on the wall said 1966. We rode to Chicago, then to a street, 15th Street, and we had an apartment in a dank, dreary building, on the third floor; there was an acrid smell of old urine in the hallways downstairs. I didn't care because both my parents were there with us and it was summer and we could play all day—only for some reason there was no grass outside this building, only packed dirt of a very black sort. We would play all day and come in and Mother would say, "Look at you—black from head to foot, clothes, everything," and we were, but we thought nothing of it, other than that baths were soon taken. Many of the buildings were run-down, some were abandoned, there seemed to be issues in the community, something had happened, and I remember Mahalia Jackson singing a song that made you bob your head and clap on beat while we were playing and living, she sang about a place called "The Upper Room," as rioting, sirens, shooting, and looting jumbled all together in my head. I saw rats and roaches. I heard gunshots. I heard my mother saying, "Dexter, stay out of that window!"

In the dreams, we lived in a shoddy, cramped building in pitiful disrepair with many other poor people, although I didn't care because wherever we were in this land of Chicago my father was with us and the rest was just inconvenient for somebody else, because I didn't care, not as long as Mother and Daddy were there. This building was like those in the projects, like Egan Homes, only taller, much, and now I was living in them, we were living in them, and somebody somewhere was saying, Don't go over there by us, my family, because of where we lived; I didn't care, because here came my father through the door. There was a grocery store beneath us, and I remember seeing people break out the glass and take things; shots were fired, bottles thrown. Molotov cocktails.

Even now when I think of the "Civil Rights Movement" I think of children in war—children who grow up under siege. In my dream, and in reality, I was like what a child of war must have been. In the dream it was always summer, hot, I loved my family, we played and we prayed. I was almost killed. I darted into the street, then it was like a giant Hand pushed me in the chest and stopped me, and I came within inches of being hit by a speeding car. Then I was all alone. Everybody else was close by, but I was all alone, like the time I was all alone at the World's Fair in New York, in 1964, when I was three years old and got lost, and a policeman found me. When he brought me back I said he was lost—I wasn't lost, he was lost.

As I now know, this really happened, these were not dreams, not at first: getting separated from my father at the World's Fair, living in the hellish conditions of Lawndale—we had actually done that, and there had been rioting and shooting, and I had nearly been killed by a car. But these were not nightmares for me. Since my father was in them, they became sweet dreams.

At four years old, Bernice was not aware of what was going on. When I study the famous picture taken by the *Ebony* magazine photographer Moneta Sleet, Jr., with Bernice sitting in my mother's lap at the funeral, the Pulitzer Prize–winning picture, I don't think she has a clue. She has blanked it all out. I sat in the pew with her at the funeral in Ebenezer. I still have the visual of the march in Memphis, the procession through Atlanta from Ebenezer to Morehouse. I was there and saw the casket and later dreamed of it; saw the pulpit and people in it; they were like ghosts to me, coming for to carry him home; yet it did not impact me the way it did my siblings.

Yolanda was devastated. Martin too. Bernice asked my mother, "How is he going to eat?" Mother repeated what she'd told me. "When you see him, you won't be able to hear him speak." One of his last sermons at Ebenezer was played; Bernice could hear him; it puzzled her; in ways, she remains puzzled. As for me, it wasn't until I reached adulthood that people saw me express much emotion about anything. A child cannot understand the full meaning of life and death.

I wonder if adults can either, for that matter.

Bernice doesn't have memories of Daddy because she was so young. So it might have taken a while for her to figure out, "Hey this is over, my father is not coming back." One thing helped me and my siblings: many surrogate father figures were there to try to help bolster us, from Uncle A.D. to Uncle Andy to Granddaddy to Uncle Harry. There were many, at first.

I had no sense of knowing or noticing this, but Atlanta had stayed calm in the wake of the assassination while the hearts of many other American city centers were burned out. I had no way of knowing that this was going on across the nation, or that this would be a part of my father's legacy, this expression of pain, albeit self-destructive, the crying that never was in some, the river of tears in others. Eventually the release would come to be expressed through sound and through music. There would be this crescendo-ing national psychic scream, the Noise, the Sound, the Big Wave— it began back then. The Hop, as in hip-hop, came in later.

Some cities have yet to recover. Raleigh. Tallahassee. D.C. Bed-Stuy. Harlem. Hartford. Wichita. East Palo Alto. Mobile. Compton. Cincinnati. Kansas City. Des Moines. Chicago. Greensboro. Pittsburgh. The Bronx. Baltimore. The Twin Cities. Boston. Detroit. Philly. Memphis . . .

Eventually from out of those gutted places would come a sound and lifestyle known as "hip-hop." It all came in the wake of the emotional wave begun when my father was assassinated. But there were no conflagrations and no fires in Atlanta. The mood there was sad, not incendiary, as it was in most other African-American communities. The mood in Atlanta was heavy, but still.

Robert F. Kennedy was campaigning for the presidency. He said, "Dr. King had a life dedicated to peace, justice, compassion, and nonviolence. It is up to us to fulfill his dream."

As I said, Bobby Kennedy had chartered that American Airlines Electra to fly my father's body from Memphis to Atlanta for the funeral, which he attended. He would be assassinated himself before the summer ended. Afterward, the famous pictorial reproduction of him, his brother John F. Kennedy, and my father sprang up on the walls of homes of the black and the poor, all across Atlanta, all across the South, all across the nation, and you, if you are African American, and maybe even if you are not, maybe you grew up with that picture on the walls of your parents' or your grandparents' home.

The purple bikes? They're still at 234 Sunset. I never rode mine again. His bike is there, just as it was. Everything is. His clothes, shoes, our pictures—everything. All his possessions are preserved for a future season. His study is intact. Mother uses it. It is functional. But would we ever be functional again? It was a legitimate question, one going far beyond my immediate family.

CHAPTER 4

Aftermath

Funeral over, repast done, visitors gone home. For the survivors, the river of life goes on, but the comforting course it takes has been unalterably diverted. Extended family leaves. You're there alone. Just your mother, sisters, brother, and conscience. Mother told Martin he was the man of the house now; Martin took it to heart, causing difficulties between him, me, and Yolanda, with him suddenly trying to be the man, with no model. Looking back on it now, I can see he was trying to fulfill the duty our mother placed upon him. Then people, male figures, came in to try and fill the void, like our Uncle A.D., Uncle Andy, the grandfathers, both, really, but mostly it was Granddaddy King. What was all of this like for Mother? Her stoical demeanor didn't change. But now roles were shifting in the sense that she now became the central figure. Almost the first thing she did was germinate the idea for the King Center. She transferred her grieving into work, then immersed herself in that.

Uncle Andy suggested that after a year, maybe we should sit down with a counselor, a psychologist. He told Mother that he thought the Kennedys had done that for their children, both widows, Jackie and Ethel. He talked about taking us to see Robert Coles, a well-known educator and psychologist. He could put us on the couch. My mother said yes, she was sure Mr. Coles was nice, but the psychiatrist she trusted was named Lonnie McDonald, who practiced in New York. They were both graduates of Antioch College. She invited Dr. McDonald down on a few weekends; he spent time with us individually. I regarded him warily, decided not to tell him of my dreams, but we continued to know him, not professionally, just to know him as a family friend, over the years. Looking back, I wish I had told him about my dreams. Maybe he could've brought me out of them. But to what? The realities of 1969, the early '70s? More to the reality of how and why my dad died? As it was, we followed Mother's lead: lick your wounds, keep moving, don't question.

As she dove into work, Martin told Mother he wished he had two mothers, one who did the work my father wanted done, and one who stayed home and was a mother. Mother looked at him with love and kindness. She was torn. We'd lost our leader, yet this man who became our martyr had told us to keep moving. He'd told us he might not get there with us, but we as a people would get to a Promised Land.

It was only much later that I even began to understand a little bit of what my mother must have gone through. She was a beautiful, gifted wife, a mother of four small children, and a partner whose life course was suddenly, shockingly changed forever in an instant. She obviously had to find a way to personally make sense of her tragedy, to find her own personal peace.

Whether she was conceptualizing the Martin Luther King, Jr. Center for Non-Violent Social Change, or writing a book, or giving a speech, or talking to us about why she was keeping on, what my mother decided to do was continue a tradition of what my father was working on before his death, because she honestly believed that his principles and teachings that address the triple evils of poverty, racism, and war could help to heal America and the world. She took time off to write a book, so we were without her for a month, but other than that, the main difference was we were now having to deal with a bigger movement, an Aftermath movement. Mother was front and center. I wasn't really fully aware of, but heard about, snippets where, let's say she was being attacked by people who were really close in, but that was even probably a few years down the road. More immediately it was family only around us—family and Uncle Andy. We as a family bonded together, were taken on outings, given a whirlwind of activities that kept us distracted.

The attitude was, We don't have time to grieve. That next summer, and every summer after that, for ten years, we spent two weeks at Camp Blue Star, in the Blue Ridge mountains of Hendersonville, North Carolina, near Asheville. All four of us went, and Uncle Andy's daughters Lisa and Paula, and Uncle Ralph and Aunt Juanita Abernathy's children, and Aunt Christine's children, cousins Vernon and Darlene, and white Jewish, disadvantaged black and white kids went too. Two weeks every summer from 1969 until 1977, we were Blue Star campers, hiking in the mountains, sleeping in cabins, sitting around campfires, sliding down Eagle Rock into the mountain stream.

Bill Rothchild was my camp counselor. He later became a rabbi like his father, Rabbi Jacob Rothchild, who was a prominent rabbi in the Civil Rights Movement and whose synagogue was bombed during the 1960s because he supported my father's efforts during the Movement. The Blue Star was the Star of David.

We were taken to the Upper Peninsula of Michigan for snowskiing by Dr. Robert Green, his wife, Lettie, and their sons Vince, Kurt, and Kevin. Uncle Bob was a dean at Michigan State and had spent time working with my dad in the Movement. I remember spraining my ankle, being lifted onto a stretcher attached to a snowmobile.

I remember traveling to Lake Tahoe, in the Sierra Nevada, at the border of Nevada and California. I remember how beautiful it was. How clear. We water-skied, and went to tennis camp. I looked down into Lake Tahoe and saw fish far below the pristine surface.

*   *   *

As I've said, Granddaddy King did not believe in sparing the rod. He was a man of the strictest discipline; maybe it came from the house he grew up in, the way he was raised, the circumstances of his leaving his home and philosophically battling his father, or so it has been said. He never spoke of such things, lest it get our curiosity up. He probably would have given us a major whipping if one of us had thought about raising a hand to him to defend ourselves. We feared my grandfather growing up because he was a robust man who came up the hard way and didn't take mess. As I grew older and got to know him better, I was more appreciative of his ethics and the way he took care of business, because he did take care of business, and you could always count on him if you were in the lurch. He'd bring a certain kind of security and confidence whenever there was a problem; he was much less frightening after my father died.

Granddaddy became a surrogate father too. He was conscientious, tried not to usurp Mother. He respected the fact that I had had a father, and he had never usurped Daddy's much more gentle authority. But he was also a disciplinarian, also a man who originally didn't believe in nonviolence. He gradually was converted, and my father had converted him.

After our father's death, I noticed something I'd never noticed before. Growing up, before my father's death, Atlanta was rigidly segregated. Black and white. Period. Then, after he won the Nobel Prize in 1964, public integration began to come into being. Amazing things happened for the state of Georgia. Of all places, Atlanta, in 1970, granted a boxing license for a fight between a journeyman heavyweight named Jerry Quarry and the former heavyweight champion, Muhammad Ali, who'd been banned from the ring for refusing induction into the army in 1967, and who, as far as I could tell, many if not most white folk disliked at the time, though I was charmed when I saw him interviewed on TV. Mother took us to the fight.

I had my own experiences of dealing with race issues; it was still a pivotal period in the Movement. Debate sprang up anywhere we showed. If we showed, it started a conversation about civil rights. People felt they had to express opinions, pro or con. We couldn't go anywhere for fun or education's sake. Children my age engaged us in debates. And I was bullied by this white kid who called me a nigger. Technically, he spit on me first, then called me a nigger.

We'd eaten dinner out one Sunday. We would almost always go out on Sundays, over to Morrison's cafeteria in Southwest DeKalb Mall. Today that mall is patronized predominantly by blacks, but then it was predominantly white. I think Aunt Christine and Uncle Isaac went with us that day, and everybody was eating dinner and relaxing. After we would eat, they would all sit around and talk, and that's when my cousin Isaac and I would go off on our own and explore. I was around nine or ten years old at the time.

Isaac and I had bonded tighter than ever after my father passed. We explored the mall. Two white kids, bigger, older, tougher than we were, smoking cigarettes, came up to us and grabbed me by the collar; it was strange because I had never experienced direct physical contact with anybody white before unless he meant me well, like Robert Culp, or Bill Rothchild. If Martin or Isaac had grabbed me by the collar I'd have been fighting back. But purely by chance and taken by surprise, here I offered no resistance, as my father hadn't when an American Nazi Party member named Roy James interrupted an SCLC convention in Birmingham by punching my father hard in the jaw in 1962. My father had dropped his hands and had not allowed the crowd at the church where he was speaking to even touch his assailant, doubtlessly thoroughly confusing his tormentor. That was a conscious act on Daddy's part. The Nation of Islam members called Elijah Muhammad "Little Lamb," but my father's heart was actually made that way. The tenets of nonviolence went beyond tactical political reasoning with him. He knew the dangers of the world he was attempting to remake. I was a child; even as a man I could never hope to have his depth.

I had spoken to whites who weren't mean, people like Camera Man, others who respected my father; since his death, there was this climate and feeling of disassociation among the peoples of Atlanta, even as integration slowly, inexorably had its way in the society. But for somebody to grab you and then spit on you and call you this derogatory name, "Nigger!" with negative force—it was foreign, shocking. I stood stunned. I might have been charmed by Muhammad Ali, but I had no sense of defending myself physically, with my fists. The big boy offered directions: "Don't let me catch yewe all walking in this mall agin, nigger!" or something. Isaac was pulling my arm, to go back to the comfort of our family, but I was rooted to the spot in disbelief. I know bad things happen sometimes to people between races, and usually it's just the terribleness of one particular person, but often we read it across a whole race of people, and I was so young then, and in my mind I remember thinking, "Do other white people hate me too?" I knew this big boy was hating me deeply, not realizing then the complexity of just what "hate" is, how closely it is associated with need, and love. I didn't know him. When he looked at me, his eyes took in all aspects of my face; then he was spitting, grabbing me. I shut down my feelings. I felt no more.

The Jackson 5 came to do a benefit concert for the SCLC, and visited our home. We played in our basement, Ping-Pong, board games, with Michael, Jermaine, Tito. Jackie Jackson was older and talked more with Yolanda, at her insistence. The person who was responsible for them visiting was Uncle Junius Griffen, a friend of my dad's who worked in the Movement over the years, then went to Motown, worked with Berry Gordy. He and Uncle Junius orchestrated that visit, and it revitalized us, or at least it did me, because I was musically inclined, to the point of being fascinated by it; the Jackson 5 were in the process of stringing together hits of bubblegum soul, as it was called, like "The Love You Save," "ABC," "I Want You Back," "I'll Be There." Because I was drawn to music—everyone I saw was drawn to music, music is where you go when everywhere else is forbidden—this seemed great to me. Martin enjoyed it. Yolanda—nothing consoled her, it seemed to me. Bernice either, though in a different way.

We could tell people were conscious of keeping us busy—we had lots of make-busy activity, though I don't know if anyone actually said, "Let's keep the kids busy."

Vice President Hubert Humphrey invited us to the White House. The White House chef made up a cake, and served ice cream. There were photos taken of Vice President Humphrey kneeling and talking to me. He seemed a sensitive man, caring, reaching out, trying to soothe us, to help with the grieving without mentioning any grieving. There we were, in the White House, the nerve center of America, and though I didn't realize it at the time, we had kind of moved on, even if we had never really addressed Daddy's murder per se; it was not uncomfortable for me being at the White House, sometime in May of '68. While in D.C. we visited "Resurrection City" for the Poor People's campaign and came back in June for the rally on the Mall.

We were always around high-profile situations throughout my life after that; we've been invited to the White House under six presidents. Another pivotal event to me came in 1972, at the Democratic National Convention. It was my first appreciation of the political process. At age eleven, I remember the details of going to Miami Beach, riding in little boats. I remember the George McGovern issue with Tom Eagleton, the VP candidate McGovern pulled in, who had to step down because of the questions about his psychiatric treatment. It made me think of Dr. McDonald, and being glad I had not told him about my dreams. McGovern was also kind to us, although I didn't sense the same connection as with Humphrey. Humphrey, I could tell, was truly, deeply, mournfully sorry. There was something instructive about Humphrey's sorrow too. Something regretful. McGovern's was different—more pity. Eagleton was aloof, distracted. He'd gotten electroshock therapy, someone whispered. These historical events stuck out. I felt blessed and appreciative that we were there. A lot of times people say, "Leave your kids at home." I'm thankful we were exposed to these processes early and continuously. And it started to have an impact on me. These were the kinds of places that my father had died for me to have the right to go to. And maybe not just to go there, but . . . what else? What else should I do once I get there, Daddy?

Marvin Gaye's album *What's Going On* was released in the spring of '71, with meaningful songs—"What's Going On," "Inner City Blues," "Mercy Mercy Me." They make me think of times after my father's death, not just in our house but everywhere, it seemed. People embraced the Sound. The Wattstax festival happened at the L.A. Coliseum in '72. Isaac Hayes was Black Moses; his statements were *Hot Buttered Soul*, and from the *Movement* LP, "I Stand Accused." He won an Oscar for the score to the Gordon Parks movie *Shaft*. Vietnam remained a bloody quagmire.

A lot was going on beneath surfaces. The early '70s were poignant; music marked the time and the emotion. Music was a comfort—maybe my only comfort. There was no pressure or disappointment from Mother. She was always our champion in terms of saying, "This is your life, so go do what God calls you to do. Be yourself. Live." These are the same values my father instilled. My granddaddy King probably was disappointed in me, but it was never to a point where I felt threatened or coerced, like, "I've got to do something, or else."

You see, our grandfather always made it very clear he wanted all of his boys, "grandboys," grandsons, to preach. And he'd ask me all the time. It got to a point where it was a running joke. He'd say, "Son, have you heard the Call yet?"

I'd say, "No, Granddaddy. But I think I heard a whisper."

And then he'd crack up, and I'd breathe a sigh of relief. "If your heart is not in it, if it's just expediency, don't do it," he said. I think he genuinely respected honesty. Certainly he wanted to see his "grandboys" in the ministry. Neither my brother nor I went that route. I don't think it was rebellion, I just think we had other interests, lived in a different time, dreamed different dreams.

My grandfather never mentioned being "called" to Bernice. Again, as God would have it, the person who, in my own humble opinion, was the least likely candidate, probably has benefited the most from spirituality. Bunny. Growing up, she'd always been shy, introverted. Could hardly get anything out of Bernice growing up. She was quiet and kept to herself, especially after Daddy died. Now you can't shut her up. These days I'll joke with her sometimes and say, "We couldn't get you to talk then; now you're like the spiritual version of CNN."

Back then she needed her silence to deal with her own baggage and issues. Maybe her introspection brought her closer, spiritually, to Daddy's legacy. I identified spiritually, but not necessarily from a religious or institutional perspective. I never wanted to wear the robes. I believe all of us have a pulpit. Your pulpit can be in a different place—a nontraditional setting. The trick is, you just have to find it. Life's kind of odd that way.

I think circumstances forged all four of us, melded us into one—or one good one, one whole one, if you will. I don't want to say we built a wall around us, but we weren't kidders anymore, as gregarious. That doesn't mean we didn't like having fun, but a combination of tragedy and always being front and center in the spotlight—any child growing up in a church where the parent is the pastor feels that kind of spotlight. All of us developed this caution, this reserve, that affected our closest interpersonal relationships. Such as they were.

Around this time, my cousins started calling me "Count." Short for Count Dracula, meaning Dexter could sleep; a lot of my sleeping would occur during the day, and at night it might not.

Don't know why I slept so much in daylight hours. Don't know where that came from. Maybe the dreams. Mother, while concerned about my sleep patterns, had her own dream. In the aftermath of our father's assassination she gave birth again, this time to the idea of creating a memorial to my father, an institution she called "a living memorial," one that would not be static, not just brick and mortar and that's all, but something to have a problem-solving aspect, to reach people, to perpetuate my father's philosophy, work, and legacy. It was an ambitious vision. It was called the Martin Luther King, Jr. Memorial Center. Initially, it was run out of the basement of our house at 234 Sunset. Mother had conceived it, and immediately she ran with it.

A few years later, the board changed the name to the Martin Luther King, Jr. Center for Non-Violent Social Change, at Mother's insistence, with an emphasis on nonviolence, training, education, and research. Mother had talked to my father during his lifetime about creating an institution that could serve as the repository for his papers and also be a headquarters where he and his staff and followers could deal with policy issues. The seed was planted during his lifetime, but it became even more important and fulfilling for her after he died.

There was this urgency in her we could sense, to create a memorial, to institutionalize his work. It all slowly began to happen. Of course, she had the instrumental support of most of her family and friends. There were some who thought she would never get it done.

At first it was a matter of raising grant money and getting corporate donations. Jimmy Carter, by then president of the United States, was instrumental in helping that along. The Ford family in Michigan also was instrumental, and I felt privileged in retrospect to have been a part of some of those first meetings, as early as 1978. I traveled with Mom to some of these fund-raising luncheons, capital-funds drives. I went to Dearborn, Michigan, to a luncheon hosted by Henry Ford and representatives from the DuPont foundation. Members of the wealthy philanthropic community were there. Ford chaired this capital-funds campaign and President Carter hosted a White House kick-off reception. While at the Ford meeting, I had a feeling, like I did before at the White House after my father died—a feeling of understanding that this

was what my father had died for, this access. Something was trying to dawn in my mind—something to do with the way people,
particularly these people, were.

I did not know at the time the history of the Atlanta University Center, how John D. Rockefeller's largesse built Spelman College, starting in 1882, when it was only an idea for an Atlanta
Female Baptist Seminary. Spelman was the family name of Rockefeller's wife, Laura, a Cleveland, Ohio, native who'd known So-
journer Truth and who'd been instructed by two of the four original
teachers at Spelman. Rockefeller noblesse oblige continued for
forty-five years. The AU Center spun out of Rockefeller-Spelman
philanthropy; dollars kept coming in to fund the growth of all the
campuses, particularly Spelman, after Rockefeller's wealth later attracted the attention of the Internal Revenue Service. This was
long, long before Bill Cosby and his wife, Camille, became wealthy
African Americans, and made multimillion-dollar donations to
Spelman.

So Mother's meeting with wealthy patrons to get support for
an institution starting in the basement of her house was history repeating itself. Although I didn't know it, there was wisdom in
Mother's fund-raising technique. She always included us in
processes. I was photographed with famous visitors who dropped
in to see us after the nascent King Center moved from the basement of 234 Sunset to the basement of the ITC, the Interdenom-
inational Theological Center, a few blocks away at the AU Center.
She was using space in their facility. It wasn't the King Center yet,
but even then we received visitors on a personal level. There's a
photo of me talking to Mother in her office, taken around '71. Marvin Gaye is there visiting with her. I can still hear his lyrics from his
immortal album, done in the wake of my father's death:

Mother, mother, there's far too many of you crying
Brother, brother, there's far too many of you dying

Though immersed in her work, Mother made time for us. She was still our mother, a working mom, and understood as a single parent the importance of playing both roles, sensitive to what Martin had said to her about wishing he had two moms. When she was gone, she made sure we had Uncle Andy, Aunt Jean, Big Mama, Uncle A.D., Aunt Naomi, Aunt Christine, Uncle Isaac, Aunt Fran Lucas, the late Aunt Fran Thomas, and my mother's sister, Aunt Edythe. And then there was the multifaceted Mr. Horton, who helped in many ways over time.

Martin and I got minibikes. Motorized mopeds. Mine was home-rigged and a hand-me-down from Martin. My brother got a Honda 70. He led. I followed in his footsteps. Mr. Horton helped us with the engines if they acted up. He ran errands, commiserated over skinned knees. He was quiet and retiring, yet always there for us. He had us work around the house. Chores. He managed the process. Mr. Horton managed the grounds, and managed us too, in a way, and did it very well. Mother had to be out of town often. So Mr. Horton would pick us up, drop us off, listen to us, do for us. Definitely after my father died, Mr. Horton was instrumental in dealing with the day-to-day.

However, before any kind of normal routine could be established, tragedy struck again.

CHAPTER 5

A Question of Faith

That's one small step for man . . . one giant leap for mankind."

Alfred Daniel King, Sr., Daddy's younger brother, died a little more than a year after my father was assassinated. Uncle A.D. drowned in his backyard swimming pool on July 21, 1969, nine days before his thirty-ninth birthday, less than forty-eight hours after Neil Armstrong walked on the moon, a week removed from the Ted Kennedy/Mary Jo Kopechne Chappaquiddick incident.

Uncle A.D. had taken my siblings and me to Jamaica for that July weekend, and two of his own five children. We'd all looked forward to it. I remember the islanders' melodious voices sounding like Geoffrey Holder—"Welcome to Jamaica, your new i-land home"—and Uncle A.D., saying, "Watch out for the jellyfish, now!" He went with us but he went back to the mainland early, to preach a sermon that Sunday. Monday, the next day, was his oldest son Al's seventeenth birthday. It was Al who found Uncle A.D. that Monday morning, floating in the backyard pool.

Uncle A.D. was a Baptist minister too. He came to co-pastor at Ebenezer and help my grandfather after Daddy was killed.

My cousin Alveda, eldest of his and Aunt Naomi's five children, didn't agree with the accidental drowning report. Uncle A.D. had been very vocal about his questions regarding my father's death. My sisters and brother and I didn't give it much thought. When I heard the name "James Earl Ray" I averted my eyes; consciously or not, my sensory equipment shut down. Not Uncle A.D.'s.

"There's more to this than meets the eye, and one day God will judge it all," Uncle A.D. said anytime the subject of my father's murder was broached. We had gotten to the point where we didn't broach it out loud. But we looked forward to Jamaica. Uncle A.D. had taught Alveda and the rest of his children—Al, Derek, Darlene, and Vernon—how to swim. He'd been on the swim team as a young man at Morehouse College, in fact was the number-one-ranked swimmer on the team. My siblings and I leaned on Uncle A.D. Now he was gone too, prompting a disconnect between me and any adult males. What was the point in connecting with someone who was dying soon?

We were still in Jamaica when we found out Uncle A.D. was dead. Aunt Naomi was with us. It was traumatic for everyone, but at that point, there was less of me there to be traumatized. We all had withdrawn, some more than others. Me more than Yolanda, Yolanda more than Martin, let's say, and Bernice far more than me. But we could relax with Uncle A.D. and Aunt Naomi, be young children again, not so somber or fearful or filled with these strange but seemingly necessary feelings of formality. We were with him on the beach, swimming in the ocean. I'd gotten stung by a jellyfish, a Portuguese man-of-war. My uncle brought me out of the water, and tended to me.

"The Reverend A. D. King, brother of Martin Luther King, was found dead in an in-ground swimming pool in the rear of his Atlanta home . . ." "Just over a year after Dr. Martin Luther King, Jr., was assassinated at a Memphis motel, A. D. King was found in his underwear, floating face down . . ."

Outside Atlanta, Uncle A.D.'s untimely death barely caused a ripple of attention. But inside our family, it was a nightmare. Alveda always suspected foul play of some kind or another.

Uncle A.D.'s death was officially ruled accidental by the Fulton County coroner.

Alveda never bought it for a second. She had sat up with him watching television the night before he died. She said he'd been unusually quiet; you know the saying—it was more like TV was watching him. Then she finally went to bed. It was mysterious, because a man who loves to swim doesn't drown in his own pool. When the paramedics arrived, she noticed there was no water in her father's lungs, suggesting foul play. Much later on, she and Jeff Prugh, a locally based reporter, later an editor at the *Marin Independent Journal* in Novato, California, went to the Fulton County coroner's office and found no medical examiner's notes on Uncle A.D.'s death. They were told, "Dr. Dillon [the medical examiner] had a bad habit. He kept it in his head."

My uncle had been investigating my father's death. We hadn't finished grieving for our father; it was hard to believe Uncle A.D. was gone too. Uncle A.D. had become one of our surrogate fathers. He'd take us places. We spent time with his children, who were close to our age. Vernon—named for his father's first pastorate, Mt. Vernon First Baptist Church in Newman, Georgia—was fun to be around: he made you laugh. Daddy liked to swim too; he'd taught me how to swim, but he was nowhere near as good as Uncle A.D. Alveda was nearly grown at the time, maybe eighteen. I was eight. Vernon cried hard. They were all devastated by the loss of their father. Until this day, Alveda, as a grown woman and mother of six, and as a former Georgia state legislator, Mrs. Alveda King Tookes, I still don't believe she's recovered. You never recover.

Burial plans were once again made at Hanley's Bell Street Funeral Home, and another King man was buried. We had to keep on living—that much was not open to speculation, theorizing, or wondering why. We had to keep living, keep forging on. It had to be difficult for my Aunt Christine, who'd lost both her brothers, and for Big Mama King and Granddaddy, Daddy King, M. L. King, Sr., who had lost both of their sons.

I don't remember Aunt Naomi's reaction when she was told of Uncle A.D.'s death. That was kept away from us. I only remember swimming in the ocean with Uncle A.D.; little lizards, like geckos, running around where we were staying, then running around inside me, it seemed. Little things crawling all over the place. Then people scurrying. Then the word Uncle A.D. was dead.

Isaac said his mom totally lost it when she found out. I hurt for her. Both her brothers dead in a year: Daddy, now my Uncle A.D. But the manner in which Aunt Christine had lost it scared Isaac. I never saw Aunt Christine or my mother lose it emotionally when they'd gone through this with my father just the year before, then . . . Aunt Christine found out at 234 Sunset. She and Isaac were in our basement. Mother was maintaining the space where the idea of the Martin Luther King, Jr. Center for Non-Violent Social Change started.

Uncle A.D.'s death damaged us all. But what really affected my spirit in an adverse way was what happened to Big Mama less than five years later.

Time had passed after my father's death and the death of Uncle A.D. We had watched our mother move the operations of the Martin Luther King, Jr. Center for Non-Violent Social Change from our basement to the basement of the ITC, then finally next door to my father's birth home, 501 Auburn Avenue, where my great-grandfather A.D. and his wife, Jennie Williams, had lived, and where their only surviving child, Alberta Williams King, Big Mama, had grown up, where she and my grandfather spent their lives until Granddaddy got a house a few blocks away on Boulevard. For the first four years of my life we lived in a house on Johnson Avenue that was down the street from where Granddaddy and Big Mama used to live.

The years between 1969 and 1974 passed with music in my

head and my head hung down. Any extroverted tendencies I might have entertained had been obliterated. I was paralyzed by the actions and potential actions of a world gone insane. Only music soothed my mind and soul and heart. Only music could get through to me.

Martin and I rode our minibikes around Vine City. The Jackson 5 had that string of hits to keep us attentive to Motown. Aretha Franklin sang "Ain't No Way" and "Chain of Fools" on radio stations WAOK 1340 AM and WIGO 1380 AM; I spun the dial and heard the Staple Singers—Daddy had loved Mavis Staples's husky contralto. I heard Sly and the Family Stone doing "(I Want to Take You) Higher," "Everyday People," "Thank You (Falettinme Be Mice Elf Agin)." Earth, Wind and Fire doing "That's the Way of the World," Seals and Crofts, then the Isleys, doing "Summer Breeze."

Being in Georgia, I began to watch the football served up to us every Friday night at high schools, every Saturday afternoon for colleges on TV, pros on Sunday. We had pro teams in Atlanta, but it was all about the Kansas City Chiefs, then the Pittsburgh Steelers winning a string of Super Bowls in the early '70s by playing players from historically black colleges like the ones around the corner from our backyard. The great baseball player Roberto Clemente was killed in a plane crash while delivering relief to disaster victims in Nicaragua in 1972. In 1974, Hank Aaron, from Mobile, in our mother's home state of Alabama, hit his 715th home run at Atlanta's Fulton County Stadium to beat Babe Ruth's record. I was thirteen, had no idea of the volume of hate mail he'd received or the kidnapping threats against his daughter, then attending Fisk University. I watched *Soul Train*, heard the Watts 103rd Street Rhythm Band doing "Express Yourself," one-hit wonder Bloodstone performing the ethereal tune "Natural High," Marvin Gaye and Kim Weston and then Tammi Terrell having a string of duets—"Your Precious Love," "Ain't Nothing Like the Real Thing." I saw blacks begin to pepper the Southeastern Conference varsity football teams on Saturday afternoon football games, even at the universities of Alabama and Georgia. Watching football was where I lost Martin. He wasn't interested. He was three years older. Three years is a lifetime at that age. Yolanda went to college— Smith. Bernice was turning eleven. Granddaddy was still in the pulpit.

Six years had gone by since my father's murder. On Sunday June 30, 1974, we happened to be together at church, me, Isaac, and Vernon, Uncle A.D.'s youngest. We were at church, dodging the unswerving eye of Granddaddy, who was still measuring us for a collar, while we were not seeing a deep, lingering sadness in him. Across Jackson Street from Ebenezer, there is a strip mall, where there were and are small stores. We were in a store called Carter's. We frequented it on Sundays for candy, novelties, and such. This was our habit. We'd go over there between Sunday school and church, get a few goodies, then make our way into church, Vernon, Isaac, and I, not as serious in our religious intent as my cousins Derek and Al, Uncle A.D.'s two eldest boys, or even as serious as Martin. Rev. Calvin Morris, from New Jersey, was guest minister that morning. Cousin Derek was seated in the pulpit. Aunt Christine and my grandfather were sitting in the first pew to the right, facing the pulpit, smiling, nodding, humming, as my grandmother, Alberta Williams King, "Bunch" (short for "Bunch-o'-goodness"), as my grandfather called her, played the Lord's Prayer on the organ.

I can remember that even from the novelty store across the street I could hear my grandmother playing—but I can't be sure.

Suddenly someone ran into Carter's hollering, "Mr. Carter! You got a gun?!"

". . . Wha?"

"They're shootin', they're shootin' over in the church!"

We raced over to the sanctuary. As we ran up the steps, what we saw was like remnants of a rummage sale: handkerchiefs, a shoe, pocketbooks, a jacket, all lying on the steps. We proceeded into the church and my eyes went directly to the pulpit. Just outside it, I saw my grandmother lying there, her head propped up in someone's lap; she was conscious. I ran toward her, but many someones—deacons—grabbed me. I was trying to get out of their grip, but it was no use. I could feel the flinty strength of their old arms and hands. I was in a vise.

I saw the blood all over her.

My cousin Derek was at the time a theological student. Granddaddy was not in the pulpit when the shooting started. He was sitting in the pew preparing to leave the service early, to fly out of town for a speaking engagement. He wasn't in the pulpit but he was still in the church. And so was this wild-eyed young black man, who was named Marcus Wayne Chenault. Chenault was a young man of medium build and complexion, with a big Afro. He wore glasses. His eyes were crazed. Insane. He had arrived in Atlanta that very morning from Ohio, by interstate bus, then proceeded directly to the church from the bus station. Apparently he had composed a list of other people from outside of Atlanta whom he also planned to murder, mostly black ministers, religious leaders. His goal in Atlanta was set, and grim—he came to assassinate my grandfather first. Marcus Wayne Chenault was a disturbed man, a pure lunatic, an antireligious and anti-Christian fanatic.

By fate, Chenault's path crossed first with my grandmother. She was a sweet woman. All I know is, I always felt so special around her. I didn't have any special name for her other than we all called her Big Mama. Everybody in our family called her Big Mama, and she was clearly the one who was the behind-the-scenes mover and shaker of her family. She got us together as a family. She was Big Mama to everybody even beyond the King family— Big Mama of Ebenezer. I felt special around her even though she had ten other grandchildren. She'd always call me to do things. I was made to feel handy as a kid. I could fix things, became industrious with my hands. Could take things apart, put them back together. Anytime she had a mechanical problem, she'd call me to come and repair whatever was broken for her, and one of my older cousins might come pick me up and take me over to Collier

Heights because Big Mama was sending for little Dexter—particularly after my father died.

I would often stay with my grandparents. Even if I or we were staying with Isaac, over at Aunt Christine's and Uncle Isaac's, we'd always go down to Big Mama's. As I've said, my grandparents lived within walking distance of Isaac's family in Collier Heights. Isaac and I spent the night there many times, particularly after my father died. I don't want to alienate anybody by saying I was Big Mama's favorite grandchild, but I felt she appreciated my handiwork. I sensed she had a lot of faith in me, too. I don't know why she would, I don't know what it was she saw.

More heartache—more, because I was not there, or not quite handy enough, when she was killed. I was there, but not physically in the sanctuary. I still feel heartache until this day. I told you how Isaac and I sometimes would be out on walkabout, most of the time, I would say, removed from the church service, the morning worship, doing our own thing, and this particular Sunday was typical—we were not in the main sanctuary and . . . I don't know why. Maybe I'm glad I wasn't there, too. I vacillate. But I felt and still feel guilty for not being there; it may be I could have done something, prevented it. But then there is another side of me which says that if I had been there, what degree of additional trauma would I have now if I had tried and failed to stop it, and only saw it happen in front of me, while being helpless? It was enough trauma being on the periphery. If I had been in there, like some of my cousins were . . .

Derek was in the pulpit. He was the third child of Uncle A.D. and Aunt Naomi. Marcus Wayne Chenault, sitting in a pew next to my grandmother, turned and shot her, then jumped up saying, "I'm taking over here this morning!"

Then he continued shooting.

He had come to Sunday school earlier that morning and blended in with the congregation. He sat through Sunday school. The only thing people noticed was he had a briefcase. Inside it were two .38 caliber handguns and ammunition. As the service started, with my grandmother playing the Lord's Prayer, he sat down by her. My grandmother was director of the choir and was always there to conduct and lead the music. The organ was between two pews. He was on the right side of her. He started shooting, jumped up, then said those words. Initially, people didn't know what it was, exactly. Some thought the organ might have backfired. People didn't react quickly because they were bowed in prayer. Then they heard the gunshots, and, not anticipating hearing guns in such a setting, looked up in shock and saw what was happening. By then, three people were already shot. Deacon Edward Boykin mortally wounded. But Big Mama . . .

Chenault had jumped up and started shooting people, then up in the air, into the ceiling; he'd turned and shot Deacon Boykin point-blank in the chest, then shot Mrs. Jimmie Mitchel, who was sitting in the same pew. She was injured, but she lived. Derek jumped out from behind the lectern up in the pulpit and dove toward Chenault without any thought or hesitation whatsoever. Chenault saw Derek coming at him, leveled his pistol, and pulled the trigger twice. *Click, click.* Misfire.

Chenault reached to get ammunition to reload. By then, Derek and some deacons were on top of him, Derek's fists hurtling into Chenault. Derek did a good job of subduing him, screaming at him at the same time. All the frustration and anger poured out of Derek then. His Uncle M.L., gone, his father, A.D., gone, now Big Mama, gone, shot right there in church. The remaining deacons who weren't holding my grandfather back on one side of the church and me and Isaac on the other, got to Derek, in the process of beating Chenault into submission. If the deacons hadn't pulled Derek off Chenault, there might have been another murder in the sanctuary.

Isaac and Vernon and I tried to get to Big Mama but were held back by a sea of gnarled hands—it seemed they weren't attached to bodies even though I knew they were. Seemed I was trying to move in outer space—everything was slow, muffled.

By then, my head had swiveled toward my grandfather, far off on the other side of the pulpit. He was bound by the restraining arms of the remaining deacons, but still so strong that he was moving the whole pile of them. "No! Don't make me leave Bunch! I can't leave here without Bunch!"

The deacons said, "No, no, no, Reverend King, you'll get hurt." He was the type of man not to care. "I got to go get Bunch!" I can still hear him. They were restraining him, but barely—Granddaddy was a big barrel-chested man, country strong, particularly with the adrenaline pumping crazily like it was then. The look on his face seemed to say, "If something happens to her then my life is not worth living."

I know that's what he felt. He said so later.

We raced to Grady Hospital. Aunt Naomi rode with Big Mama in the ambulance. We walked into the ER, then the OR, as if compelled, as they wheeled Big Mama in. They began working on her on a long white table. We all stood there while they operated; a nurse shooed us out saying, "Please, let the doctors work." My grandfather, Isaac, and I went over to see Chenault, who also had been brought to Grady for treatment. Even though he was in custody, we were allowed access; this may not have been the wisest thing. We waited for Granddaddy to make a move. Once, when Granddaddy was a boy in Stockbridge, Georgia, a cruel landowner beat him up for refusing to fetch water while he was carrying a bucket of milk and butter for his mother, Deliah. He'd gone home bloodied. When his mother saw this, she asked him who did it, went down to the white man's farm, jumped on him by the barn, fought him, drew blood. He told her to get off his land. She said, "You can kill me, but if you harm one of my children, this is my answer." A mother this physically brave was an inspiration to Granddaddy.

But now I heard him asking the murderer of his wife, this Marcus Wayne Chenault, a question. Looked him right in his face and said, "Why did you shoot my wife, son?" Called him "son."

That stunned me. I looked at Granddaddy, usually so stern. A lot had gone out of him.

Chenault said, "I came to get you, and when I get out of here, I'm going to get you."

My grandfather said, "Son, I'm going to pray for you. You need help." He forgave him. I witnessed this. And this began then to work on me, set a subconscious tone for things later in my life. I believe this moment was the culmination of the non-violent influence of our father on Granddaddy's life, his conduct, his sensibility.

My feelings then were in direct conflict with the way I was brought up by my parents. When my father was killed, my mother said, "You know, Dexter, you shouldn't hate people. The man who did this was sick. And this is a sick society. But you must learn to forgive. Not to forget, but to forgive. You must. Or you will become bitter."

My father forgave Izola Ware Curry, who stabbed him with a letter opener in the chest and almost took his life in a Harlem department store while he sat autographing books. The stabbing weapon was a quarter inch away from his aorta; had it pierced the aorta, he would have drowned in his own blood. My grandfather didn't know his wife was dead, not at that moment with Marcus Wayne Chenault. Only that it didn't look good. Chenault turned his head to the wall.

We all walked back to the OR. They told us they couldn't do any more.

The pain made him grimace, wince, moan, and wheeze. He aged a decade in one afternoon. I saw him do it. I was thirteen. This traumatic experience helped shape my future—to see my grandfather this way, to have heard him say what he said to Chenault. At the moment he said it I didn't understand it at all. I didn't understand what was so bad about bitterness. Sometimes bitterness might leave a good taste. I wasn't alone in my confusion. Isaac lost it emotionally. He began questioning the doctors.

"Y'all didn't do all you could do! Y'all know y'all didn't . . ."

I tried to calm Isaac. No good. He looked at me. "What's wrong with you, Dexter? He killed Big Mama!" He tore away from me. We went to where her body was on the table and said our good-byes. It was sad. But I didn't cry. People said something was wrong with me because I never cried in those moments. Only Bunny never questioned it. Isaac was crying, Vernon was crying, Derek was crying, Martin was crying. I understood what was going on in terms of what death meant. I had been in close proximity to this latest murder, yet I was just kind of . . . detached.

Was I feeling guilt, anger, sadness, fear? Guilt. And later, even more guilt. I kept thinking, "If only I had been there. So stupid! If only we hadn't gone to Carter's between Sunday school and Morning Worship, if only I'd been more like my father, or even more like Derek . . . If I'd been there, maybe I could have done something." I lapsed into the dream state again, where I was there, and I saw Marcus Wayne Chenault pulling out the .38 pistol, and I leaped through the air and caught the bullet meant for Big Mama. I caught it in the chest . . . but there was no pain . . .

A short time later we gathered in my grandmother's house, the family gathering place there in Collier Heights. We were all there—those that were left. M.L. Sr.'s and Big Mama's progeny, the families of their sons, M.L. Jr. and A.D., and their daughter. Christine. There were Alveda, Alfred Daniel, Jr., Derek Barber, Esther Darlene, and Vernon Christopher—my Uncle A.D.'s and Aunt Naomi's children; Isaac Newton Farris, Jr., and Angela Christine Farris—the children of Aunt Christine and Uncle Isaac; then us— Yolanda, Martin III, me, and Bernice Albertine, children of Martin Jr. and Coretta. Uncle Andy Young was looking at Granddaddy in shock. How could he not be broken? We gathered at the river, the home of my father's parents. I stared at photos—Granddaddy, Big Mama, Aunt Christine, Uncle A.D., and "Uncle M.L.," as my cousins called my daddy. Three of five were gone violently. What kind of man wouldn't ask God, "Why?"

Later I said this to Mother, but instead of the shock and revulsion I expected from her about this blasphemy, she merely nodded and said, "Your father went through it."

Went through what? I asked. Questioning God? Yes, she answered.

She told me that when my father's grandmother died of a heart attack at the family home where he'd been born, 501 Auburn, he had experienced the same guilt, because he'd sneaked away to watch a parade, and he felt maybe if he had not done that, if he'd stayed at home, he might have been able to help her.

"She was the epitome of a Baptist preacher's wife," Granddaddy said of Big Mama. The question I asked was, "Why would a loving God allow this? Why would God, if God was good, take a woman everybody loved? She threatened nobody's way of life, harmed no one." We knew Daddy had enemies. Even if my grandfather had been shot—I would have been more prepared.

What really set it off was when my little sister Bernice said what I was thinking: "If you're not safe in the church, where else are you safe? If you can't go to church and not worry about getting killed, where can you go?" The experience was horrific for my family, particularly, as I recall, for Bunny, who was already in a shell. Damage had been done to me; my grandmother had been the glue of my life.

We went into the master bedroom, the family and Uncle Andy, for three or four hours. There we fleshed it out, our emotions, fears, frustrations. It wasn't heated—no confrontation between anybody in the room. It was purely emotional. Just wave upon wave of it. And so many tears. A river of tears, for it wasn't just Big Mama being mourned. Uncle A.D. and my father too. I can still hear the wailing, still feel the heat rising up in my throat choking me, taking my breath.

But no tears came from me. Not from Dexter. I couldn't figure out how this could happen to such a sweet person, how she could die such a violent death. Her faith was strong, and her belief in us was as strong, and her fellowship was strongest. The abrupt loss made us all question ourselves most of all. Near the end of the four-hour session, my grandfather said, "I think— I think that I have to—we have to—forgive this, and forgive this man. Even this. Do you all follow me?"

I thought, "No sir, I don't." But I said nothing.

There was uncomfortable silence around me, then a soft "Yes" and "Yes sir, Daddy" and "Amen, Granddaddy." As he prayed, you could feel trembling, hear wracking sobs—but also feel the bond. When he'd finished, Granddaddy looked up, beyond us, and said, "Now I want you all to leave. Leave me now. But remember, don't let anybody make you hate."

In time, my grandfather's way and words that evening helped us overcome useless feelings of vengeance. Even though I didn't realize it at the time, hearing him say, "I cannot hate this man," moved me. I had to honor that. Uncle Andy was there for support, advice, and consent; the sentiment from them both was, "You can't let him bring you down to the point of hatred. I can't hate this man. You can't either." This was more like my father than my grandfather. My father had a profound impact even upon his own father. Even long dead, Daddy was still our Rock of Ages.

I felt for my granddaddy because he had lost two sons. First-born son and namesake: gone. Second-born son: gone. Wife: gone. All gone, within a six-year period.

He said, "I'm here for y'all." Then he switched, was talking like he wanted to go "to his reward," as he termed it. "Maybe my work is done and I need to go on home." Then, a reversal again: "But now I've thought on it. I still have you. I have my daughter, my grand-children to live for." And so he did live on for us, for ten more years. One of his sisters, Woodie Clara, came and lived with him the next year and cared for him. As we were leaving that night, he said, "Keep the faith, and keep looking up. Also be thankful for what you have left." If he could say that—I can't measure his suffering, and if he, an elderly person, not as physically strong as he once was, could endure this, have it taken out of him like that and still have faith and move on, then the least I could do was move on too. But as what? To what?

CHAPTER 6

Soul Survivor

For the next several months, Bernice would stare at pictures in our family photo albums, then tilt her head toward me birdlike and ask, "I wonder who's next?" She also developed these notions in her mind that she was supposed to be this perfect person now. Which you cannot ever be. It was like a setup, really. My father was the standard for all of us to live by and live up to. He became the standard because he was so exceptional in so many ways. But how can you live up to the standard that by definition is so rare, so exceptional, that it is only met by a once-in-a-lifetime human being?

My mother says that when Bernice was born, my father said Bernice would be the most well-adjusted. Bernice articulated for me these unspeakable feelings of dread. I couldn't get mad at her or impatient with her, for I'd had the same feelings. First Daddy. Then Uncle A.D., who had taught Bernice to swim. Then Big Mama. Bunny said she started to think that death was after my family. She'd sit there on the living room couch, look at pictures, and try to figure out who was next.

I myself was preoccupied with death for a long time. And

Bunny's preoccupation helped drive mine; I thought about her when I took a job at the Hanley's Bell Street Funeral Home.

I ended up working there, in 1977—at the funeral home that had buried my father. I was afraid of death, so maybe I needed to get closer to it, put myself in an environment where I could better understand it. Instead of running from it, run to it. And that was my way of addressing my fear of death, getting a job working in the funeral home. My Uncle A.D. had conducted services with the same funeral home once upon a time; I didn't know that until I got the job.

At that time, Hanley's buried many members of Ebenezer. The proprietors were members of Ebenezer, and my grandfather encouraged patronizing them when the time came. They'd buried members of our family back to Granddaddy's father-in-law. It was a big deal for me to drive the hearse. I was a mortician's apprentice. I was afraid at first but kept reminding myself I was doing it to overcome my fear of death, and to explore my interest in mortuary science, so I handled the corpses and watched as my bosses filled them with fluids and dressed them so that their families would say they "looked good." Seeing them in the pre-embalmed state, I knew better. Death was ugly. And noisy. Gases would build up in the corpses, and escape through every orifice. Sometimes through the mouth. You haven't lived until you've been alone in a mortuary with a corpse sounding like it wants to breathe again. Once there was a ripping thunderstorm, dark as night in the middle of the day, and the other employees were out on call. I was alone, having a sandwich for lunch, with the squeaky ceiling fan my only company. I heard a boom from behind the door leading back to the embalming room. A tree limb banging against the shutters, or shutters slamming against the building, I thought. I took another bite of my sandwich. *Boom-bam . . . creeeeak.* For all I know, that sandwich is still on the counter. Unless whatever made that sound came out and ate it. I'm kidding, but it was serious then. I was standing outside under the awning in the rain when the hearses returned. My bosses at Hanley's had a good laugh. The experience of working in the mortuary did help me overcome my fear of death.

Jimmy Carter, the governor of Georgia, was part of our survival. I think we were part of his too—in a political sense. Traditionally, members of the King family went to every Democratic National Convention. Democratic honchos hadn't forgotten the presidential election in 1960, after my father's arrest and imprisonment, and the hand my grandfather played in the election of Senator John F. Kennedy as president. So we were invited, on the off chance that something funny might wind up happening again one day. We were invited in '72 in Miami and '76 in New York. So we went. He never took any credit for it, but Granddaddy was also helpful to Jimmy Carter's being elected president in 1976.

Governor Carter, in the run-up to the campaign, had made a public statement that almost destroyed his candidacy before it began. In Atlanta's Central City Park, he made an innocuous statement about ethnic purity that some interpreted as racist. It's not what he meant, but it came across that way. My grandfather bailed him out. Granddaddy stood up at a rally, supported him, and said, "This is a good man, so don't hold that misunderstanding against him. Don't try to repeat what he said, he had a different context." He repeated his confidence in Mr. Carter from the pulpit at Ebenezer, and the rest is history. Some inside the African-American and Jewish communities were getting ready to blister Mr. Carter behind the "ethnic purity" statement taken out of context. If those two communities hadn't voted for Carter in numbers, he wouldn't have won the 1976 presidential election.

The outcome was that my grandfather had direct access politically to President Carter. He could call him at the White House and actually get him on the phone. President Carter saw him as kind of an unofficial "adviser." If Carter had an issue of relevance to the African-American community, he would not hesitate to have Daddy King tell him what he thought about so-and-so, straight up, in that down-home southern way. Carter seemed to genuinely respect him. And my grandfather became bodacious in the heady atmosphere of this kind of political legitimacy at such a rarefied altitude. He may have forgiven Marcus Wayne Chenault, but for his remaining years he was not going hat in hand to politicians or elected officials. Not anymore. The Secret Service didn't daunt him. This all coming after Big Mama died, there was no one around to rein him in, no one he felt shy or humbled around. We were in New York City during the 1976 Democratic convention; at the Sheraton Center, going up to the Presidential Suite to see Governor Carter. He wasn't president yet, but he was a candidate and had Secret Service protection—a must for all presidential candidates since the Robert F. Kennedy assassination in Los Angeles in 1968.

Granddaddy said, "I'm here to see the governor."

The Secret Service agents sneered, as if thinking, Who is this thick old black geezer? "Sorry, no one can come through here."

Granddaddy did his thing, rolling out his name in an avalanche of syllables.

Next thing you know—"Oh, come in, Daddy King!" That Jimmy Carter has a smile on him, doesn't he? Point being, Granddaddy didn't balk at obstacles. If you know his history, what he had been confronted with in his life, all along—being in his presence and watching him operate gave me a lot of pride. One thing he taught me was, always go to the top, if you can. If you got a problem, deal with the top man, top woman, top person, top dog, the one in charge.

He had a methodology, a way of working things out so you just felt empowered, you felt confident, you felt safe. Granddaddy was a compassionate human being, would bail out people all the time. Members of the church, whoever. You know, "Give this man a second chance!" He would go down to the court, talk to the judge. He had relationships with everybody—sheriffs, judges. These were white, old-line southerners, yet they respected him. They'd come out of the Jim Crow South, but realized this was a man to be reckoned with, a man who had a large congregation. He didn't do his ministering as a threatening man; he befriended people. Watching him taught me about how to operate in a climate of tension. This lesson was invaluable to me. I didn't know how close Granddaddy was to the end of his bright path.

When he officially retired as pastor at Ebenezer in 1975, my grandfather brought in Rev. Joseph L. Roberts as pastor. William H. Gray III, Bill Gray, pastor of Bright Hope Baptist Church in Philadelphia, later a congressman and now head of the United Negro College Fund, had recommended Joe Roberts. In November of 1974, five months after Big Mama was killed, shortly after Marcus Wayne Chenault was declared insane and institutionalized, Granddaddy recommended Rev. Roberts as his successor. Rev. Roberts was raised in the African Methodist Episcopalian Church, then went to a Presbyterian undergraduate school, Knoxville College, then to Union Theological Seminary and Princeton Theological Seminary. My grandfather turned it all over to him, effectively breaking the string going back to 1894, when his father-in-law, A. D. Williams, had become pastor of Ebenezer.

No one else in our family was ready to enter the ministry, much less to assume the pulpit at Ebenezer. Derek was a student, Martin would soon wind up at Morehouse College, still trying to keep up with my mother's charge to be the man of the house. I was fourteen, with no such inclinations. My grandfather had high hopes for my cousin Al. Maybe also for Isaac. Maybe also for me. But in his wisdom he could see it would not be happening soon, if at all, certainly not before he was ready for his final angle of repose.

He couldn't leave Ebenezer at the whimsy of factions of deacons. His thoughts about a possible successor from the family stopped with the consideration of his grandsons.

My grandfather liked Rev. Roberts's preaching style. He was also impressed by academic credentials, even though he was a fire-and-brimstone Baptist preacher himself, full of cadences and emotions, and he liked the rolling thunder call-and-response of a congregation to get where he wanted to be in the pulpit. Ebenezer became a different place. It became different once Big Mama was killed. Granddaddy retired and a man I'd never seen was in line to be pastor. My father's voice, with its lifting, rolling cadences that used to warm spirits, was gone.

But other music was still there.

Music had taken root in me early on. My interest was always there, from my earliest memories. Mother's roots are in music. She was classically trained at the New England Conservatory of Music. Mother always had us in musical processes, learning to play instruments, singing. Growing up we all had piano lessons; later we all were in our school bands. And my father, well . . . his whole preaching style, coming out of the Baptist tradition, was musical, metered, mathematic, but then it was also refined by his own persona, his own ability to put things together that made sense and were lyric and epic. He was a composer.

There was a pure powerful seduction by rhythm and musicality in his speech. Later I picked up on deejaying. On one level, it was a way to commune with my peers. On another level it was a way to commune with my father. For outside my sisters, brother, and cousins, I had few peers. I was apart, distant; if this was some kind of royalty, it was accursed royalty, with violent death.

In 1974, after an acrimonious but professionally run campaign, Maynard Jackson took office as elected mayor of Atlanta. A Negro, a colored man, a black, an African American, was the mayor of Atlanta. "You're gonna make it after all . . ." I didn't consciously watch *The Mary Tyler Moore Show*, but its theme song was still in my head. Not really good music, but music still. For a long while after Big Mama was killed, it didn't look like I'd make it after all, or at all. Who cared if I didn't? I saw what the end looked like for me, in a line of caskets at Hanley's Bell Street Funeral Home.

I got kicked out of the house. By that I mean my mother did not let us rest on tragedy; we couldn't stop and lick our wounds for a long time, into oblivion, or grieve listlessly. We had to lick our wounds and keep going. She told me, "You're going to do something constructive with your time, Dexter, and you're not just going to sit around the house. Go learn something, get a job, do something." She had grown up in the deep country, where it's about earning your keep; you've got to do something constructive, to help develop values in your own head.

Also that summer there was a CETA program, where you learned a trade; kids and just about anybody were paid nominally to learn a trade, an example of a good government program. I was making $5 an hour at age thirteen to learn a trade. We all had a choice of photography, silkscreening, and brickmasonry, and a couple of other options that were so enticing that I forget them now. I took up photography, and found I could really sink my teeth into it. An organization called Southern Rural Action administered the CETA program at a school that was converted for this purpose, where you could come and learn these trades. Teaching the photography course was a high-fashion photographer from San Francisco named Clint, a black man, respected in his craft.

I met many people who went on to become today's network photographers and videographers. We learned composition, framing techniques, point of reference, background, darkroom techniques, everything. With the money I earned, I got secondhand equipment. My involvement snowballed. We'd go out on assignments. I was in this program when Big Mama got shot. Some of the young people in the program were taking photographs at Big Mama's funeral, on assignment; it was kind of weird, I went from behind the camera to in front of the camera. I didn't want to pose. I was vulnerable, as you are only when someone close to you dies. I went through trauma while also engrossed in learning a trade, meeting new people, most of them older than I was. They seemed to be sorrowful as their shutters clicked and motors whirred at the stunned faces of me and my family.

Photography was an interest, whereas music was a love. However, photography became more than just interesting when I saw I could make a bit of a living at it. It was also an escape. Go behind the viewfinder and hide. I never stopped to think of where my fas-

cination with it came from before; never even recalled my fascina-
tion with Camera Man, Mr. Flip Schulke, who would come to our
house when my father was alive and document our home life, or
who was in church that day—was it when my grandfather called
me and Isaac out, and somehow we got out of it? All I know is,
once I got my hands on a camera, it felt kind of like Bloodstone
singing "Natural High."

Soon, if you saw me without my camera, you thought something was wrong with me. It was my constant companion. And
since my other constant companion was my cousin Isaac, I brought
him in, taught him how to shoot, develop images. I built a darkroom in our basement, set it up from money I earned from the
CETA program. Soon I was spending twelve hours a day in the
darkroom. I even put a bed down there. That's how into it I was. I
would sleep in the darkroom, adding to my reputation as "Count."
I found satisfaction in being able to create something, a product, an
image. I became obsessed, fixated. Take the shot. Develop the
print. See the fruit of your labor. I used a 35mm single-lens reflex
camera—my first camera. It was secondhand, of course. We did
not have much money, nor can I ever remember us having much
money, not when my father was alive nor in the years afterward.
But I made some money with photography and had my own cash
before plowing it back into more darkroom equipment. It started
out as a hobby, but because people wanted copies and prints of
my images that I took of them, I had to start charging. As I started
charging, it became a business. I brought in Isaac. I needed help.

Soon we were overwhelmed by business. Our grandfather was
supportive of industry from his congregation, let alone offspring,
particularly his grandchildren.

"So-and-so owns a funeral home and I know y'all don't want to
support him, particularly, since everybody wants to go to Heaven,
and nobody wants to die, but we all got to go at some point, so go
see Brother So-and-so in your family's hour of bereavement need."

Or, "Brother So-and-so's got a used-auto dealership, you need
to support him." This was part of his technique of growing

Ebenezer back in the day, after my great-grandfather died in March of 1931. Hanley's Bell Street Funeral Home had handled that burial. If new members with businesses were successful, it meant bigger offerings and tithes placed in coffers at Ebenezer. It's no different now. "My grandboys Dexter and Isaac have a photo business, so when y'all have weddin's or other occasions you need photographed, call on them. Let the church say, Amen."

Soon we were shooting nearly all the weddings at Ebenezer and spilling over into other churches. Soon we couldn't handle the demand. We grew ourselves out of business. Fourteen, fifteen, and sixteen years old, and doing heavy-volume business. K&F Photographers—King and Farris—became successful. Even longtime pros around town knew us and embraced us.

Along with the photography business, I had also started deejaying at parties. It kept a little change in our pockets without us having to ask our parents. It was thrilling. Challenging too.

Music, when it came along, hit me different. More. Find a way to do what you love for a living, and you'll never work another day in your life. I don't remember Daddy saying it to me, yet when that saying comes to my mind, it comes in his voice. I recruited Isaac again, taught him to work the mixer and turntables, later how to blend. Don't ask me how, but I think I would get attracted to something and I would sink all my attention into it. I didn't understand why I had difficulty doing this with text, in class, reading history books, literature, learning all that. Anything creative, or working with my hands—that seemed natural for me. I enjoyed it.

The deejaying was an outgrowth from growing up in a musical family. I loved the swing and flow of music; I think I enjoyed seeing entertainers and entertaining people, making people respond, making them be happy. Making them feel energy. Like Daddy. Part of me needed to gravitate to feel-good things. Aretha Franklin singing "Dr. Feelgood" was a feel-good thing. Things around me were so serious. Everybody saw my dad as serious, especially after he died a martyr. And he was a serious man, but he also loved to play, to sing, to clap his hands and enjoy himself, but there were only a few places he could, because of his public persona.

Eventually the photo business dissolved and Isaac and I concentrated on K&F Sound. It wasn't a change in interest: a greater interest in music was always there. Isaac and I also had a major loss. I left equipment—larger-format cameras for portraits—in our basement. They were stolen. I don't know until this day what happened. I was going on a job, grabbed for my equipment, and—gone. I had to borrow equipment to shoot my last job. Does everybody have an experience where you think you have your belongings in a safe environment, only to find your stuff gone?

I liquidated my darkroom equipment.

I never could liquidate my ears, which even now love the sounds of music. We started out deejaying parties, but ultimately turned more to audio engineering. I loved music. I have always wanted to be closer to it. I've always wanted to recapture the feeling of when I listened to music. Listening to good music of any form—whether it be jazz, blues, big band, reggae, country, rhythm and blues, hip-hop of the best sort, or classical, which Mother insisted upon, or the finest, most moving music I ever heard, the sound of my father's voice delivering a sermon—it can tilt my head to one side and close my eyes in rapture until this day. I wanted to be a part of the process of making something like that, originating it; that was my response to what was happening around me.

Later on, I had a conversation with the late Lee Atwater, Republican National Committee chairman. Everybody was asking him why a country and blues guitar player was managing George Bush's presidential campaign in 1988. I talked to Atwater at Bush's inauguration. I happened to sit next to him. He happened to start talking. He said musicianship transcended expediencies one made for politics, he said politics was just his job. Music was his love. Being a musician helped him as a political strategist in terms of understanding how things harmonize. Anybody you talk to who's a musician can relate, from whatever point on the political compass. He seemed quite anxious for me to understand this point about his political efforts.

I was always exposed to music. Mother made sure of that. I played trumpet. Then I learned to play the bass, electric bass guitar, a popular instrument in many Baptist churches. In fact, most popular musical acts, ones with African-American talent certainly, came up out of the church, one way or another, since time began in this country. One of the members of an R&B group called Brick gave me bass lessons at Johnson's Music Studio, which was run by Cleophus Johnson, who also served as band director at Morris Brown College. I would get together with guys in the neighborhood, and then we were gigging here and there, but for some reason I did not stay with it. I think part of it was again the focus, a lack of concentration, of focusing on getting my chops in order, playing R&B and Top 40, mostly R&B, and, of course, when I was playing the trumpet, that was all kinds of music. Mother insisted that we all take piano lessons growing up, but I didn't do as well with that. I didn't stick it out, and of course now I wish I had, for the sake of composition and also reflection and private solace. Ah, most grown-ups say they wished they'd stuck with the piano lessons their parents gave them, don't they? My approach to music may not have had to do with my passion but may have been related to my strange inability to concentrate, or to stay focused, to sit there and grind it out, to practice and do the lessons. Whatever— music was my one great love.

Even at that young age, I was an old head in what was soon coming to be, the hip-hop nation. Just what is that? I would call it a phenomenon, which first was manifested audibly by the rappers up in places like the Bronx in the late '70s and early '80s— Grandmaster Flash and the Furious Five, Kurtis Blow, Afrika Bambaataa.

Then in the '80s the explosion came, where all children had to have "rhyming skills," the ability to mimic drums or other musical instruments, and also to tell a story in a metered, rhythmic, even poetic way, even though the emotions they expressed were not always about love. How could they be? These were the children of the generation of African Americans who had had the hope let out of them like the air out of a pricked balloon, with the assassination of Daddy and other people who seemed to be just trying to help them. This was the end result of all that.

This was music. Hip-hop culture later came to embrace everyone and everything from Lauryn Hill, formerly of the group the Fugees, to certain hairstyles, to clothing, to a general sensibility of life. I think that sensibility of hip-hop has to do with honesty at all costs.

Of course, I couldn't quite put it together like that back then, what was coming, in the form of this new hip-hop culture and sensibility. Neither could I even begin to imagine how it would affect me, and all of us, as Americans, or even that it was coming at all. At the time I couldn't see that it was coming, or that it would also represent and encompass me. Not just yet I couldn't.

In life, as in music, sometimes, when you're improvising, you just . . . let it happen.

One night, long ago, when Daddy was still alive, we went to Yolanda's elementary school for an event called "Great American Music Night," where different kinds of "American" music were celebrated. Only they didn't play any African-American music: no blues, gospel spirituals, R&B, jazz—nothing. My father said it made him sad. It was supposed to be an American celebration.

They ended the program by playing "Dixie."

It's funny, but I hardly remember that night at all.

CHAPTER 7

Schooled

I attended Galloway School. Isaac went over to Oglethorpe Elementary. The Galloway School was an integrated private school/academy based on the open classroom concept. Classes were not graded. You got credit or no credit. Pass-fail. A small school, it had been started by the headmaster, Mr. Elliott Galloway, whose son was an Olympic track star, Jeff Galloway. Galloway was highly rated academically. What interested my mother about this school was it was open, it was more progressive and open-minded—and it was integrated. It was always important to my mother that my father didn't die in vain, that what he'd fought for we at least lived out. That was critical to her.

So every one of us, her children, went to Galloway School, except for Yolanda. Yolanda went first to Spring Street Elementary, then to Henry W. Grady High School. Martin and I also attended Spring Street Elementary School, I for kindergarten through second grade, Martin through fifth grade. Bernice went to Galloway through seventh grade, having attended the Montessori School before that. The Abernathy kids, Ralph and Juandalyn and Donzaleigh, were still at Spring Street when we left for Galloway. I stayed there through ninth grade.

Galloway was located in north Atlanta, in affluent north Buckhead, in an area known as Chastain Park. The school was actually next to Chastain Amphitheater. At the time there were about five hundred students, K through 12. Class sizes were ten students, maximum.

Initially, Galloway was fine. It was me that wasn't so fine. Galloway lacked a certain structure I may have needed. Maybe the lacking was in me. Galloway was structured in three levels. Early, middle, and upper learning, almost the same as elementary, middle, and high school. Upper learning started at eighth grade. Once in upper learning, all bets were off; it was so open you could smoke cigarettes in class if your folks gave you permission. A lot of people called it weird.

As I mentioned, you didn't get graded. You either got credit or no credit. The upside of this was that you literally had some ten-year-old geniuses walking around doing calculus because they weren't discouraged from it. That was the upside of the freedom. The downside was that if you did not or could not self-manage, if you needed structure, your learning might suffer.

In my earlier years at Galloway, I was hanging with everybody else. I was having a little extra success in math. I liked math. I took math books everywhere. To church. I'd sit there reading algebraic equations and word problems. I loved word problems. But around seventh grade, I started losing even that math focus. This turns out to be when many black boys in general begin having trouble in the school system. There may be some general trend—society no longer sees these young black males reaching puberty as cute mascots, but as threats.

My attention span, my ability to reason and focus, was becoming more of a problem. I had anxiety attacks. Sweating. Fearing something bad was going to happen, yet not knowing exactly what, which made it worse. I couldn't sit still in a classroom and listen to the teacher—I was constantly jumping ahead or around, frustrating the teachers because I would stop their roll, ask, "Why is this, why is that?" and they would get irritated. I was treated like "the black," a special "black" kid.

African Americans had at the time progressed, if it can be called that, from "Negro" to "black." At Galloway, we were different from other blacks, to the white kids. Galloway was 98 percent white; of that number many were Jewish. But there was a feeling, gleaned from others, that I was different.

"You're a privileged black, aren't you?"

The inference was, You can't relate to these other "blacks," can you? I'd be having lunch and talking about a football game or a new record album or something and suddenly and unwillingly I was involved in commentary on "black" issues and had to defend my background. My school chums' parents obviously had said some things at home that the kids would regurgitate in school.

One of the issues at school was Maynard Jackson being elected the first black mayor. A lot of things happened in 1974. Jackson took office as the first black mayor of Atlanta. He was elected in '73, but took office in '74. He showed up at my grandfather's home to pay his respects, always with his bodyguard. My siblings and I had activities, but we never went to pistol ranges, never went skeet shooting, never went hunting. Police were integral in my development, because when you don't have a father you substitute people who are more visible who represent a male presence. Maynard's bodyguard took time to play with us. Maynard's bodyguard became chief of police. His name was Eldrin Bell. I remember admiring him. At that time he was a sergeant.

I also had met Maynard Jackson. My family knew his family, and he knew who I was, and I knew who he was. He wasn't really that close to any of us then, but there was always a cordial family respect. His family grew up here, but mainly in his younger years; he was away for some time too, then came back. He was important to me on a symbolic level. The fact that I had history with him made me feel special about him. He was much more important to me than he was to most of the kids at Galloway—or to their par-

ents. At Galloway in the seventh grade I would get into these debates with other seventh graders over them saying he was not
"qualified" to be mayor. It made the hair on the back of my neck
stand up. You're hearing twelve- and thirteen-year-olds saying,
"Well, it's a shame, he's not qualified," as if they were authorities
on political parties and pressure groups. Here I am, thirteen, defending full-grown man Maynard Jackson.

Didn't Maynard have a long history of being in the city government at that time? Yes he did. He was vice-mayor before he was
mayor, I said. On the city council, I said. Came up through the
ranks, I said. Morehouse man, I said. I said all that, to much eye-
rolling among my classmates. Those were my comebacks. Clearly,
"not qualified" was their emotional response, given matter-of-
factly, tossed off like science—science of spin. Attacking Maynard
was emotional, self-serving, not supportable by fact, primal, and
racially charged. All the stuff that would usually be ascribed to
black folks. Pot calling the kettle black. What disqualifies Maynard?

"What? . . . Well, he just isn't," they would insist.

I pointed to the skin of my own hand. "Is this what disqualifies
him?"

I was constantly getting in debates and arguments over this
kind of thing. Occasionally there might be a kid who would say the
"n" word casually, not to me, not in a charged way, but just around
me, and I would have to speak on it. Maybe twice it happened. But
it did happen.

There was this one kid—Rogers Baker Wolfe, I'll call him. He
was more maladjusted than the rest of my schoolmates. He wanted
me to feel different, to feel bad, to be inferior, and to be happy
about it.

"Hey, Dexter King, you hear about what the blaaaacks did yesterday?" Rogers Wolfe might say. As if I was responsible. When the
Atlanta child murders—the mysterious murders of twelve prepu-
bescent black boys in West End and other inner-city areas—began
at the end of the decade, I wondered about Rogers Baker Wolfe, if
he was taunting any innocent blacks about that.

At Galloway, there were a lot of affluent kids whose parents were heads of corporations, that kind of thing. Most were cooler than Rogers. I got invited to bar mitzvahs. Children who invited me into their homes came to ours. Mother said, "If you go into their homes, they come into ours."

In many ways I had both worlds, if not the best of both worlds, growing up in Vine City, a black working-class neighborhood. I had relatives in middle-class black suburbs; I was going to an avant-garde school with white children of industrialists and professionals, exposed to views that amused the white middle-upper class and drove the white working class. Most of my playmates at home were lower-income, from broken homes, but with extended-family support; by day, I was dealing with people who were from well-to-do homes economically but who might have been in broken homes emotionally or on other levels. A lot of kids I knew were dysfunctional for different reasons. I saw it all—thirteen-year-old alkies or addicts at Galloway. Drugs were in Vine City, but not the worst kind, not yet, not yet the crack cocaine that finally leveled it.

On one hand, some of my classmates at Galloway were wealthy, but on the other hand maybe their parents were not there, not hands-on. Even when families were together, they weren't together spiritually. I was exposed to kids in the 'hood who were from broken homes but were genuinely good people, spiritual people, who didn't have the means to rise and had to pin their hopes on the following generation. Till this day I feel comfortable in any environment. I could hold my own back then. I accomplished this by trying to appear calm and saying nothing. Let others make the mistakes first. Elliott Galloway always seemed to me to be an optimistic person. He was not imposing physically. Everything about him was medium. Medium height, medium build. Tweedy, just a little bit. Reminded you of an "all-American" type person. An all-American type guy who was always up, just very optimistic, very extroverted you know, kind of a cheerleader type. Loose collar. Just seemed very accessible. Could get serious too. Interactive.

When he got serious, he'd put on his glasses. Then you knew he was serious. He didn't wear them all the time.

In 1976, I transferred to Frederick Douglass High, a predominately black public high school. Nearly three thousand students attended Douglass. Martin had by then graduated from Galloway and gone to Morehouse. Bernice and I left Galloway a year after he did; I wanted to go to Douglass because Isaac went there. Bernice left Galloway because I did. Isaac was going to Douglass for his second year. I joined Isaac in entering tenth grade. Bernice went there as an eighth grader.

I also wanted to play football; there was no football team at Galloway.

For you to know how important football was to a young man at the time in Georgia, think of how important basketball is to a young man in an inner city today—then double it. Or go to Atlanta today during football season and see how much coverage is given over to high school football in editions of the *Atlanta Journal-Constitution*. The high schools get more ink than the NFL Atlanta Falcons. Then, and probably now, there was a social order and acceptance to playing football, a communal sense I desired, wanted to be a part of, wanted to experience.

My mother seemed to be open to Douglass. After all, my father had gone to Booker T. Washington High, another public high school. I don't remember any resistance one way or the other. Douglass. We knew it was a good school academically in terms of its rating; it was west, over on Hightower Road, now renamed Hamilton E. Holmes Drive after one of the two black students who integrated the University of Georgia, at the foot of Collier Heights. I think she was comfortable with Douglass because she knew my Aunt Christine would not be sending her kids to a school that was underachieving. Aunt Christine was a college professor at Spelman. Still is.

Douglass is on the west-by-northwest side of town. If you're going toward Six Flags, I-20 West. The surrounding neighborhood had an interesting mix if you could discern it; though it was nearly 100 percent black, you still had kids from all walks of life, from the projects to the wealthiest black kids in the city from Collier Heights. People also started moving into Cascade, which had been all white traditionally; white flight came when a few blacks started moving in. Pretty over there. Not built by blacks. Collier Heights was founded by blacks.

The Atlanta I grew up in at the end of the 1970s was a busy city. Growing. Since John D. Rockefeller had bought all this land on the near west side of town for Spelman, Morehouse, and Atlanta University, and since the Methodists had moved Morris Brown College from over Auburn Avenue way to the AU Center, along with Clark, the west side was different from most inner cities. The colleges themselves brought a professional class—instructors and administrators. Movement outward toward the suburbs on the west side was overwhelmingly black.

Something was always being built in Atlanta in those times. Topographically, streets changed to accommodate construction. A two-way street became one-way to accommodate growth. Highways expanded. I was always out traveling. I drove to school the spring of my last year as Atlanta turned luxuriant, verdant green. I appreciated that the city was well-kept. Clean. You didn't see a lot of trash on the streets, things that make a city seem run-down. In Atlanta, I always felt I was in a clean, fresh place and a pretty place just purely from an aesthetic point of view. In terms of attitudes . . . that was another story.

I always saw football as about being a member of a team—a way of being accepted and getting respect. I always saw the sport as a chance for a camaraderie I hadn't known for years—being able to interact on a level with my peers while growing up. In high school, I wanted to identify with others my age, not be apart from them, to be down with the fellows, the peer group. What's more important to a teenager than to act, think, and dress like those of his generation? Very little I know of. I think football gave me that.

Maybe it was a macho thing too. I know it was a tough experience; some of the players didn't readily accept me, not at first. Maybe it wasn't because I was the son of Martin Luther King, but because I was fresh meat, somebody who wanted to join and had to be initiated. They tested me because they wanted to see if I was real. I would always be tested to see if I was a real person or the saintly son of a saint; it's one of the burdens of my particular legacy. When I first got to school, the B-team defensive coach took a liking to me and put me on the squad. Coach Montgomery gave me a chance at running back and linebacker. He saw potential in me. Put me on first team. When the season ended, he brought me up to the varsity. All advanced players were brought up. The B-team was JV.

I was in tenth grade. It was the first day in the locker room with the varsity football team at Douglass High, the Douglass Astros, me, Dexter King, one of the royally cursed King children—I was a 'Stro! Just as I was feeling I was part of this great thing, here come the three biggest guys on defense. They jumped on me and basically "initiated" me—let me know who was boss. I then also found out that I could hold my own too; that sometimes when you fight back, it hurts less than if you just let someone pummel you. Afterward, through the shiners and bloody lip and everything, the smiles were warm and sincere and the experience led to a different kind of bond. After that episode there was a newfound respect in their eyes that I had earned by my own actions, not from the passive notion of being the son of the prophet of the Civil Rights Movement.

They said, "He real. He King's son, but he real. He ain't plastic. He bleeds. I seen him bleed."

I ultimately became captain of the defense as middle linebacker. Yet that awareness was always there. "Hey . . . son of Martin Luther King!"

There was no getting away from it.

Football wasn't the whole school experience, though. Not everybody rallied to football necessarily to embrace me. Some used it to ridicule me, critique me, maybe to see what I was about in responding. I was for them intriguing. Sometimes I felt humiliated; the way they'd chide me in the cafeteria or hallway. Walk down the halls and you could see them pointing, whispering, not caring to be discreet. "Martin Luther King's son," pointing. Another one would loudly say, "No it's not." "Yeah it is." "Ain't." "Bet a dollar that's him." And then they would walk over to me and stop me and say, "What's your name?" Just like that. No hello. No warm fuzzies.

I might say, "I'm Dexter, nice to meet you."

"Yeah? Dexter what?"

"King."

"You lying. Your name ain't no King. Your name King f'real?"

When I'd say, "I'm Dexter King," the other one might say, "No you're not."

"Yes I am."

"No, you're not, 'cause if you was, you wouldn't be here with us."

I'm saying, Hold it. Saying that to myself later on, after the fact, because I'm speechless in the situation as it is happening. I don't know how to respond. For the longest time I walked around thinking that in the predominately white environment at Galloway School I wasn't totally accepted, and had to debate whether Maynard Jackson was qualified, or whether Hank Aaron deserved to be mentioned with Babe Ruth, or whether black people can do math and science, endlessly proving myself, having to always take a "black position" on a "black issue." Now here I was at Douglass, thinking I'd be comfortable, only I was having to prove myself again. From then forward I realized I didn't really fit in anywhere.

Even some of the teachers at Douglass High might say, "Your father was up above all of us." I'd say, "He was one of the people." But they'd always have the last word. About my father. This would become a life trend—people telling me what my father was and wanted, having the last word about my father. "One with the people. Not one of the people." He did everything he could to have us belong, and yet people would not let us. We were trying and Mother was trying. It wasn't phony baloney. And it was a long time before I started to say to myself, "So what? So what that you don't fit in anywhere? Who does? What's so great about fitting in places that need changing anyhow?" But those weren't my thoughts back then.

That happened throughout school, into college, even today: being a part of a "living legend," as if people don't know how else to relate to you. I didn't have many peers I could hang out with because where do you find somebody else who's the son of a pope? Where do you congregate? Where do you go?

When people judge you, it's subjective. You are always being compared to this more-than-a-man, once-in-a-lifetime phenomenal presence. So who's to determine what's right and wrong about you? Nothing is right enough. Conforming was a problem. Conform to what? Compared to what? When I started deejaying parties in high school, of course people found that odd. I should be doing serious things. Couldn't do something because I was good at it or enjoyed it, but weren't these the privileges of youth? In photography, I shot the homecoming events, parades. Sometimes I'd get in trouble because I'd pass photo proofs around and end up in the assistant principal Mr. Hill's office. This gentleman later became principal at Douglass for many years. Mr. Hill took his job seriously, and more so because he had the children of Martin Luther King in his charge. He sat me down and said:

"Ah, Dexter. You know you are in violation of the Sherman antitrust act. You have a monopoly on selling photographs and you are disrupting class." And I mean, he was serious.

Photography, deejaying, and football all helped me commune with my peers. Without those activities, I might have been even more lost. I got to feel normal, even if it was from behind a camera viewfinder, a turntable, or the face mask of a football helmet. That was as close as I could get. My senior year, we won the high school football championship of our region. We were a good team, one of the top teams in the state of Georgia. We went to the state championships and got to the quarterfinals, where we lost to Griffin, Georgia. In Atlanta, our region, we were number one. High school football was significant to me; I contributed to something real; I believed my father might have been proud; I had a chance to spread my wings at Douglass, clipped as they were. I found out I was athletic. I joined the track team, and put the shot. I made the tennis team, played singles and doubles. What else could I do in life?

Since his name was Isaac N. Farris, Jr., and since he bore small resemblance to me, he could disappear. He said he had the best of both worlds, access to the world of notoriety, but at the same time he could step back from it. Especially in the earlier years. Everybody in school knew who he was, son of the sister of Martin Luther King. And things were happening. Somebody would make a death threat against us, cops would have to come to the school, things of a strange nature. Happened more than once. Who would be next?

This began in '74, before I came to Douglass. Around the time of my grandmother's death, we got a kidnapping threat. This was the era of the Patty Hearst kidnapping by the Symbionese Liberation Army in California. All kinds of kidnapping threats were going on. Hank Aaron's daughter was threatened with kidnapping while she was at Fisk, right when he was threatening to break Babe Ruth's home run record. An editor at the *Atlanta Journal-Constitution* named Reg Murphy was kidnapped. The King family got a threat. Police posed as teachers at Galloway.

We grew up in an environment of house and church bombings, shootings, murders, jailings, beatings. We were desensitized in that way; we knew there was always a possibility of danger, but we didn't walk around looking over our shoulders. Not consciously anyway. My brother had just started to drive, and when we'd ride places, there'd be a cop car following us around, which was awkward. You go to a high school function, you've got a cop car following you. It cramps your style. And there was always security around; how awkward it was to live like that. Subliminally, you begin to think people were out to get you.

Dating was difficult. Basic things. Girls would not be shy, but rather were wary, not because of me, but rather because of what—

and who—I carried with me. There was one girl I kind of fell for. If there is such a thing as love at first sight, this was it. It felt natural once I started going out with her and getting to know her. Her parents were in the ministry. Her father was even a prominent minister; it was in keeping, I thought, in light of Granddaddy and Big Mama. Actually her parents were friends with my grandparents. I thought that was even more natural. I was on a high every time I was with her. It was all perfectly innocent. Then she told me she felt like she wasn't good enough for me. She cut it off. This crushed me internally. I pretended not to care.

After that I held back. A lot of girls I liked never really gave me the time of day anyway. One said, "You'd make a good husband, but not a good boyfriend."

What?

Another girl said, "Nooo, I don't want to go out with you— no thank you. The FBI may be watching." Or the girls' parents objected on similar grounds. One father said, "I'm not burying my baby because she was standing too close." People were afraid, or intimidated, or superstitious. "Your daddy may be looking down at us." If it was bad for me or Martin, I can only imagine how much worse it was for Yolanda and Bernice. Just another step along the old tracks of our tears.

These experiences made me realize that no matter how much I tried to blend in, I was never going to ever be able to do it. It was part of our legacy. Some of the rejection I took personally; maybe the girls really didn't like me. I went through that for a period, but then I realized, no, that wasn't really it, what they said is what they meant. Some of those girls, as I got older, made a beeline back to me, because as worrisome as the whole thing may have been, the girls later realized that the idea of being with me wasn't so bad after all. My response was, You didn't want me then, so why now? But in truth I said it to protect myself from future rejection. I was just still numb, a jumble of contradictions.

Uncle A.D.'s daughter, cousin Darlene, died while out jogging in 1976. She vomited and choked on it and suffocated. My cousin

Alfred died similarly in 1986, while jogging, of a heart attack. Darlene's death was another chunk taken out of my grandfather—out of all of us. In the back of our minds we could not help but think, Who would be next?

Where the King Center is now on Auburn Avenue, there used to be an open lot. As a kid I played in this open lot, which was on the east side of Ebenezer Church. This is where the King Center now stands. The King Center was constructed in phases. We watched it all come up out of nothing—the reflecting pool and arched, covered walkway known as "Freedom Walkway." Next the administration building went up, then adjacent to it, Freedom Hall was constructed. The construction of the center was rewarding to Mother, because it was her insurance that her husband's message and spirit would endure. There were people, well-intentioned people, who thought it could never happen. Even Uncle Andy had talked about how he didn't believe it could happen. Building a multimillion-dollar anything is going to be difficult, whether it be to Martin Luther King, Jr.'s memory, or not. Many Americans—white Americans—were still trying to figure out if Dr. King was friend or foe.

It wasn't hard for me to figure.

Jimmy Carter, along with Henry Ford, helped galvanize the effort. Granddaddy King was pivotal in raising funds for the King Center.

CHAPTER 8

This Little Light

of Mine

My college training, especially the first two years, brought many doubts into my mind . . . I revolted too against the emotionalism of much Negro religion . . . shouting and stamping. I didn't understand it, and it embarrassed me. I often say that if we, as a people, had as much religion in our hearts and souls as we have in our legs and feet, we could change the world.

—Martin Luther King, Jr.

Some people are fine doing the routine, following a tradition. They are capable of it, fulfilled by it, and the circumstances on which their routine or tradition was built do largely remain the same. Such was not the case for me. I think of Bernice and Yolanda and Martin, and each, in his or her own way, was fine and good following traditional steps. I was not. If it reflects badly on me, I can't change it now. I can only go on from here. I use the comparison of the sacrament and the ceremony. To me, sacrament is what's in your heart; ceremony is what people expect you to do about it. A wedding is the ceremony, but the love that you share with your companion is the sacrament. You do the ceremony for others, not for you; society, the world at large, needs to see proof to feel it's validated. In God's sight, you're there anyway. I wanted to find a connection to something inspirational. I looked for it in a book, in a classroom, but didn't find it there.

The fruitless search was never more evident than in my years at Morehouse College, a place of wonderful traditions, mostly. There's no great disappointment where there's no great love. If I was an actor like Will Smith, a hooper like Kobe Bryant, a ball-player like Hank Aaron, a producer like Quincy Jones, I wouldn't even have needed high school; you just go on to the next thing you're good at, were meant to do. But being the son of Martin Luther King, Jr., put extra oomph into my feelings of failure when I didn't follow his exact footprints.

I didn't graduate Morehouse, but I did matriculate there. Had I been named Dexter Smith or something, and school hadn't worked out, then I would have just left. Being who I was, I couldn't just leave. I still felt like I'd accomplished something by the time I left Morehouse for good. It isn't like I hate the memory. It was more a good feeling, actually. At least I knew what I wasn't.

It started with graduating from Frederick Douglass High. That year, 1979, there were three graduations in the family. Martin graduated from Morehouse. Yolanda graduated from NYU, the MFA program in theater. "We've arrived!" I can still hear her chortling. She was not the same Yoki after our father passed, but she could still be exuberant.

I couldn't join in her feelings. People were telling me, "Oh you got no choice. You're going to Morehouse." Great-granddaddy A. D. Williams was in the Morehouse class of 1898, the second graduating class of its existence; Granddaddy M. L. King, Sr., was class of 1930; Daddy was class of 1948; Uncle A.D. was class of 1950. Pressure never came from within 234 Sunset, yet despite that everybody assumed, "Your mom and grandpa won't let you go anywhere else." Sure, Granddaddy King wanted me to go to More-house. But he wanted Dad to do a lot of things he didn't do either. Mother said, "Son, you don't have to go there. But you must go somewhere."

I had at least three football scholarships. I almost ended up at the University of Southern California. If I'd chosen USC, I could

well have had a minor pro football career. The coaching and re-
cruiting staff at USC didn't exactly hound me, but the offer was
there if I wanted it.

If I stayed in Atlanta, I reasoned there would be some obvious
advantages. Football didn't interest me that much after high school.
I thought I was interested in electrical engineering.

People always ask young people, "What is it you want to do?"
And in my opinion, all but the very lucky are thinking, "I don't
know, what do you want me to do?" In high school, I was in a club
called JETS, Junior Engineering Technology Society; then there
was also being the handyman for Big Mama.

Morehouse, like all the colleges in the AU Center, had dual-
degree programs where you could take classes at AU Center and
Georgia Tech. In five years you're out with two degrees—sounded
good to me. I chose Morehouse. I said, "If I stay here, I'm not
going to play sports, because as far as football goes, Morehouse
isn't that well-known for it, so I figure I'm not going to waste my
time fooling around." So I got into the engineering program and
quickly realized it wasn't what I wanted to do. I'd heard of young
people who started off in engineering and ended up in law school,
for instance. I didn't feel bad about it. There was plenty else to
feel bad about.

My brother had a collection of jazz LPs, vinyl, in his campus
dorm room; and he had every reason to escape to them via head-
phones. He took the first wave, the brunt of expectations at Morehouse for the sons of the school's most famous alumnus. The
pressure on Martin, being Daddy's namesake, was enormous. My
first exposure to Lonnie Liston Smith and contemporary jazz fu-
sion came because of Martin at Morehouse. I hung out in his room,
getting my mind expanded by Lonnie Liston Smith, vocals by his
brother Donald Smith, doing "Expansions" and "Give Peace a
Chance" off the *Visions of a New World* LP. Music lived and moved
and grooved and grew inside me. I didn't concentrate on it. It just
was.

In high school, I believed if I didn't go to Morehouse, it would be scandalous. *Jet* editor emeritus the late Robert Johnson; *Ebony* editor Lerone Bennett; Maynard Jackson; Julian Bond; Olympic gold medalist Edwin Moses—all went to Morehouse; and in attendance there at the same time as my brother, Martin, was a guy named Spike Lee. I didn't notice him a lot, but I'd seen him. Always thought he was somehow different. Everybody did; it was an impression we all had; Spike was kind of ahead of his time. I think the word is "innovative." Not a Big Man on Campus type. His persona was more tied to coming up with creative pursuits. Because his was not a mainstream type of persona, he had a cult following— his troupe, if you will. Always had people hanging out with him, kind of an entourage. I think he still works with some of those people till this day. I never really got to know him in terms of working in that inner circle. I was on the periphery, a high school kid, the kid brother of Martin III. I didn't stand out. I don't think anybody knew he was going to be the Spike Lee he is today. At that time, who was thinking that far ahead?

I was going over to see Martin at Morehouse, hanging out, picking up the campus vibe, deejaying parties still. At one point I had two or three mobile units; people working for me. My first memorable encounter with Spike was when he was directing the Morehouse homecoming coronation, like in his movie *School Daze*, only this was real; I helped do the sound, audio engineering, even though I was still in high school. Spike Lee finished Morehouse as I was about to enter freshman year.

I noticed the barrier still existed, even at Morehouse; the barrier was that people didn't know how to relate to me and Martin, whether to be down home, or serious, or more formal. I didn't know how to be with myself, after always having to deal with "What does the family of King represent?" We don't have royalty in this country, as African Americans. Don't have it or need it. But maybe, like most people, secretly we do kind of want it. We want our version of it. We need positive myths; all people do.

One thing that got through my thick head at Morehouse was that some of the students and faculty needed to see Martin and me as scions of the royal King family. But that also meant that those people didn't really want to see or get to know the real us, two young men trying to figure out who we were like every other college student in America. I tried to do well, but maybe I didn't try hard enough. Or maybe it wasn't in me. Better to have people think I didn't try hard than the alternative—that somehow I didn't have the equipment.

College life was still fun. Even I knew that. I managed to be less inhibited, worried less about the responsibilities of being Dr. King's son. I wanted no part of it. I'd seen what it got you. And so I became the black sheep of the family. Didn't fit the mold. Doing my own thing and being unconventional. Deejaying, and a preacher's kid—PK, that's one name I got called at Morehouse.

Isaac came to Morehouse a year after I did. I never went to him specifically with any of my frustrations. We were always in each other's heads, so I didn't have to. His situation was similar to mine. After all, his mother, Aunt Christine, taught at Spelman. Seemed as if we both had to live out other people's ideas. We were constantly talking through things because we were dealing with some of the same issues. Some people seemed to be successful at college and yet became what we called "professional students"—there were a number of them at the AU Center schools, who, for one reason or another, wound up staying in undergraduate school five, six, seven, eight years. Not that they were stupid; they liked being there—the three squares, the casual academic environment, the new batches of coeds every year, the safety of the college campus and the avoidance of the workaday world. They were in their own way institutionalized. Others may have bright minds, but the regimentation of academia, for one reason or another, doesn't reveal their strengths. I don't know why, but academic regimentation didn't reveal me. I did know that. I wasn't the first one in history. I happened to be the first in my immediate family.

It was not the best idea for me, to follow the family male scholarly theme in the first place. We—Isaac and I—should've gone away to school. Maybe to the army. But the armed forces weren't options for me. The son of the prince of nonviolence, an infantryman? Wouldn't do. Then I was constantly being asked, "When are you going into the ministry?" Or "Pre-law? Hm?" We come from five generations of ministers. Granddaddy's mother and father had been functionally illiterate; when he first came to Atlanta, there was not a high school or library where blacks could go. Like most black southern families, mine believed vehemently in education, believed in it because for so long they were denied it, in some cases they could trace back only a generation or two privileged by it. It affected Martin III at Morehouse. He was called out as Martin Luther King, Jr.'s son lots of times, but with the piano playing of Lonnie Liston Smith consoling his ear, he made it through.

Aunt Christine was on the faculty at Spelman. Granddaddy had served on some of the boards of the institutions in the AU Center, namely Morehouse and Atlanta University. Since Daddy's death, there had been plans to build a bronze statue of him in front of the Morehouse administration building. Eventually the memorial was built.

Maynard Jackson had been mayor of Atlanta. Now Andy Young was gearing up for a successful run at being mayor. Contrary to what segregationists always said, Atlanta was still there after integration—not only was it there, it was also bigger and better than ever.

In 1981, my third year at Morehouse, Uncle Andy ran for mayor and was elected.

I had always thought that I might pursue a career in politics; maybe even become Georgia's first black governor. I was interested in the arena, and it would serve the family legacy. But later, I saw how my brother got treated in politics. He was a Fulton County commissioner in 1986. Isaac was his campaign manager. I helped on his campaign by organizing a fund-raiser that Robert F. Kennedy, Jr., attended at which the singer Jennifer Holliday performed, at the home of Michael Lomax, the chairman of the Fulton County Commission. Martin did get elected and served two terms. I admire Martin. I know deep down he wants to help humanity. I know he cares. But I saw how he got dragged through the mud because he wasn't Daddy. I said, "Not me."

I did have a need, as my father did, to be understood and gain understanding. I had trouble getting it out of books, as my father did. He didn't do it so much at Morehouse; he was an average student there, didn't take off academically until he went to Crozer Theological Seminary in Chester, Pennsylvania. I can't fathom how he did it, analyzed and translated philosophers like Immanuel Kant or G. W .F. Hegel or Jean-Jacques Rousseau, Søren Kierkegaard or Henry David Thoreau or Reinhold Niebuhr. He had done it.

I wanted—needed—to contribute in life. Like most young men, I had not yet found my mission and I didn't have the same interests Daddy had. By the time he was twenty-five he was ready to pastor; by the time he was twenty-six, political machinations or not, back door or not, his idea or not, he was the leader of the Montgomery bus boycott, and everybody from Mahalia Jackson to Kwame Nkrumah to Dwight Eisenhower to Jack and Bobby Kennedy to Richard Nixon was in his sphere of influence. I needed space to experiment and figure out who I, Dexter, wanted to be. But this need seemed to always put me at odds with a society, and well-intentioned people, who wanted me to be what they wanted: the second coming of a King. Outside of the family, I didn't even have a friend, let alone a best friend.

I think there were only a few people that Isaac and I bonded with. One was John Carson. He was from Stockton, California, a town outside San Francisco. His plan at the time was to follow in his father's footsteps. His father was a doctor. John was like me— didn't make friendships easily. Another person with whom I bonded was Phillip Jones. I met him in the spring of 1980. There was a girl I especially liked. He was dating her, only I didn't know it. I was trying to date her. He didn't know that. I'd frequently visit her at Spelman. As I was coming out of my campus dorm one day, this guy approached me. I didn't know he was coming to read me the riot act. He said, "Say, what's up with you? Do you know you're trying to talk to my lady?"

I took the initiative.

"Hi, I'm Dexter King. And you are?"

He told me later the way I did it was disarming. Said he couldn't bring himself to even say anything about his girlfriend. We hit it off, became friends instantly, spent almost a twenty-four-hour period nonstop hanging out, though he was a senior and I was a freshman. The girl was from Tennessee. Very attractive lady. Don't know what happened to her. Phil and I spent the day and night talking and walking around. We went to the music room and he played some of his songs on the piano, asked me what I thought of them. We hit it off because our interests were aligned; we were musically inclined. We could talk on any level; that impressed me because there weren't many I could do that with. He seemed to warm to my interpretations in the field of music. It's funny, I can say that and see it clearly now, but back then, I didn't even think of music as an option of what to do with my life because I knew people would not have found it "acceptable" for King's son. It was not an academic discipline as I had approached it. Phillip was a musician, a good composer, and I liked that we could talk about issues, politics, growing up, hanging out; there was substance, but also an ability to have fun. The fun was important; the seriousness was draining; there's a side of me, a little boy that wants to play, wants to be expressive. Being around Phil, hearing him, watching him, helped that side. There's a process of composing that teaches you about life. I wanted to learn about life.

Some of the buddies I had were Isaac, Vernon, Ralph, and John Carson, James "Chip" Carter, and Clarence "Bumpy" Cox III. I do

know there were not many people I could really be "down" with at
Morehouse. With Phil, I was down.

The summer of his graduation, we went into the studio to produce a record. This was the first production where we hired the
artists, we hired the musicians, we were producers. And I felt . . .
right. I felt alive. Just maybe I had found my calling.

We were at the Democratic National Convention in New York
in 1980 when Phil's mother passed. She committed suicide. I'd
seen and met her at his graduation—an attractive woman. Her
name was Loretha. He remembered that she cried over the TV in
1968 when my father was assassinated. She was an alcoholic. An
angel when she wasn't drunk, Phil said, a biochemist who'd been
trained at Meharry. But she was sometimes attracted to violent
men. She was violent with Phil when she got drunk. Split personality. He didn't even know he was being abused. When she wasn't
drunk, she'd tell him how much she loved him.

At the convention, Granddaddy gathered us in a circle, and we
held hands and said a prayer for Phil's mother. Loretha had done
the same thing with him when my father was killed. He said, "This
is my family now." I could relate. My grandfather brought him into
the family prayer circle and prayed for Phil, so it was memorable
and tragic at once, and formed a bond between us that will last
forever.

That next fall, I was on my own again. School was not working
out. While my father could argue the relative merits of philosophers, I could not; but I could tell regional differences in musical
preferences among the school enrollment. I took advantage of my
rep as the person to work with for music. It got to the point I was
so busy deejaying I had to hire out help; in some cases, had three
parties going on at one time. I had mobile units I'd send out; two
other guys who worked with me, plus Isaac. One is now a federal
law enforcement agent, and the other is a dentist. But they all
worked for K&F Sound Productions and were dedicated and loyal.
We had a thriving enterprise.

In the summer of '80, we auditioned a couple of female singers. We even flew one girl in whom Phil knew from his earlier days at Morehouse. She'd been at Spelman a year, and had gone on to become an *Ebony* Fashion Fair model. We had songs written, hired the studio, engineers, musicians. The song went nowhere. This was before Kenny "Babyface" Edmonds, Antonio "LA" Reid, and the music industry descended on Atlanta in the '90s. We learned the hard way. You can have the talent, the song, the arrangement, a good product, but it's held against you if you do something independent. You're penalized for not going through normal channels; if you're outside the system, the system keeps you outside. It was a learning experience; same in politics, same in music. We never took no for an answer, but eventually Phil went back to New York. The next time we got together on a serious project would be years later.

My problems with school worsened. I would try to read something, and I would struggle to comprehend it. I would have to keep trying over and over again, and even then I had trouble retaining it. It wasn't until years later that I discovered the reason why. I was guarded about admitting this challenge; I still am even now; guarded because of early recollections in '72 when I was at the Democratic convention in Miami, as an eleven-year-old, and saw Tom Eagleton stepping down as vice-presidential nominee because he'd seen a psychiatrist and had electroshock. I thought, "Man, I've got to deal with these issues. People will say I'm nuts. Mother will be shamed."

I was in a catch-22. I needed help, but I couldn't afford to be seen as needing help. How could King's son be less than perfect?

At that time, Morehouse's administration asked students to choose a major at the end of sophomore year, as a part of the liberal arts education process. I had more episodes where I couldn't focus, buckle down. Going to class, following up assignments, schmoozing the professors—the basic functions of college academic life seemed to throw me. Some of my professors were concerned and wanted to help, but others were happy to heap the incompletes on me, and others simply gave me F's even when they knew I was in the process of completing assignments, or trying to. No matter what their reaction to me, everybody saw clearly that this particular King communicated well, could tell you what he thought, seemed intelligent, ran this successful K&F Sound operation, yet they couldn't pinpoint why he was not following up. It had gotten the best of me; it was increasingly difficult to accomplish anything, and the shame of it, the shame, as Martin Luther King's son. Hey, I had problems just getting up in the morning; chronic fatigue, where I would just sleep. I might sleep twelve hours, no problem, and always had a hard time waking up.

Those professors who didn't take the time to really talk to me were offended and insulted: "Well, who does he think he is?" I even had some people tell me, "Look, if you think you're going to get through because you're King's son, you better think again." But I didn't think that. Scholastically I was bad all on my own. Figured they'd already made up their minds about me. I couldn't articulate why I was having problems, felt embarrassed because people were comparing me all the time with my father, comparing me to this singular great finished product.

How could I get up before children and say, "Get an education," if I hadn't completed mine? Even in high school, periodically I'd have some academic problems, but for whatever reason I was able to manage them better. Maybe because of the physical activity, the high school sports in some way helped me mentally, helped clear my mind. I was a walking illness without activity. Maybe that was it. I'm sure there was some practical reason why I couldn't sustain in academics.

I got a party-boy reputation to go along with the black sheep hook. People knew I wasn't performing in class and they also heard, "DK's deejaying tonight." People couldn't reconcile it. It wasn't that I was dissing one for another. Deejaying paid, and academics it seemed I could not do. It was not ability for one as it was lack of capability for the other. The music was more fluid and did not require any textual analysis. The classwork required a connection between analysis and execution, a thought process. Deejaying was sensing what you and others were feeling inside.

I enjoyed the latter because I had to learn about the different cultures too. D.C. people wanted to hear a certain kind of music—go-go music played by the godfather of go-go, Chuck Brown. The New York brothers by then wanted to hear Grandmaster Flash and the Furious Five, or Kurtis Blow; Chicago and the Midwest wanted to hear house or dancehall; brothers from L.A. wanted to hear the solar sound. Then you got into different styles of rhyming, early hip-hop, the stage being set; there was a connection between it and me—it was exciting, thrilling, cutting-edge, inspirational. The classroom seemed cobwebby, constricting, strangling by comparison. Music permeated me; I could read the crowd and see, "Okay, tonight I got a lot of brothers from D.C., so I'm going heavy on the go-go"; or "I got some brothers from New York, so I'm going house." Or, "Hey, the rhyming . . ."

Whatever the flow was, I felt it, I was always alert to it, you couldn't plan that far ahead of time, so you didn't have to read up on it. No homework. It required only reaction, a sense of what you heard, of what was going on around you, a sense of what was "out there," in the streets, in people's faces, in their hearts, what they responded to. You couldn't script it out and you couldn't learn it in a class on Western civilization. In class, it was all numbing regimentation—numbing to me, anyway. I disliked the distance of the subject matter from the culture at hand, and from my own personal history. The music made me feel good and useful, somehow, as if . . . as if I was making a thing right that needed making right. The only place I had problems was with the structured environment of a college classroom. I asked myself why, why did I have this problem?

I got plenty of "Well we are very disappointed in you, young man."

Everybody approached it traditionally. They saw me as a failure. I always felt my symptoms and knew my problem, I just didn't know why. Nobody could tell me why—why I didn't do well at Morehouse. Why I didn't finish. Maybe this is another reason why the music, the Sound, meant so much to me. I wanted music to be worth it. I wanted to be worthy.

CHAPTER 9

Wrecked

I went to work in 1982 for the Atlanta Police Department. I started out as a community service officer, poised to become a police recruit, then changed to corrections officer, all under the umbrella of the Department of Public Safety. My motivation for joining the police department was that I thought I could help people who were victims of the criminal justice system and pay my dues in public service, which I felt was a prerequisite for any elected office I might pursue in the future. I was still dealing with Morehouse too. I took some time off from school to get established in public safety, but I still had the intention of going back.

I'd been wanting my own place, so Ralph Abernathy III and I became roommates.

Ralph had been living in the Kappa house, I'd been in a good old dorm. We moved into a renovated duplex in the West End, on Beecher Street. Ralph initially went to Benedict College in South Carolina before he transferred to Morehouse. My mom had said, "If you don't want to stay on campus, I've got a house here that's paid for, you can stay here. But if you want your own place, you pay for it."

Cool, I'll get a job. I still had K&F Sound Productions, but with me not really being at Morehouse anymore business wasn't coming in like it used to. So my mother was saying, "If you want your own apartment and a car, I'm not going to fund them. Particularly when you're not a great student." What it forced me to do was go out and look around at options. The police department was hiring. They had a program called "Community Service Officer," kind of a prerequisite to recruits if they wanted to go on into the department. I started out there. The pay was decent, you worked for the city so you got "bennies," benefits. It was consistent work, and you didn't have to have a college degree.

I was intrigued with law enforcement as a child because I'd often been exposed to it; growing up, there was always a police presence, always somebody providing security, looking all tight, precise, competent, calm, responsible. When I was younger and we'd go places with my dad, there were these police escorts. I played with plenty of sirens in my day. Like that last little tour we took in Georgia, in the last week of March 1968, me and Dad and Martin. The cops might take me out and show me all the gadgets in the police cruisers.

Meanwhile Isaac was becoming a political animal, working in different campaigns, like Walter Mondale for president, the Andy Young mayoral campaign, helping Uncle Andy get elected in 1981. Uncle Andy was a veteran of the system now; I also wanted to help that process.

The man heading the department at that time, J. D. Hudson, was in the group of the first black policemen in Atlanta, which my grandfather was instrumental in making happen, so there was a connection. When I stood on the carpet before him, he was anxious to take me under his wing.

But he never let on then. "Are you going to shape up, Dexter King?"

"Yes."

"Yes what?"

"Yes sir."

*   *   *

I started out as a police department community service officer assigned to the identification section/crime scene unit working in a support role for those who were photographing and lifting fingerprints from crime scenes. I was then reassigned to the SIS (Special Investigations Section), which included the organized and vice crime unit, the intelligence section, major crimes unit, and narcotics. As a practical matter, I later decided to switch from the Bureau of Police Services to the Bureau of Correctional Services, which was a relatively simple administrative change in that both were under the Department of Public Safety.

The police investigator who was doing my background check seemed befuddled—"You're Martin Luther King's son?" He didn't get it. A lot of other people had that look on their faces too. "What's the motivation here—what's your story, King boy, like you think you can just come in here and get a job here because of who you are? You here to blow the whistle, wear a glass shield?"

The investigator turned out really cool in the end. He overdid his job in terms of talking to neighbors, friends, and everybody. They gave me no special treatment. If anything, it was the opposite. After he went through the background check, I think he gained a newfound respect because he saw I was serious, wasn't looking for any favors. I was ready to cut it, do the job, go through the rigors of whatever that meant I had to do. Eventually my cousin Vernon started working as an officer too, assigned to court detention.

The academy was near the prison farm. The physical training was no problem. I'd played sports. The training we went through for corrections was not nearly as intense as for police. We had to go through it only as it related to arrest techniques and firearms training and awareness of laws and basics. It was not the full-blown extensive training that a police officer goes through, but I'd just started out on this other road. I wanted a taste before a bite, before I went the way of the late Tom Bradley, former police officer turned mayor of Los Angeles, and joined the regular force. A lot of it had to do with J. D. Hudson being supportive, working with me.

I started off on late-night watch. I don't care who you are, how famous—whatever as a rookie, you work graveyard shift. It so happened that I got a nine-to-five assignment soon after that, working Monday through Friday; I couldn't ask for more, but from the grumbling I heard secondhand, some of my coworkers could. I was "J.D.'s famous boy," they said. King's son. Coon's son. I heard it all, one way or another. It crossed my mind that resentment might make an officer slow backing me up. I didn't dwell on it. Just do the job.

It got to the point where I'd done all I could do there; the next step was to pursue promotion to superior supervisory officer, like sergeant, lieutenant, so forth and so on, and maybe I could have risen through the ranks. But as far as change to correct some of the systemic injustice, I saw ceilings. That had to come from a political or legislative standpoint, from someplace beyond me.

But it was good exposure. Corrections was run like a paramilitary organization, like any law enforcement and public safety agency. I learned chain of command, discipline, process. It was the closest I could get to military training without being military, which would've been opposed to what my dad was saying. I'd always had a curiosity about the military. By exploring a career in law enforcement, I'd decided to act on my own curiosities for a change. It had a cost. I'd come by the King Center on Auburn Avenue after work, still in uniform, sidearm on, to see Mother. Some people, board members—on one occasion in particular, Gerry Allen, now deceased—would say, "How can you come in here, in this building, with a weapon?" I thought about the plastic toy guns, and Daddy.

This happened not once, but time and time again. Some people seemed to take pleasure in repeating the same line with the same grave tones and the same half-hidden smug smile.

For whatever reason, I was able to separate that this was a job; it didn't make me not my father's son. That's always been a subconscious consideration of each of my adult acts, although I'm not clear whether I'd faced that reality then. I never had to use my sidearm. I was trained to do it, and I didn't see it as diametrically opposed to nonviolence, as long as the greater good prevailed.

Sometimes an inmate would step up to me and say, "If you didn't have a badge and gun . . ." Typically, once they understood that I didn't hide behind a badge and gun, the inmate changed in demeanor. Many officers did hide behind that badge and gun. Made them tough guys quick. I saw it happen. And sometimes you had to be tough. Make no mistake.

Working in that environment did much for me in terms of learning about the criminal justice system, seeing society through that lens. When you were going to a crime scene or to a domestic situation, you were learning how to communicate, developing skills to use. When criminal, near-criminal, or violent things are happening around you, you have to be up on your toes. You have to think quickly; what do you do? A lot of thinking on your feet. Ultimately for me, the streets weren't the answer. I ended up at the Bureau of Corrections. I was assigned to the prison farm, then the jail, then ultimately to the transportation unit, which handled mostly prisoner transport. It was interesting, instructive, especially when I was in the prison or jail bringing in offenders. I took on another personality, dimension, and dynamic with my coworkers and with the prisoners. The conversations I engaged in were from both sides of the bars, from a crazed inmate who challenged me for "screwing up my world, got King's face looking at me from the other side of these bars," to some bystander at the King Center who said, "Aren't you Dr. King's son? Why are you wearing that uniform and badge, carrying a gun. Don't you preach?"

A fellow officer once asked me, "Why are you here? Trying to take my job? You a spy?"

Funny thing was, the prisoners were supposed to be the enemy, but in more cases than not, they were my defenders. They saw I wanted to be fair. If a real crazy came into the lockup and started cutting up, and stepped to me, the prisoners would most often take care of it. "Don't want to mess with him, fool. He looks out for us."

I was firm, but fair. Even if the guy was a lunatic, they would "sane him up," as they called it.

One crazy they didn't manage to "sane up." This hostile inmate almost bit my thumb clean off. He was strung out on drugs, had shot his girlfriend. I was transporting him from court over to jail; he barricaded himself in a corner, and it took four or five of us to get to him. Dope had turned him into an animal. The way he was acting, he wasn't on heroin or cocaine, it was methamphetamine or crack, probably. I reached down to lift him; he growled like a dog, his neck snapped his head toward me like a striking snake; next thing I know, I'm in Grady Hospital with an IV in my arm for a week. The doctor said, "If a rabid dog had bit you, we would've given you a shot, sent you home. But a human bite is the most deadly there is."

The injury was not that major—a chunk of thumb just hanging there by a sliver of skin. He'd chomped down good. They'd covered it up with a balloon wrap, put an IV in my arm, then my arm in a sling. I looked like a casualty of war. I remember the face of the inspector when he came by to get an incident report, how shaken he was by what he saw.

The same prisoner, when I took him to court a few weeks later, was sober, apologetic, down off his high—he was out of his mind at the time of the bite, didn't know what he was doing.

Initially some fellow officers felt awkward, until they got to know me. One of them said, "It's like trying to run Hell while watched by an angel." I said, "I'm no angel." Most of them were very supportive.

This was before things got really bad with the drug scene. You had a lot of people there on traffic charges. DUI was big at the time. Mothers Against Drunk Driving had by then mounted an effective legislative crackdown. You had situations where you had somebody on DUI in the same environment with somebody charged with armed robbery or murder. The lockup is no place for the faint of heart, I can tell you with some authority now. I would never want to be in jail on the side of the bars my dad used to be on. There is little about it that strikes you as noble when you're in there. Maybe after you get out you can look back on it that way, but jail is no place for the good. The good can't stay that way long in jail.

One of my high school football teammates came in on a murder charge; he had murdered his girlfriend, whom I also knew. I had to handcuff him, take him in, process him. It was bizarre—the way he looked at me, the way there was nothing to say but the formal language of incarceration.

Another time, a cop I knew came in on a rape charge. Occasionally you would see people you went to school with, women who came in on prostitution. You were like, "No, I can't believe it, she was an honors student!" "Oh no, not her!" "Oh no, not him!" I'd talk to them. "What happened, why did you do it?" What I found was that even with people who'd committed the most heinous acts, more times than not, they didn't know what they were doing. They snapped. There were a few occasions of premeditation. But I'd say the vast majority had just lost control.

Then there were some there just out of ignorance. They needed guidance and help. I had experiences with people who would come back after they got out of jail and thank me. They'd say, "Hey, I appreciate you taking the time to talk to me." I did my job, never crossed the line, but if they said, "Please, tell me who do I need to talk to?" I'd always answer. Part of their problem was fear of the process. Some had never been incarcerated. I'd say, "These are your rights. You can talk to the public defender. Your warrant was incorrect procedurally." My job was to make sure their rights were kept; that their rights were protected while in custody.

I tried to treat them all like human beings. Some appreciated it. One guy was going to hang himself. I talked him out of it just by listening; that was all it took to get him to face the next day. I often got the feeling if somebody had just listened to them beforehand, so many crimes could've been averted. In that case, it was a white guy who'd broken up with his girlfriend. He wanted to hang himself. Jail is depressing. I said, "Hey, it ain't that bad. It's not worth dying over. Don't give the people who put you down the satisfaction of seeing you live down to their opinion of you." Maybe he heard me, but anyway, he lived, walked out of jail later on, giving me the thumbs-up sign. Just my taking time to hear his story was half the battle of his gaining self-control. It wasn't what I said so much. Most people, if you give them an ear, that solves half the problem. That helped me to develop a better sense of dealing with people on the edge, and bolstered my own confidence.

It was rewarding and challenging.

However, I was just an officer, a private, so to speak, and had to make a choice. Was I going to take the examination to be promoted or not?

I was there because I wanted to learn; you can't affect a thing unless you know it, how it works. You have to get in there and see it. I never want to seem like a guy talking about things from afar, so I'd worked hard and learned a lot. I'd been there and done that, I know security issues, the criminal justice system from a practical level. I got what I needed out of it. A lot of what I needed came from the head of the bureau, who was both a mentor and a father figure.

J. D. Hudson was a stern man. Not a big man, but a presence—his voice, his way, and his manner. He came from college—the College of Hard Knocks. Hudson was an ex–police captain and homicide detective whom Maynard Jackson brought in to run the Bureau of Corrections, under the Department of Public Safety. There had been a lot of pernicious racism in the department, so Maynard broke it up and created a separate Bureau of Corrections with jurisdiction over the prisoners, because there'd been everything from suspicious prisoner deaths to contraband being sold, guard to prisoner, to officers beating false confessions out of people. Maynard put Director Hudson over the operation and said, "Clean it up." Hudson was no-nonsense. He reminded me of my grandfather in some ways.

So I think he too was disappointed when I told him I felt I had to muster out, yet I think he also knew there were other things for me to do. He said so. I don't know if I believed him. But he said things to me that stuck with me until now. I talked to him about how I felt traumatized by losing my father, and how maybe that was one reason I wanted to spend some time on the force. But now it was time to move on. He listened to me. When I paused, he asked me if I was finished. I said, "Yes . . . yes sir . . . I think so."

J. D. Hudson sighed and said, "Listen here. You don't need to be feeling sorry for yourself. You know how many other people lost their fathers, just on April 4, 1968? Do you want me to go through a census records check, just so you can see how many died that day, and how?"

I squirmed in my chair. "No. No sir." I'd never thought of it that way before.

Hudson said, "You come from better timber than that. Some people don't even know their father. Do you understand what I'm saying to you? You can't use your father being killed, or not being here for you, every time you have a crisis, as some kind of an excuse."

He said I was fortunate to have had not only a great father, but a great mother. And I knew that. I'd had two parents, together, for a number of years, and I should be down on my knees thanking God for having such parents for any length of time. He said, "You be thankful for what you got, and what you had." It was like a figurative ass-kicking, in a good way. I'd heard similar comments, but never as strongly and logically worded and never from a man I respected so much. Back in high school, I heard it from the principal, Dr. Lester Butts, but at that age I wasn't mature enough to hear it right, the way I heard it from Director Hudson. J. D. Hudson came across to me as not only a father figure, a disciplined figure, an authority figure, but also as a peer figure, a work-related figure. Hudson was a man who related to and cared about me, a man who had walked in my shoes, who knew loss, lived with loss, survived and overcame it with tough love. He had many "adopted children" working in the bureau who were the sons and daughters of prominent Atlantans. He took us all under his wing. I cherished him and that experience.

One summer between '82 and '84, I was cruising along the freeway between Buckhead and Midtown. I was alone, having dropped off my date after a semiformal fund-raiser for the United Negro College Fund. I was in Martin's brand-new amber-colored Pontiac Trans Am. I always borrowed Martin's cars. Couldn't wait for him to get another, so I could have it.

Here I was driving south along on I-85 near the Brookwood Connector when a transfer truck swerved right in front of me, fish-tailing, to avoid another vehicle. I slammed on the brakes, yanked the wheel opposite; the Trans Am spun out of control. The rear of the truck tailed over, almost took me out then and there, cut so close to the bumper that the only thing that kept us from having impact was the Trans Am spinning out. The Trans Am hit the re-taining wall on the right side of the freeway and the front end was flattened into a standstill from a 65 mph brake-and-turn, ejecting me thirty feet away, the rear end of the car coming to rest facing in the direction from which I had come. I went hurtling through the night air, having been ejected through the driver's side window, which was rolled up at the time. I went through a closed window—shattered the glass and went right through.

It was one of those life-altering experiences where people talk about seeing the white light; it was a near-death experience. Right before impact I said a prayer because I knew it was over. There was a slow-motion calm to the sequence. Oddly, a smell went with it, like . . . after rain. Or like the smell right before a thunderstorm. And white light. And the voice. A clear channel to the heavens. That's what it felt like. I experienced being taken out of harm's way. It's like some angelic presence took me out of the car. Physi-cally, what happened to me was virtually impossible.

I was in a low-slung car, and I'm not a little man. I'm big-boned like my mother, and six foot one. Martin doesn't hold it against me, but it was his car. I'd torn up a couple of his cars before this, too.

The first thing I thought after the light dimmed and the rain smell went away was, "Man, Martin's gonna kill me." It had gotten to the point where he was wary anytime I asked him to let me drive, grumbling as he handed over the keys. I was fitted rather snugly into the cockpit of the car. As tight as I was in there, my body literally left the cockpit at an angle, right angle, left turn, through the glass, and right through the driver's side window. I was catapulted through the air, curled in a fetal position, like I was still behind the wheel, but twirling in the air outside. I could see all of this happening, somehow.

What blew me away was how I landed in a ditch of sand on the right side of the freeway. The highway was under repair so there was a lot of debris. How was it that I landed dead center in this ditch and didn't go headfirst into the concrete divider, or over the divider into the path of oncoming traffic? A miracle.

I landed sitting upright, as though I was still driving. Two feet either way, and I would have flown into concrete or the speeding steel of onrushing cars on the other side of the divider, and would not be here talking about it. When I hit the sand ditch, I hit it as if I was still behind the wheel. Literally sitting still in that posture. Upright, in a three-piece suit. Right on my butt. *Bam.* I looked to the right of me and my brother's car had to be a good twenty to thirty yards away. Totaled. To show you how powerful the impact was, one of the headlights was ten feet to my right. Other debris was nearby. That's how far I was ejected. I stood, felt for my body, and mumbled, "Thank you, Lord."

I couldn't believe it; until this day I have trouble explaining how everything was intact. Even my glasses were still hanging inside my jacket pocket. Yet my shoes were not on my feet. I'd been wearing loafers. I wobbled over to the wreckage of the car and peered inside.

My right shoe was resting on the accelerator.

I was literally snatched out of my shoes. Later, somebody took pains to tell me that Daddy was also snatched out of his shoes when the bullet hit him on the balcony of the Lorraine Motel.

My other shoe, the left one, ended up a quarter of a mile down the freeway.

I was standing on the side of the freeway, still getting my bearings together after I had walked around. There were witnesses, rubberneckers, Good Samaritans, passing by when it happened. A few stopped and asked if I needed any help.

A white couple stopped. I said, "I think I'll be fine; if you could just call the authorities because this is a dangerous situation." The accident had occurred at a blind curve in the freeway just outside of a covered overpass and in not a good spot visible to following traffic. They said, "No, no, you need to go to the hospital." If you saw the totaled Trans Am, you'd say, "This poor guy didn't make it out of there alive. No way." Even the cops were freaking out when they found out I was the driver. And the cops did not arrive quickly, because the accident created a chain reaction of crashes. I was witnessing the chain reaction. My car sat on that blind curve on I-85, heading south.

I could see these other people pulling up. Dominique Wilkins, for one. He was one of the Atlanta Hawks pro basketball players at the time. He drove by in a Jaguar and he and somebody else looked over as he was easing around the car. At that point, other collisions had occurred; it had been kind of a mini–chain reaction, actually, and I had heard brakes squealing, then silence, then crumpling impact. I guess Dominique was a good driver; he had avoided the mini-pileup and driven around. As he eased by, Dominique said, pointing to what was left of the Trans Am, "Whoever was in that— they didn't make it."

I was standing there trying to talk, and it was almost like they couldn't hear me, either I looked too unmussed and couldn't have been involved, was just a bystander, or—this occurred to me, for a split second—maybe I wasn't there at all in the corporeal sense. It was like I was watching them but I was out of my body and they were watching my demise and I couldn't say, "Hey, I'm okay." It was the strangest thing. I was standing on the other side of the accident, watching, trying to let them know I was okay. I could hear them, but they couldn't hear me.

It was like I was in a *Twilight Zone* episode. Then suddenly back to the land of the living. A woman driving behind me hit her brakes to keep from hitting my car, then got hit. I knew her from college. Her mother worked at Morehouse; she was a student at Spelman. She was upset because the person who hit her didn't have insurance. The woman was shaken, she was having a conversation with me and herself. "Dexter, that you? Dexter, they don't have insurance. What are you doing here? Can you help me? Where's your car?"

I said, "Over there."

She looked over at the wreck and gulped. "Oh . . . Dexter . . . you okay?"

Everybody who saw the car freaked. "You're walking?" she asked. "You can't be walking." By this time, it was like a tailgate party on the freeway. People were out of their cars. It took the ambulance forty-five minutes to get there. If I had been seriously hurt, it would've been too bad.

She immediately shifted from her worries. "You need medical attention. You don't look like you need it, but based on that car . . ." She made me sit down until the ambulance got there. When the ambulance finally arrived, I told the EMS guys, "Go ahead, I'll meet you down there, 'cause I need to collect all my stuff and wait for the cops to come and do the report." The cops were having to work accidents all along the way until finally they got to me. The glass was shattered out all over the car. My briefcase and all my stuff were strewn all over the freeway. I wanted to collect it. I must have looked insane, or like some kind of ghoul, walking amid this wreckage, bending to pick up papers, pens, other items.

"You're the one who was driving this car?"

"Yes."

The cop's eyes widened as he looked at me. "Hold on. You mean to tell me you walked away from that?"

"Not really. I got thrown away from it."

". . . Have you been drinking?"

"No. No sir. No I haven't been drinking."

"Good. Then you should be able to tell me how in hell you walked away from that."

"I have no explanation for it." I knew the old cops' tale: when people walk away from major accidents, they've been drinking; people who walk away are often intoxicated. The officer recognized me when I told him my name. He rushed me to the hospital, blue lights blazing.

Shock? Worse than that. The doctors thought I was mentally disturbed. They could not believe my condition. The resident looked at me and said, "What's the problem," and I explained I'd been in a wreck. He looked at me like, "Right. Sure." He said to the cop, "This guy okay?" and then motioned to his head. I said, "I know they don't teach you this in medical school, but there's a higher power, and there are such things as miracles. I was ejected from the car. Out of the window. It was rolled up at the time."

Everybody thought I was crazy; either I had made it up or I was on narcotics. I tried to explain: "There are such things as miracles. They don't teach it in medical school." It bothered me, the way it was being denied that I'd been in an accident. The ER resident was probably thinking, "Okay, full moon, Saturday night—who knows?" People who work the ER or the cophouse will tell you, full moons and Saturday nights—that's when the wild stuff happens. They get crazy action then.

I was x-rayed; everything checked out, except I had an ankle that was so badly sprained that it swelled to twice its normal size and felt broken. That was it. No internal injuries. I was off my feet for several weeks, ankle bandaged up. If you could say any good comes out of tragedy, my mother literally nursed me back to health. She cared for me like I was a kid again. There's nothing like a mother's tender loving care. Aunt Christine came by, and after wagging her finger at me for my recklessness, she said, "Dexter, God is saving you for something."

Although I had been at fault only once before, that was my fifth total wreck. But this was the last major car accident I ever had. It did something to me, inside. It made me take my life into my own hands. Before, I'd put it to chance. This was a life-changing experience. I realized maybe God didn't have it in for me; maybe I had to help myself. I changed from living aloof, to saying, "Okay, now you've got to do what you've got to do."

My grandfather died in 1984 of heart failure. As I'd gotten older, I'd begun to appreciate him more. And then he left us. This played into my scenario that everybody close to me ultimately gets taken away. All these events caused me to start looking for root causes and cures for any symptoms I had. I was a walking symptom of something. I didn't find any answers until I looked for myself, did my own independent research. Things you finally know and directions you finally go in are often not the things you are told to do, but things you find out for yourself, through living, and through, somehow, not dying.

So it was the combination of things—the wreck, leaving the Bureau of Corrections, and Granddaddy's death—that made me realize that I needed to take control of my life. I was the only one in my family who had been given a reprieve when faced with certain death. I had been miraculously delivered out of the clutches of "Who would be next?" and I was intent on finding out why I was saved.

CHAPTER 10

Answers from Within

I began to try to learn if my problem was me, or something inside me.

I didn't know what was going on with me internally, from a medical/chemical and neurological standpoint. I was disabled and tortured by something, all through those years since I'd been born to Mother as her "battlefield commission," delivered in post-traumatic stress syndrome. It hadn't been just the bombing when Yoki was less than two months old, it was bomb after bomb: those churches and residences in Montgomery after the success of the bus boycott; Uncle A.D.'s house in Birmingham in 1963, when he was ministering there. The bombers didn't rest on their laurels; they bombed Sixteenth Street Baptist Church and killed four little girls in Birmingham, and they kept bombing or burning. How many small rural southern black churches were burned in the '90s? Thirty? At times, in the '50s and '60s, it seemed they wanted to bomb us back to the Stone Age.

Izola Ware Curry had stabbed my father in the chest at a book signing in 1958; there'd been a trumped-up income tax evasion trial in Montgomery; stress on stress until my parents moved to

Atlanta in 1960; conflict between my father and grandfather over the direction Dad should take, whether or not we should live in Vine City; presidential politics of 1960; turmoil before Dad's being jailed; how he was jailed, sent to Reidsville State Prison.

Mother endured all this. After delivering me in January of '61—because I was premature and on the advice of the doctor, who was concerned I would not get enough nourishment—she took a shot to stop the flow of milk, so I wasn't breast-fed. Doctors didn't know to recommend breast-feeding over formula then, although Mother could handle it. She had breast-fed Yolanda until the house in Montgomery was bombed, then they moved so much and there was so much stress that she went to the bottle. Martin was breast-fed for months then supplemented with formula. I was a straight formula baby, all formula all the way. So was Bernice. No mother's milk at all. Some things you can't overcome. Not without help. We need what Mother Nature intended to give us. Later, I'd suffered undiagnosed problems, physical ailments, maladies—you might call them shortcomings. I had food allergies, environmental allergies, a cornucopia of ills.

I knew I had issues in terms of health and wellness as it related to my moods changing. I just subconsciously chose not to do anything about it. I'd known since Mother took me to the sleep disorder clinic in Memphis when I was twelve. We went to Memphis Baptist Memorial Hospital, where they wired me up. I had wires coming out of my head, out of my neck, my chest, the EKG, the brain-wave monitors, all that. Almost from the minute I fell asleep, I entered the REM stage, right away I was dreaming within fifteen minutes—not normal for most. Most people enter the REM stage much later. I experienced rapid eye movement almost immediately. They couldn't figure out what it meant. It's one thing to fall asleep and go into the REM stage immediately. That might be an exception; but I'd go to bed at night when I was six, seven, eight, nine years old, wake for breakfast, eat, and a half hour later, I'd be back to sleep. Even though I'd just slept eight hours, I could fall asleep again after breakfast and enter the REM stage.

What developed was this pattern of dreaming all the time. I've told you my dreams were fun and engulfing and engaging—and often about my father. It's almost like I didn't want to wake up because when I was in the non-dream state, things weren't as pleasurable or secure. I would get upset when I was rudely awakened or disturbed, because I would feel like I was being pulled away from my dream.

Then as I got older I had problems deciphering, concentrating, focusing, sitting for any period of time. Not until I was twenty-eight were my troubles diagnosed as attention deficit hyperactivity disorder; people like me can read a thing over and over and still find it hard to comprehend. Even when I'd kept rereading, it wouldn't sink in because I couldn't focus. I'm not sure when the doctors became able to diagnose it. I know they couldn't in the 1970s, when I was twelve and thirteen and having the sleep problems, the concentration deficit.

In my younger years I had whined a lot; the whining seemed to be a need for attention. I'd ask repetitive questions, the same question over and over again: "What did you say? What did you say?" We were visiting cousins in Louisville and they broke me of this habit by putting me in a blanket and running me up and down the hallway until I stopped. "Aunt Naomi," I'd repeat the name, "What did you say, Aunt Naomi, what did you say?"

These experiences, and that of my cousins calling me "Count," as in day-sleeping vampire, not making it through Morehouse College; not being able to hold classroom concentration—were all tied up together. Triggering much of it were food and chemical allergies and environmental factors.

Now, once you accept that this malady exists—and it took a while for me to accept it—and when you research the people who experience this, you find that their diets, certain foods, certain metals, products, food coloring additives, affect them. For me it was a host of things, from dental materials in my mouth to my favorite foods. But I didn't know I had an illness. Today they call it the "invisible disability." Somebody's got one leg shorter than the other, people can see it, you allow for it. This is something where people say, "Oh, it's all in your head. You're making it up."

Environmental toxins aren't made up, neither are those unlucky people who react or who are sensitive to them. Environmental toxins and allergies can do bizarre things to you.

I was walking in the wilderness. Back when I grew up, they really didn't know how to address those kinds of things. They'd just say, "Those are bad kids." There was a welling up of shame in me when I found out. But it's just a learning disability. I've been told that public relations mogul Jerry Della Femina told *Modern Maturity* magazine in 2000 that as a youth he couldn't read a map, do simple addition, subtraction, multiplication. He compensated by being creative, seeing things differently. When I heard that, I knew it was what I'd been feeling for years, was why I loved working with music so much, but was never able to say—I guess because I didn't know it was all right to say it. It was hard for me to focus and concentrate, so I had ups and downs. I tended to be attracted to things that didn't require a lot of attention, but that wasn't a firm rule, because when I was working in public safety, it required focus, and for whatever reason, I was able to maintain it. So I went through periods where sometimes I was able to manage it better than others, but the real turning point was when I went vegetarian. For good.

The change finally came, or started, when we were sitting in the reviewing stand of the King Day Parade in Atlanta, in January of 1988. I had to leave and go to the hospital because of an acute headache pounding away, throbbing, there on Peachtree Street.

I left there with what my maternal grandmother would call "the blind staggers," a headache so debilitating you can hardly open your eyes. The emergency room physician told me the only thing they could do for me was give me painkillers and a decongestant. He said if it didn't work they'd have to drill a hole in my sinuses to drain them. That did not sound like fun. I said, "I have a better idea." I remembered something I'd heard from Dick Gregory, who wasn't one of my old "uncles" from childhood but rather a figure we'd met and befriended. He'd said something about diet, sinus, dairy products, things that cause mucus and buildup and sinus congestion. I said I was going down to Dick's place in Florida, Fort Walton Beach. I was in bad shape. The pain was so bad I'd been given Tylenol 4 and it didn't help. So in near-desperation I went down to Dick Gregory's for two weeks. The first week, I stayed in bed and fasted. Juice and water. Within five days, the sinus condition subsided. I regained strength, felt different. Once Dick got there, we talked. It was like a retreat. He met with me, talked to me about diet. From that day forward, I made a commitment, I was only going to eat raw foods, preferably vegetables. I could only sustain it for about a month at that time, but I felt so good not eating cooked food that I didn't want to mess it up. I felt better—euphoric, clearheaded. I wanted to stay on that plane.

I learned to have faith in holistic methods; maybe the efficacy of any system is believing in it. The traditional system was just going to further medicate me, or drill holes in my head, not deal with the problem, but only the symptoms. All this came full circle on January 30, 1988, my twenty-seventh birthday. I became a strict vegetarian. And from that day forward, I started learning and evolving more and more, health-wise. I learned as I met with alternative health practitioners, dealt with spiritual counseling, and delved into other aspects of holistic alternative health care. And I finally began to learn about me.

I found I have a neurological chemical reaction or chemical illness that affects me from time to time. It was worse when I was younger, but today my altered way of life makes it manageable. Traditional medicine doesn't have a clue as to how to address this "invisible disability"; a lot of the ADD kids you hear about today are called Ritalin kids. Doctors tried to put me on Ritalin as a child. Mother wouldn't allow it. Some medication is worse than the symptoms.

I developed a passion for health and nutrition. My unconventional, nontraditional, unorthodox approach raised questions. People looked at me funny. I'd hear, "Brother from the South talking about he don't eat no meat? He's crazy." Some think "vegetarian" means you don't eat red meat. No, it means you don't eat chicken or fish either. I'm a strict vegetarian. My diet consists of fruits, vegetables, grains, nuts, and legumes only, and has for the last fifteen years now. Back then I also began to take blue-green algae supplements. Blue-green algae is a sea vegetable—like any green or vegetable except it grows underwater; it's very nutritious, has all of the minerals and vitamins. It's considered a whole food complex, which means that it has all of the nutrients that I would get if I ate a meal. Our American diet is devoid of a lot of enzymes and vitamins and nutrients that help the system fight off disease.

Now, as Americans, we're so brand conscious that we don't even read ingredients. I began to read every label of everything I picked up. I wanted to know what's in it, because nine times out of ten if there was a word you don't know, that's something you don't want to put in your body. I got a book on additives and ingredients so I could look up things. I happily, joyfully turned to eating raw vegetables. Finally, something that could be done to help bring me focus. I felt myself getting fitter, less congested, more alert. Alive! I'd eat fruit, but too much fruit wasn't good for me either; sugar made me lightheaded. I didn't want to risk this newfound clarity.

When you're born, the foundation you get from breast milk is key. I didn't get the foundation laid properly. But the human body is so magnificent that it will overcome deficiency. It might not end up as strong or as resilient as a body that got it all early. I had to compensate. I didn't know this until I did my independent research.

All that time before then, I was physically and mentally foundering. Before, people didn't know; they just said, "Dexter's lethargic. He's in a daze. He's off in the ether. What's he on?"

An American diet is so full of things that our bodies weren't necessarily meant to handle. Having a weak foundation in its ecosystem, my body wasn't fighting things well. My tooth enamel was compromised, partly from the formula I'd been fed. I'd get cavities, craved sugar, sweets. Once you get that sugar in your system, you're corrupted. You always want it. We're an addicted population. Again, some people can handle some unnatural things better than others. My body craved naturalness. I didn't choose vegetarianism to make a statement. It was survival. I was going downhill fast. If I had not become a vegetarian, I might not have made it this far. It was through alternative medicine that I found answers. The compassionate part of me wants to enlighten people, but there is a conflict: I've seen what happens when you try to change not even a whole society, but just one person. Though my lifestyle has much to offer, I can't put it out there as a cause that I will champion. It just simply has saved my life.

What bothered me the most about Granddaddy's death is that he still had a sharp mind, but his body gave out. It gave out because of conditions most think are typical, expected in the aging process. What I learned in my research is it's not a given, not absolute: you can affect aging. You can grow old and not be in pain, not suffer. Diet, lifestyle, stress, and emotions must be managed. If Granddaddy had tried the diet and lifestyle I adopted, he might've lived longer.

My mother is a strict vegetarian. Has been for many years. I brought her into it. It was like pulling teeth getting her to change, at first. "Look, if you change now, you won't have those problems later," I said. "Hmph," she replied. At first. Her dietary changes have significantly improved her health. If my grandfather, with all his wisdom, along with a lot of other great elders in our society, had only cultivated better dietary habits so they could have been around longer, who knows what they could've accomplished? We say "prime" is one's youth, but it's later, I think. We put our elders out to pasture because their bodies break down. I didn't get a chance to share my dietary revelations with Granddaddy. As I've said, we lost him to heart failure. But I could help Mother. My maternal grandmother in Alabama, Bernice Scott—her mind left, but her body was still there. Good country living helped her have a better physical ecosystem. Alzheimer's took her mind. She died at ninety-one. My grandfather Scott died eventually, at age ninety-nine. So maybe Mother will be around awhile too. We need her.

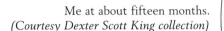

Me at about fifteen months.
(Courtesy Dexter Scott King collection)

Family photo, about 1963.
Front, left to right: Alfred Daniel, Jr.;
Yolanda; Martin III; Vernon on
Mamma King; Alveda; Isaac, Jr.;
Daddy King with me; Darlene;
and Derek. Back, left to right: Daddy,
Mother, Aunt Christine, Uncle Isaac,
Aunt Naomi, and Uncle A.D.
*(Courtesy Christine King Farris
collection)*

On Santa's lap, around 1962,
with my brother, Martin III,
and sister Yolanda.
*(Courtesy
Coretta Scott King
collection)*

My sister Yolanda with our family pet, Topsy, Martin III, me, and Bernice pose for our Christmas photo, 1964. *(Courtesy Coretta Scott King collection)*

Daddy at home with his two sons on Johnson Avenue. Left to right: Martin III, Daddy, and me. *(Courtesy Coretta Scott King collection)*

My father was always fun to be with. Here I am enjoying playing on the swing in the backyard with him. *(© Flip Schulke—courtesy Dexter Scott King collection)*

Our last official family portrait with my father, 1966. Left to right: me, Yolanda, Daddy, Bernice (sitting) with Mother, and Martin III. This photo was taken in the study at Ebenezer Baptist Church. *(Courtesy Coretta Scott King collection)*

April 9, 1968, my father's funeral at Ebenezer Baptist Church in Atlanta. Front pew, right to left: Mother; Bernice; Rev. A. D. King, Daddy's brother; Martin III; Yolanda; cousin Isaac Farris, Jr.; me; Granddaddy King; Mamma King; Joel King, Daddy's cousin; and Aunt Christine and Uncle Isaac Farris. *(Courtesy Coretta Scott King collection)*

At Grandfather and Grandmother Scott's home in Marion, Alabama, Mother's Day, 1969. Left to right: me, Yolanda, Grandmother Bernice Scott, Grandfather Obie Scott, and Martin III. Front: Arturo Bagley and Bernice. *(Courtesy Edythe Scott Bagley collection)*

The Galloway School class photo from 1969–70. That's me in the fourth row. *(Courtesy Dexter Scott King collection)*

Camp Blue Star in North Carolina. A photo of my cabin mates. I'm in the second row, center, in the sunglasses. *(Courtesy Dexter Scott King collection)*

At a dinner honoring Daddy King at the New York Hilton on October 12, 1977. Left to right: me, Bernice, Daddy King, Mother, Martin III, and Yolanda. *(Courtesy Coretta Scott King collection)*

With my grandfather Rev. Martin Luther King, Sr., affectionately known to family and friends as "Daddy King," along with cousin Vernon King (far left) and J. D. Hudson, director of the Bureau of Corrections. I would learn much from my relationship from J.D. *(Courtesy Dexter Scott King collection)*

A meeting with President Ronald W. Reagan in the Oval Office prior to the Rose Garden King Holiday signing ceremony on November 3, 1983. Left to right: Martin III, Yolanda, the President, Mother, Bernice, and me. *(White House photo—courtesy Coretta Scott King collection)*

Me as producer of "King Holiday, Sing, Celebrate" recording session with Run-DMC and Kurtis Blow in 1985. *(Courtesy Dexter Scott King collection)*

President George H. Bush shaking my hand following a White House signing ceremony. Also in attendance that day were (left to right) Christine King Farris (Daddy's sister), Mother, Bernice, and Martin III. *(White House photo—courtesy Coretta Scott King collection)*

Nelson and Winnie Mandela visit the King Center during a stop on his U.S. goodwill tour following his release from prison in South Africa. Left to right: Bernice, Winnie Mandela, Mother, Nelson Mandela, Martin III, and me. *(King Center photo)*

Phillip Jones, one of my closest friends, and I talk with Stevie Wonder following an awards dinner in Beverly Hills, California. *(Michael Jacobs— courtesy Dexter Scott King collection)*

My brother, Martin Luther King III, and I participating in a ground-breaking ceremony with (left to right) Senator Edward Kennedy, Mrs. Ethel Kennedy, and President Bill Clinton at the Robert F. Kennedy–Martin Luther King, Jr., Peace Memorial in Indianapolis, Indiana. *(White House photo—courtesy Dexter Scott King collection)*

In March 1997 I traveled to Tennessee to visit the detention facility that held James Earl Ray, the accused assassin of my father. He would confirm my belief in his innocence—a belief I'd formed after reviewing evidence prior to our meeting. Seated in the background is Ray's attorney, Dr. William F. Pepper. *(IPM/Cornell McBride)*

My family meeting with President Clinton in the Oval Office to request that the U.S. government reopen the investigation into my father's assassination. Left to right: Bernice; Martin III; Mother; President Clinton; me; Minion Moore, assistant to the President, director of political affairs; and Ben Johnson, assistant to the President, director of One America Office. *(White House photo—courtesy Coretta Scott King collection)*

During a tribute in honor of the life of Dr. Betty Shabazz, following her passing, her family is recognized at a King Center event. Left to right: Dr. Niara Sudarkasa, Shabazz family friend and former president of Lincoln University (PA); Attallah Shabazz; Qubilah Shabazz; Ilyasah Shabazz; (blocked and behind my mother) Malikah Shabazz; Mother; (partially hidden) Malaak Shabazz; Dr. Maya Angelou; and me. *(Courtesy Coretta Scott King collection)*

Congratulating Ms. Oprah Winfrey on receiving the King Center's "Salute to Greatness" Award in 2000. Left to right: Dr. Maya Angelou, Mother, Ms. Winfrey, and me. *(King Center photo)*

Martin III, the birthday boy, Mother, Bernice, and Yolanda at a surprise party for my fortieth birthday. *(Courtesy Ambassador Andrew J. Young)*

CHAPTER 11

Legacy

It was 1985, the year after my grandfather died, that we prepared to celebrate the first national King holiday in January 1986, which, after much effort and acrimony, was signed into law by then-president Ronald Reagan on November 3, 1983.

I wanted to give my own special gift to my father and his legacy. I felt that if it involved music, my passion, I could hopefully take his message to younger generations. I decided to produce a record. I called Phil in New York.

He had the musician contacts, he was a talented composer, he could help me pull it together. Phil agreed, and immediately started getting together a group of artists—rappers, initially, which at the time was very avant-garde and controversial. But we believed that rap and hip-hop would become very influential in our culture. We felt it was the crest of a new wave and that if we could do something cutting-edge like this with the song, kids would listen and maybe even hear the ideas of my father. The first person we approached was Kurtis Blow. Kurtis got excited, wanted to involve other people.

These were the beginning days of "rap," initial stages of the whole cloth of hip-hop as a new culture. We went to a young music entrepreneur named Russell Simmons and got some of his artists involved, including his brother's group, Run-DMC. It just snowballed from there. Initially, it was to be a rap song, but once the New York artistic community found out about it, they wanted to get involved. So it evolved to a rap/vocal/R&B song—really a chorus, with rap. Every day a new verse was written to accommodate another artist who had agreed to help, whether it was Stephanie Mills, Whitney Houston, Tina Marie, or New Edition.

We had to turn down LL Cool J, which I regret in retrospect. We didn't have enough room. He was just starting out. Today I can't believe some of the people we had to turn away. We had fifteen or sixteen acts, doing it on a shoestring. Studio time was donated.

We got various groups to help us until a record company picked it up. We jumped out there on faith. At the time I was the director of the office of special events and entertainment at the King Center. It seemed like the best place for me to continue to nurture my love of music and the arts while still attending to the serious mission of Mother's life after my father's death. The King Center is the embodiment of the work and sacrifices of my family, and my soul needs to support it. But my heart always dreamed of a life in music.

I was by then viewed as the black sheep of the family; this project didn't reverse that perception. I don't mean I was viewed in a bad way—I wasn't a rebel, it was just that I was more out there than some thought I should be. I was visible socially—informally versus formally. I didn't follow the path of being groomed, accredited, blessed. I'd moved toward the King Center, toward the legacy, for the first time with this job. I didn't want to let down my family, but I still wanted to be me.

This record project helped to raise money for the King Center and to create awareness around the new King holiday. It was exciting, going into the studio, recording these artists. Until this day, when I see Michael Bivins, or any of the former members of New

Edition, they remember. Ricky Martin was in Menudo then. It was like a "We Are the World" production. We had many of the hottest young artists, and the music video was financed entirely by Prince. Music industry veteran Clarence Avant served as our senior adviser and contributed financially. Polygram eventually picked up the record for distribution. However, we soon realized that we had set up the deal in a way that did not provide enough financial incentive for the record company to aggressively promote it. In hindsight, we would've been wiser to have structured it so that everybody got a little bit of something, profit-wise; that would have been more of an incentive for them to push it through the channels, and onto many more radio station airplay lists.

A lot of radio stations would not even play it once we had it pressed. I'd get on the phone with some of the black radio program directors and they'd yawn. Phil and I produced, recorded, marketed, and promoted this record. We'd done the legwork. But in the end, whenever I'd call these radio stations, they'd claim that because it had rap in it, they couldn't play it.

Remember, this was 1985, going into 1986. Rap was still mostly underground. Ours was one of the first projects to incorporate rap into mainstream values or icons like Daddy. It would be years after before rap and hip-hop exploded. Now, seventeen years later, you can't close a record deal, make a commercial, or record a movie soundtrack unless you have rap and hip-hop in there somewhere. But at that time, we met with a lot of resistance.

In subsequent years, around the King holiday, many radio stations would play our song, even through the '90s.

The title of the single was "King Holiday, Sing, Celebrate."

The lyrics went something like, "Once a year, we celebrate Washington and Lincoln on their birth dates, now a third name is added to the list, a man of peace, a drum major for justice . . ."

The chorus: "Sing, celebrate, sing, sing, celebrate for a King, celebrate." The first verse started out with New Edition. "Who do we thank for teaching us that we have the strength to love . . ."

Tina Marie came in: "We thank the prince of nonviolence . . ." Then Stephanie Mills, Whitney Houston—a great blend.

We conceived this thanks to many, particularly Mother and the commitment to making the King holiday a reality by the consummate musician, Stevie Wonder. Stevie composed a song, "Happy Birthday to You," and put it on his *Hotter Than July* album in 1981. Now that song is sung nearly as often as the traditional "Happy Birthday" melody. Stevie was front and center of a march in Washington to help ensure there'd be a King holiday to celebrate.

We were invited to the White House again in 1983, for the signing of the King holiday legislation by President Reagan. Martin and I were quiet as we entered the White House. George and Barbara Bush, the vice president and his wife, reached out warmly, like they were accustomed to seeing black folk as people beyond whatever they had to do publicly to retain political currency. Like Humphrey, Bush was kind. I watched the faces of my mother and siblings brighten when Vice President Bush took personal time with them. President Reagan used thirty pens so those present could get to keep one and say that that was the pen he used to sign the legislation.

Vice President Bush took my brother and me to his desk and showed us where all the vice presidents of the United States, dating back many years, had carved their initials in the drawer. Then Mr. Reagan was ready for us to come into the Oval Office; from there, after formal hellos and a few stories, we walked out to the Rose Garden for the signing. George Bush reached out to me, and Barbara Bush had a downright grandmotherly warmth. With both of them, you felt like you were talking to real people. I appreciated this, especially since we were already beginning to feel public slings and arrows, backlash, I suppose from my father being so sanctified in the public memory and from the battle to make his birthday the first American national holiday to honor an African American. We were already taking hits for being just the family of Martin Luther King, Jr., and not Martin Luther King, Jr., himself.

It was an honor, no doubt, yet we'd had to demand it.

President Reagan was nice, but seemed a little aloof. But George Bush? "Come on in here! What's going on? Let me tell you about this. Let me show you that." That was one time I felt we were at an important moment in history, where somebody went above and beyond the call of duty. The Bushes could've just come for the ceremony. They also seemed to be interested in the sacrament. It didn't come across as contrived. I sensed that these were caring, decent people. I have always appreciated their attention, especially after Granddaddy's death, when we got condolences from the Bushes, and Vice President Bush attended the funeral.

It was the fall of '88 when my mother called us together as a family to go on retreat. By now she'd been head of the King Center for twenty years, and through her hard work, and the help of Maynard Jackson and Andy Young when they were mayors of Atlanta, and Jimmy Carter when he was governor of Georgia and president of the United States, and captains of industry like Henry Ford, the DuPonts, and others, the Center was built and completed on Auburn Avenue, adjacent to Ebenezer Baptist Church. If ever Atlanta had a historic district, this was it.

At the countryside retreat, Mother raised the issue of succession. The King Center board of directors had been raising the issue with her; it was important for any organization to have a line of succession. At first I was barely listening, then for some reason my ears started burning. It was the way Mother was looking at me. Expectantly. Me? Not me. Not with my rep, my history.

We were in a cabin in the northeast Georgia mountains, the tailpipe of the Great Smokies, sitting in a circle, and Mother first put it out there—in essence, Who's interested in taking this on? By then Yolanda was fully into acting, directing, producing, into the life of theater, drama, film, the arts. She shook her head emphatically. "No way," her look said. "Not here." In fact, her mouth said it too. Yolanda has never ever been particularly shy.

Martin had entered politics.

By then Bernice was pursuing her calling to the ministry.

We gazed around the circle and everybody wore the same expression: "Not me, it's not me, don't look at me," rolling our eyes at our mother, but in a good-natured way. Then everybody kind of looked at me. Bernice and Yolanda came out and said it. I don't know if they had worked it out beforehand. First Bernice: "Dexter, you know we need you to do this . . ."

"It has to be you, Dexter."

I seemed to be the one who took the most interest in the Center, they said. Plus, I was the "why" guy. We all had gotten a little bit of something from our father. Yolanda got his sense for the dramatic, for the theatrical, and his great feel for people. Martin got his name and his ability to canvass and to be diplomatic and to advocate, and also his moderacy; Bernice got his deeply rooted spirituality, his religiosity, his philosophical bent, if I can put it that way, and, I must add, his oratorical ability.

What did I get? Outside of a resemblance to both parents? Well, in the first place, the uncanny resemblance is something, isn't it? But also, I think I got Dad's disposition, and patience. He was the same way. I may feel upset about something, but I know it's not going to help matters to go do something that makes it worse. Even though to a lot of people, that's gratification.

It wasn't a question of whether or not I wanted this responsibility anymore. It was a question of how best to accept it. I knew that, at least for now, this move was my destiny. How can one argue with that? I had always had a sense of process from a grassroots, jailhouse lawyer perspective, watching my mom in board meetings, reading the minutes, being on the board. I probably got the best kind of training by practical experience. But I also knew that it meant continuing to put my dreams of a life in arts and entertainment on hold—indefinitely. I had been seriously considering moving to Los Angeles around the same time; really trying to make a go of it. Through my work on the King Holiday record and my position at the Center, I had developed experience and relationships in music and entertainment. But duty called, and for the love of my family I responded. I was reminded of the way my mother must have felt when she chose to postpone her musical career after graduating from the New England Conservatory of Music to return to the south with my father to continue to challenge the prevailing social conditions.

It was the spring of 1989, and I'd just turned twenty-eight. I was not scheduled to come in and officially take charge until April. The King Center board wanted it to coincide with the King assassination "anniversary," April 4. I had an installation service, five hours of formality in the old sanctuary of Ebenezer Baptist Church, where so many of my memories were. It was a big celebration, with people from all over. Berry Gordy came and donated Motown master tapes of some of our father's speeches. There was a real anointed feeling. It humbled me. It was a period where there was much hope and good intentions. But you know what they say about the latter. People important to me came: Phil Jones, friends from Los Angeles, some of my acting friends like Sheryl Lee Ralph. Tavis Smiley came—he at that time was working with Tom Bradley, part of a young political group. Isaac was there. My friend Jennifer Holliday sang. Adam Clayton Powell IV came, as well as other sons and daughters of the Movement.

Barbara Williams Skinner was serving as the chief operating officer and executive vice president of the King Center. Barbara was very active and prominent in black leadership circles, particularly in the D.C. area. She had worked with the Congressional Black Caucus, been in different circles, and had a longtime relationship with my mom. Some members of the board felt that Barbara needed to be packaged with me to make this, and me, credible. Because of the way it was presented, I think, to other people, it raised more questions than it answered. When the torch was passed in the ceremonial part of my installation, Barbara appeared on the platform to receive the torch with me. That in and of itself sent a message.

Is this man standing on his own two feet, or is he being propped up by Mama?

I didn't understand it then, but in subsequent years I came to. What made it worse, the same person who made these requirements, who said he supported me, later switched the resolution and made a statement to the media when I wound up resigning five months later; he said, "We never really expected Dexter to be in charge. In fact, he was a president in training."

President in training?

It's always been about Mother, but I was an easy target. What I have come to find out is that people who had been gunning for my mother for years took it out on me. I've had people tell me that I got hit so hard on a lot of issues because there were long resentments from years back. Human nature, petty jealousies from the most stunning, disappointing quarters. And in the black community, you have issues because of her being the "First Lady of the Movement." I have such a hard time with all these people always saying, "Dr. King . . . our leader . . . my man . . ." and yet stabbing her in the back the whole time. I was just like some boxer in there trying to duck punches, and getting hit, but I didn't at the time know much of this was premeditated. I didn't recognize Machiavellian behavior. That was my failing.

Why can't I just go on and live and be happy being selfish? This is the conflict: not only do I know the way the system works from what I've experienced, but I also saw what it did to Dad. And I was not just the kid who's scared, and saw that his dad was assassinated. We'd gotten to the mountaintop and seen not the Promised Land, but rather the truth, the very matrix itself, and we as a family seem sometimes to have a heavier burden now than we did before.

Somehow I thought that I would be able to just help, and I still believe this, maybe it's just my fallacy, but I hang on to the fact that I can still do this—help out—and at the same time be Dexter, protect that part of me that's mine, that's private, or that just wants to get home safe at the end of the day. There's a side that does not want to necessarily belong to the world. I've seen what the world can do to a good man, then not look back, except to put him on a pedestal once he's gone. I'm reminded of all these noble athletic teams named after the noble red man. We have one in Atlanta—the Atlanta Braves baseball team. When did these Native Americans become recognized as noble? After they were dead. There was a time in this country when the only good Indian was a dead Indian.

The media has always portrayed my father in this very serious light, as a public icon. Do you bring him down off the pedestal and humanize him, or do you keep him up on the shelf? Maybe you keep him on the shelf, humanize the family, the wife, the mother, the children, the daughters, the sons, do what comes natural, obliterate them, since they're still living. Maybe you go beyond that, in this insatiable celebrity- and media-driven society. Maybe you don't just humanize—maybe you humiliate too. History puts Dad on the shelf, not people. The truth is, too many see history as largely irrelevant, passé, so they put it on the shelf until it's convenient for their purposes.

In Isaac's words, I "had the biggest pair." Unlike me, he could get away with saying something like that publicly, in a relaxed, informal vernacular. Actually, my father would've probably gotten a kick out of that description. But I felt I had an image to live up to now. Isaac was probably less guarded, but between the two of us he probably needed to be less guarded.

There was another, less obvious dilemma. Once my father's cause came into prominence, a lot of local connections were almost severed, with the exception of my grandfather. When my father was growing up, his family was plugged in locally. I must be honest, it's almost a shame to say it, but after he came to prominence, a fear developed. In Atlanta in the '50s and '60s, there was a large section of black society, including the preacher-teacher class, that felt, "Hey, we're straight. We don't necessarily need to integrate." It probably was the James Crow Esquire example of separate but near-equal, meaning the infrastructure for some blacks in Atlanta wasn't such a low-grade thing. Houses in the black community, for blacks who could afford them, were as nice as houses in some white communities. Blacks could buy nice cars, there were restaurants here serving them. No need to go over to Lester Maddox's place to get met by an ax handle. Black chefs here were as good as white ones. There were places in Atlanta for talent to express itself. The colleges, education, even on lower levels, the schools, were as good as the white schools. People here weren't anxious to upset the apple cart. Many of them were fine with the status quo. The extension of that today is in people who write editorial columns saying they see the King family as an embarrassment, like something of another era, something that is no longer needed, a sort of civil rights history exhibit.

There was and is lingering resentment because of this history. There were a lot of successful, intelligent, well-to-do people, right there on the King Center board, who had resentments. My grandfather didn't encounter it as much. My father? That's another story. Don't get me wrong, I'm not saying everyone liked my grandfather. He was a driven man. Such men are never universally liked. The resentment I'm speaking of against my father was from his generation. Don't rock our boat. You might spill our champagne. We don't need you anymore. Go on home now, preacher and children alike. And this mentality was about to land on me, on us all, and land hard.

CHAPTER 12

Betrayed

All my mother wanted was for the King Center to do its work, spread the legacy of my father's methods, carry out his mission of peace and brotherhood, and be a repository for mementos and artifacts of his life. The King Center was finally about to be completed as an edifice, a place where the people of the world could commiserate and peacefully reflect near his remains.

Nothing angers Mother quicker than for someone to say she was an ornament my father picked up. She'll tell you in a minute that she began to earn her stripes as an undergraduate at Antioch College in the late '40s, early '50s. She spoke out on human rights issues from the beginning. She spoke out against the Vietnam War before Daddy. She went to Geneva in 1962 for a disarmament conference—Daddy encouraged her, but she'd supported conscientious objectors since they were some of her fellow students at Antioch.

Mother—think what you will of me, her wayward third child. Some board members had their own motives. So my being elected to the position of president was a real soap opera. We had to line up votes before a January 1989 election. Mother and I went around, met with board members, soliciting their support. Some I met with one-on-one; some she met with me. One in particular, though not on the board now, is still close by. He told us we had his support. Broke down in tears while meeting us in a suite on the upper floor of a downtown Atlanta hotel the day before. The next day the rest of the board members waited downstairs to take the vote. He was looking at me, talking to Mother and me about how much character he knew was in me. He asked if I had any skeletons in my closet.

I said, "No," and quoted the Bible: "When I was a child, I spoke as a child, I thought as a child, I acted as a child. But when I became a man, I put away childish things." He broke down and said, "You have something more special than somebody who has a degree or credentials." That stung. It always stung back then. I didn't know to let my sincerity be my credential. I was still insecure. "Okay," I thought. "I didn't graduate from Morehouse, I'll never live that down in some circles, but how long will it be held over my head?"

I think his concern was genuine, but I also think he didn't have any backbone. The next morning, he tried with the attorney to hamstring me by changing the resolution. I'm being brought in as president and he's trying to change the language on the resolution behind the scenes, so that when it's agreed to, a legal glitch would make me a puppet, a figurehead.

Fortunately, the King Center's attorney, Archer Smith, alerted us. There was, then and always, a lot of legal action around the King Center and my father's legacy, in the form of the King Estate. Whether one was asking Boston University for the return of a portion of my father's papers, or asking USA Today not to publish my father's speech without permission, or any one of a dozen legal disagreements, attorneys were always working, either for the King Center or on behalf of the King Estate, two separate entities. So it was Archer Smith, who had always been loyal to the family, who blew the whistle. We found out on the morning of the meeting. We were in a suite, in a hotel downtown, Mother and I sitting there while we were being converged upon by eight to ten people who did not have our best interests at heart; we did not meet them all at once, but one or two at a time. The board meeting was convening downstairs in a meeting room. We were up in the suite when one of the prominent board members, a businessman, came in saying, "We don't have the votes," telling Mother, "If you don't have the votes and if you go forward, you're going to be embarrassed."

Mother—I'd never seen her like this. She was near tears. She looked at me, through me, and I don't know what flashed in her mind—her deceased husband, their lives, twenty-one years since his assassination, twenty years working to make the King Center vision come alive, and now—"They've betrayed us," she whispered. I saw her face in mine.

She told the man, "I've gone around and met with all of you; I was told I had the votes. Now you are telling me, today, at the eleventh hour—no? There's a credibility gap. A big credibility gap."

I can still see the hurt on her face—that sweet, full, butterscotch angel's face I've seen above me all of my life. I have to be honest. Those people became my enemies for a while for hurting her. I kept telling her, "They aren't with you, Mother. They're here for their own purposes." She began to take her earrings off and then put them back on. She does that when she's either nervous or has something she wants to say. Maybe she didn't want to see it. I don't want to say she's naive; that would be putting her down. I was naive. But that was changing. She has good intentions and takes for granted that other people do too. It's a country trait, it can be a downfall. She believes in the goodness in everybody. I tend to be more skeptical. I've seen what happens. But then, so has she.

Mother said, "There's a credibility gap." Another board member ignored her, saying, "If you go forward with this nomination of your son as president, then I'm stepping down."

These votes of no confidence made me more determined, whereas before I might have been a little unsure about stepping in, fearing that I was doing it because my siblings and mother elected me. Now it was more personal. A faction of the board was not going to have me under any circumstances. They were fighting to the death on this one. Finally somebody else came in, another wealthy, prominent Atlantan; he called off the dogs and said, "We need to let this one go."

People downstairs were getting wind something was funny, because we hadn't come down yet. The nomination and voting should have been taking place. At some point Uncle Andy came up and said we had the votes; he and the wealthy, prominent Atlantan had twisted a few arms. I don't think Uncle Andy knew what was going on at the time. He was always true-blue ever since that April day when he stood on the balcony of the Lorraine Motel in Memphis pointing toward where he thought the shot had come from. Also when he was a congressman, and later a UN ambassador during the Carter administration, and after that, as mayor of Atlanta; now he was downstairs dealing with the grassroots portion of the board, the King loyalists. Sure, there were some people in the loyalist crowd who may have had general concerns about an unproven person coming in, but if Mother said, "I believe this is the right thing," they weren't going to question it. They may have said, "Dexter, what's your plan for this?" But I had eight to ten board members against me who were telling me, "Look, you're not qualified, you don't know jack, and we're going to show you don't know jack." I was very hurt by the lack of support from people who I had not only looked up to but who, frankly, had also benefited from the efforts of my family.

We all went downstairs, the vote was taken, and I was elected. Nobody voted against it. People who were against it had left the room because they didn't want to be on record. At that point they had shown their cards. The sad thing is that some of these people, I could have worked with them then, and in fact later did work with some of them. These are black businesspeople who were known across the state and country at the time, but they just could not deal with me alone—couldn't trust me without an academic pedigree that was familiar to them. "If it was Martin, we'd support it," I was told.

So I was confirmed, but there was this undercurrent of contentiousness that went on past the January confirmation, even past the April installation ceremonies. Some wealthy board members feared I was going to come out and confront all these people, and stir things up, and try to wreak revenge. I never was going to do that. I kept it to myself, and my mother and siblings. The general public never really knew about this.

Someone on the board put it out that a rift had come up between my mother and me. It was tense between Mother and me sometimes, and really, as much as anything, that is what also led to my resigning as the titular president and head of the King Center that following August.

The board called me in one day, after having discussed with Barbara Skinner her departure. There were professional differences between the board and her, and she was moving on. They didn't tell me or consult with me on that. Why would they? I was the ultimate target because I stood between them and Mother. This was the last straw for me. Since Day One I had had numerous battles with some board members who had never supported me and who wanted to micromanage the King Center. Even more important, I was not being allowed to carry out the vision I had articulated for the Center, which was to bring my father's message of nonviolence to new generations of young people who needed it most of all.

I said to myself, "The mature thing to do is get out of the way, you all can have this." I felt like, "If it means this much to them where they're going to go through all this stuff to hurt me, to hurt my mother, to hurt the King Center, then hey, they can have it."

Some people said, "If you were just a little more diplomatic," or "If you understood you have to kind of work your way into it." In other words, they were saying, Stay and be a figurehead and eventually you'll get it. I was president reporting to the CEO. Mother was CEO. Then there was the board chairman. Then an "oversight committee." I had a title with no means of accomplishing anything, I only had the liability of being in charge, ceremonially, emotionally, and spiritually if something went wrong.

When I resigned from the King Center in August '89, I was devastated. I felt betrayed, torn. I felt then that while Mother hadn't caused the problem directly, she had indirectly. At the time I didn't understand that she was an innocent bystander. I was suffering to even have to question whether or not my mother had a hand in my leaving. I now don't think she did, but at the time I was still hurt. Some of her people had betrayed me. After I left, I went through other experiences that opened my eyes, matured me; eventually I saw her hands had been tied, but at the time, I felt like she had cut me adrift—not willingly, yet it had happened. These were her people, as I saw it. There should have been allegiance from them to her, at least to the point where if she had intervened, they wouldn't have been able to confront me in the way that they did.

Mother and I had verbal knock-down-drag-out arguments about it; I felt betrayed by her, and told her so. My father and grandfather had had the same kind of philosophical arguments as well. And my grandfather had had similar arguments with his father.

I had been told that we at the Center would be able to work together to get things done, so I had tried to work in their structure, against my better judgment. I felt it was flawed. I don't know if it was anybody's fault. The structure was not practical or workable. But we tried it anyway; the experiment didn't succeed. Mother fell victim to what some people were saying about me: "What credentials does he have?" Mother, once she's firmly behind something, will support it ardently, and she did support my coming in. However, she didn't know how to appease or placate those voices of dissent that were bringing to her attention these "inadequacies" on my part, as they saw them.

Mother was concerned about appearances. I was not a traditional candidate, but then neither was Daddy. I'd never, ever com-

pare myself to him; but let's face it, on some level he was not a traditional leader. He was a C student at Morehouse, an average student by most academic standards, and became a true scholar only
later. He reached heights of understanding I can't hope to equal,
emulate, or imitate; yet his grandparents were functionally illiterate. So how do you judge a man? By where he's from, or by where
he's going? How do you judge a person's efficiency without first
giving them an opportunity to be efficient, to fail, and to try again?

I don't fault the board now. They put pressure on Mother, put
her in an awkward spot, she was caught between a rock and a hard
place—I'm her son, she supported me, but then she had people to
answer to, some out of the Movement. My hope was she would've
somehow been able to see beyond the past to our future; as a mom,
I knew she'd support me, but I wanted her to validate me, to believe that I knew what I was doing. Not just support me because
I'm her child, because the legacy needs heirs, but because quickly
I'll know what I'm doing, I'll bring something fresh, modern to
bear. But on the other hand, would she know that from past experience?

Those other factions preyed on that doubt. They pushed her
hot buttons and knew exactly how to get into her insecurities. I
could tell when they had talked to her. I could hear it in the tone
of her voice, her discomfort.

"Mother, what is it?"

"It's . . . nothing."

When she says "nothing," it's usually something big.

Once I saw that everything I was trying to do was being shot
down, I knew I had no support. At board meetings there had been
confrontations; there was open, deep hostility that these older people had for me, particularly older black males I didn't know. Some
of those who found my presence objectionable were my father's
peers. All of them knew my father, but weren't necessarily of the
inner circle. I resigned in August of 1989, but remained on the King
Center board. Resignation was painful, but the bigger trauma

would have been not to resign. Mother's getting caught in the crossfire—that threw me.

I was living alone in a townhouse in Midtown Atlanta by the end of '89. I did not look back; but I could not look forward either. I was stuck in a place of hurt, anger, and confusion. My old friend Phil Jones, my loyal confidant, friend, and collaborator, went through all of this with me as a sounding board, and was probably the closest person to me. He knew the dynamics of it all. Now he was like my consiglieri. He'd sat in on some proceedings, was a person who understood what went on from my point of view. And he stuck by me. I could talk to him. He became my closest adviser. The choice I made—not going public or creating a scene—was no choice. The press was looking for a story behind my leaving. I would not talk to anybody. With a newly minted King national holiday, the last thing we needed was scandalous infighting. The media tried to make it about a rift between me and my mother, but it wasn't. The real rift was with these board members. But I didn't go public, so I couldn't defend myself. I felt bad that my leaving the King Center presidency was portrayed as Mother's and my having problems.

By November, I was in a funk. The only thing that saved me, outside my friendship with Phil, was that I'd met a woman who became my girlfriend, a woman who was at the right place at the right time for me. I'll call her Good Natured. I met her at an event. I fell head over heels in love with Good Natured, such as it is within my ability to fall; I took her through all of my ups and downs, which is my habit—maybe it is the habit of all men. She'd roll with the punches. I was on some kind of journey of self-discovery and she was there with me, going through a shedding of the old skin, a metamorphosis, a slow, painful one; she was there and went through it, good and bad. The relationship ended after two and a half years, got to a point where our main issues—well, I don't even know why we broke up, to tell you God's honest truth. Sometimes I wish we hadn't. It got to the point where we were constantly at each other's throats over any- and everything. But I never questioned whether this was somebody I deeply cared for. Still, we didn't make it.

I started doing therapy during that period with someone who wasn't a traditional therapist, meaning she wasn't a psychiatrist or psychologist, but a spiritual counselor and an alternative health specialist. She helped me to realize I had issues I was still dealing with in regard to Daddy's death. "Dexter, you must come to grips with your father's death in order to move on," became her mantra. When I was younger and went through that phase, meeting with therapists, I never got any answers I could use. This was the first opening where I was dealing with psychological, emotional, spiritual needs. I was in year two of my vegetarianism; I was in the zealot stage, I was learning, I was self-righteous about it. This was another reason why the relationship with Good Natured soured; I imposed it on her: "You've got to be a vegetarian, you have got to eat this way." The things I love, I smother. Part of it, I learned through counseling, is because of the trauma of Daddy's death; he and Big Mama and Uncle A.D. gone. I developed a protective shell, where I was not giving of my heart because of too much pain. I held on to my heart. There was this control thing, not knowing how to open up with the people closest to me because I'd been hurt, afraid anybody who got close to me would be taken away. I wouldn't let anyone close. That was my protection. I was told this over and over. It just wasn't really crystallizing.

Before that, I thought it was everybody else's problem. I thought it was Good Natured's.

I didn't realize I was pushing her to some of these places and causing her to lash out. I was controlling and creating my environment. We Kings were always so stoic, so necessarily stoic, after Daddy's murder. I watched my mom and she seemed so stoic and strong; me never really emoting or crying was no accident. Obviously emotions were touched. For a long time after we broke up, Good Natured and I didn't speak. The relationship ended badly; there was no communication. Later I tried to reach out to her, but she'd been hurt. Said she had to shut me off in order to protect her feelings. Once I realized the hurt I had caused her was my fault, I reached out to her to apologize and ask for her forgiveness. But she had already forgiven me long before so that she might move on with her life. I can say today that we are on good terms. When we talk now about it, it's almost like yesterday, and it's been many years. I feel fortunate that I was able to get out of denial for a while with her. I was walking around oblivious to the fact I was carrying baggage.

On January 11, 1990, Mother unveiled the Behold monument. It was not on the King Center grounds, but just across Auburn Avenue, on the National Park Service grounds, near a small mini-amphitheater. The plaque says it is a tribute to her late husband and an enduring inspiration to all who fight for dignity, social justice, and human rights. The sculptor, Patrick Morelli, was inspired by scenes from the '70s TV miniseries *Roots*, the scene of actor Thalmus Rasulala, portraying the Gambian father, Omoro Kinte, lifting his newborn son Kunta to a star-studded African night sky and reciting these words: "Behold, the only thing greater than yourself." The statue itself is of the "baptism" of the infant Kizzy, by her father, the slave Kunta Kinte, played by LeVar Burton.

Across Auburn Avenue stood the King Center administration building; that side of the street also holds old Ebenezer, and my father's tomb in the middle of the reflecting pool. Across Auburn is the Behold monument, and soon there would stand a new multimillion-dollar Ebenezer Baptist Church; Ebenezer Horizon Sanctuary; then also the King Visitor Center set up by the National Park Service for the 700,000 tourists who visit the King Historic District each year. Up Auburn Avenue a bit on that same side of the street is the King Natatorium, the swimming pool. Above Boulevard, on the same side of Auburn Avenue as the King Center, is Fire Station No. 6. Across from that, shotgun row houses, private residences; across from them, Daddy's birth home, 501 Auburn Avenue. I often drove by his birth home. It was demanded of us, furthering this legacy. But even though physically I was refreshed, spiritually I felt hollowed out, banished, betrayed, and, somehow, a betrayer. There was only one place left to look for help.

CHAPTER 13

Brightly Beams
Our Father's Mercy

Bernice was seventeen when she heard the Call. My grandfather had always looked for it to first reach Martin III, Isaac, Derek, Al, Vernon, one of his grandsons, the Call that for various reasons he and then both his sons, my father and Uncle A.D., had received, in their different personal circumstances and lifetimes.

I never got it. Isaac never got it. Martin never got it. Derek got it, and Vernon got it. Meanwhile, Bernice got the Call clear and strong. She says an inner voice told her she was going to preach like my father. For years she resisted it—for eight years, from when she first got the Call before age eighteen until she was twenty-five years old. When she was a younger woman she saw and felt and thought that preaching was something for men, mature men at that. No wonder she would get that impression, since she was in the South, since she was in Atlanta, since she was in the Baptist Church, and since she was in Ebenezer Baptist Church. Quadruple whammy.

I wouldn't call it sexism so much as obliviousness; the same factors that might have helped cause my grandfather and his sons to take up the calling were impacting her, as a woman, a black woman in the South. Many mothers and grandfathers of earlier in the century in the South wanted their sons and grandsons to "hear the Call," to take up the Bible and the way, because, first, it was one of the few ways a man could speak his mind and then still be held safe against powers that would kill or otherwise mute a "Negro" who was outspoken about the heinous crimes being committed against those of his flock, and, second, it was a way to make a living, a way out of no way, before segregation ended. Some of the same factors held true for women nearer the close of the century. But Bernice was, as my grandfather would've said, a woman who was "God-troubled." He died aware of her calling. Wish I'd been there when Bernice told him, to see the happy look on his face.

For whatever reason, it was Bernice who got the Call; not only that, it was the right Call, according to her talents and gifts. She had an ability to reach her zenith through preaching, to move an audience via spoken word, to minister, even though she claims to have no memories of our father. Granddaddy was dead. He'd found no successors among his grandsons.

I was in the congregation for Bernice's first sermon. She gave it at Ebenezer, on March 27, 1988. She called it "Getting above the Crowd," and based it on the story from the Book of Luke, about Zacchaeus, a short man who climbed a sycamore tree, the better to see Jesus. Fittingly, she gave this message in the sanctuary at Ebenezer, where I had seen my father and grandfather speak so many times. Bernice had fasted for seven days before she gave the sermon. She seemed to me to be in another realm that Sunday. She is unique. Bernice is singular, unto herself; her individualism would be a strike against her later on.

We all were there that Sunday—Mother, Yolanda, Martin, me. A light shined in Mother's eyes, a light I had not seen in a long time, as it did in the eyes of many of our cousins and extended family. When Bernice spoke that day, I could see she'd inherited much from our father—certain hand gestures that startled me in their familiarity. I'd not seen them in so long—a certain tilt of her

head, a lilt in her voice, strategic pauses, drawing out words—
seeeen—or making multisyllabic certain words, the opening twist of
humor, even the looks on her face that were exactly the kinds of
looks that my father had. It was eerie. I think Bernice was oblivious to these similarities.

Bernice came in knowing how to preach, but she needed to
learn how to pastor. Rev. Roberts advised her to take her appren-
ticeship elsewhere, because she had grown up in Ebenezer and
might benefit from outside experience. She took his advice and
went to minister at the Love Center at Greater Rising Star Baptist
Church in southwest Atlanta. She became an assistant to Pastor
Byron L. Broussard, and she dealt primarily with youth and
women's ministries. It seemed strange not to have a King somewhere in the pulpit in Ebenezer.

My spiritual crisis had begun with my father's death, and continued with my uncle's death and my grandmother being gunned
down. Ever since, whenever I have had a question of faith, Bernice
has helped show me the way.

What about my other siblings? Were they proud of Bernice, yet
disappointed in me? I'm sure they were caught in a difficult position. I think they never understood why I had to leave the King
Center. Mother didn't really understand it, and they seemed to follow her lead. There may have been a feeling that maybe I walked
away from it because I wasn't mature enough to handle the pressure, didn't have the stuff of Kings. I didn't ask and they didn't say.
Later, once they saw subsequent events and we'd talked about it,
they understood. We couldn't always talk about it initially, it was
just so heated that it became more of a divisive conversation than
a productive one. So we just kind of steered clear of it as a family.
I think there was this feeling that maybe I brought some of this on
myself, but I never felt that way.

Bernice confided in me that she had also had dreams. She
dreamed of our father, back when we had that retreat in the north
Georgia mountains in 1988 and Mother asked if any of the four of
us would volunteer to succeed her at the King Center. Bernice

dreamed that Daddy appeared and expressed concern about Mother and the King Center; that she needed time for herself. Suddenly Bernice saw me appear in the dream and at that point she awakened from her sleep. She later concluded I was the one to succeed mother.

Bernice told me she'd had another dream since our retreat. In her dream, Daddy was sitting at his desk. Bernice was sitting across from him. He reached across and held her hands. Then she said I came in, and our father smiled and looked at me and said, "Dexter," and put Bunny's hands in mine. Bernice said in her previous dreams about our father, he was chasing her, gliding after her. But now she had no fear. When she told me that, it humbled me. Scared me a little too.

Bernice asked me to trust the Bible. I told her I didn't know it as well as she did. Now I had an opportunity to learn more about it, through my eyes and hers.

I came back into the King fold around '92. I told Mother I still wanted to have involvement with the family, with the legacy, but from another perspective. Consulting with my best friend Phil, I began to focus not on the King Center but the King Estate, the business and cultural side of the legacy. They were separate— licensing, intellectual property, creative projects—an open book. Bernice left the Ebenezer fold. I knew I must work with the King Estate, must not give up on the legacy, must be true to it. The question was, how?

CHAPTER 14

A Moving Image

My mother had always dreamed that a big, important movie would be made about my father's life to honor him and his message, much like the movie *Gandhi* had honored its subject. In 1992, Spike Lee released *Malcolm X* through Warner Bros. studio. The film was launched amid a firestorm of publicity. Everywhere I went people asked, "When is a movie about your father coming out?" Not to take anything away from Malcolm X's story, but I had to agree that a movie about my father made sense. Movies are central to our culture—they're the way into the collective consciousness and a way to continue for each generation. At one time it was books, radio, newspapers, billboards. Now it is television and movies. And music. We had the story. We had the fascinating character. We just needed a way in.

For what I had in mind, I'd need help, big-time—somebody who knew the ins and outs of the filmmaking business. Two associates would back me. One was Phillip Jones. He became key to virtually all the plans of the King Estate and Intellectual Properties Management (IPM), the company he set up.

The other was Michelle Clark Jenkins, a New Jersey native

who had graduated from Princeton in 1976 and had gotten a law degree while working in New York for Time Inc. She had been a business affairs manager for HBO, and had worked in several divisions in what was later to become Time Warner. I first worked with Michelle when she was at HBO and she produced the video for the King Holiday record. Later, she would come to Atlanta, at my request, to run the King Estate.

In 1990, Michelle Clark Jenkins took a job offer from Bob Johnson, head of Black Entertainment Television, to go to L.A. and develop films at Tim Reid's production company. One of the first projects they worked on was *Once upon a Time When We Were Colored*. She kept in contact with Phil, and he aligned her with me after *Malcolm X* came out. That was how we came to be in L.A. together, trying to get a film made about my father.

"So we're talking biopic," Michelle said. We had nerve, thinking it could be done. But Michelle knew the terrain and thought we had a good shot. Through her I learned that the film industry felt there had been so much out there on the subject of Dr. Martin Luther King, Jr., and the Civil Rights Movement of the '50s and '60s that the story had been told. We felt there hadn't been enough told.

There's never really been a feature film made about my father. *King*, a '70s TV movie with Paul Winfield and Cicely Tyson, was only adequate. I have respect for Cicely and Paul as actors, and Ossie Davis, and the other key people who were in it, but the story was too one-dimensional to me. That production was an Abby Mann made-for-TV movie in 1977. The overall texture was lacking—a lot of it had to do with the technology then. Just seemed like it was a little rushed, maybe.

We were on the set for that. It was shot in Macon, Georgia, and all of us children had some extra roles. Yolanda actually had a speaking part. She portrayed Rosa Parks. That turned into an uneasy experience because what the finished product ended up being was not what we'd believed it would be. Abby Mann was famous for the long-running TV series *Kojak*. Paul Winfield played Daddy.

Everybody I've ever seen portray Dad, they sort of overdo his piety. It's like they're forcing a presence on you; it's actually their perception of that presence being forced—that's not what he was. That wasn't his approach. His was natural, a presence that spoke for itself. My point is, we just felt something was needed: the right person had to be involved, and we needed not only to have somebody who got it creatively, but who could also get it done. This was twenty-five years later, a new day.

The whole purpose of the many trips I made to L.A. during this period was to identify a director, a studio, a producer, and a "bankable" star who could "open a picture," and who would be not only willing but eager to do a definitive King project. The whole point was that we always felt there had not been a definitive film done. There hadn't been a film about Dad's life showing not so much the icon or the serious, public, celebrated person, but rather the man in terms of a very interesting and gripping story. It had never been done.

So we felt like we needed someone who could do it justice.

The first person Phil and I thought of was Spike Lee, the old homecoming coronation director at Morehouse who in the intervening years had become the controversial and internationally famous film director. He had shot *Malcolm X* starring Denzel Washington, and I gathered it was not easy to get funding, not easy in any way. Phil called Spike. Spike didn't bite—either it wasn't a challenge to him, or he was tired because it had taken such a monumental effort on his part to get *Malcolm X* made.

Michelle set up meetings with movers and shakers in the Hollywood scene. It was just Michelle and me. I stayed with her and her family in the foothills of Pacific Palisades, between the beaches of Santa Monica and Malibu. In the down time I'd sit and look at and listen to the breakers rolling in, looking westward, and for the first time in my life I knew peace. This place was calling to me. I was serving as the administrator of the King Estate, away from the political machinations of the actual day-to-day operation of the King Center.

*   *   *

We met with Frank Price, a former head of Columbia Pictures, who still had an office on the lot, and had kind of "godfathered" director John Singleton. He broke a lunch date to meet with us and was very accommodating, and it made me feel like if we could come up with a director, a script, and a star, we might get a studio interested—maybe the studio he was aligned with.

Then we started meeting with what's called the "talent."

We met Ed Zwick at his office, in Santa Monica. I was impressed that he was the only one who met with us—by then I'd learned that Hollywood types are usually bracketed by yes-men whom they treat awfully no matter how many times they say yes. It was just Michelle, him, and myself, and I really liked him; that one was really my initiative. I had asked for Ed Zwick, really liked his approach directing *Glory*, and while in the end I felt *Glory* was a tragic movie, it was a triumph of historical re-creation and dramatization as well. It moved me. Very few movies have done that.

Glory was a good movie, but again, in Hollywood translation, it didn't do big box office. Michelle said that was because you didn't have repeat business, where, in particular, fourteen to twenty-five-year-olds went to see it four or five times. The ending was depressing; one viewing was enough.

Ed Zwick was polite, quiet, didn't ask a lot of questions but had a few, was an unassuming person, laid-back, seemed very interested; but then, everybody we met with was interested. Not one person said, "This isn't something I'd be interested in," or "It's not up my alley." Michelle and I approached it more like we were feeling people out, wanting to get different perspectives.

We met with actor/director Bill Duke in a restaurant in the Valley, Burbank, I believe, just Bill, myself, and Michelle. Bill had an assistant who was kind of around the periphery, but she wasn't actually sitting there during the meeting. We saw her at the beginning and at the end. Bill Duke had directed films like *Deep Cover, A Rage in Harlem*, and *The Cemetery Club*. He was about to join the faculty at Howard University as head of its film department. He was very passionate about our proposed project, really seemed he wanted to do it himself, but he also felt it needed to be done right. His whole thing was, "You can't hurry it—you don't want to rush through this. This needs to be done by somebody who really gets it." I agreed with Bill Duke.

Duke's opinion was that we couldn't allow people on board if they were just looking to take advantage; he also believed in having an African American in the process, if that person was among the best producers, screenwriters, or directors; somebody who knew how to make a film. He felt we needed to make sure "Dr. King" was portrayed strongly. He kept saying, "People need to get his full impact. Many think he was just some kind of wimp when in fact he was a revolutionary with a transcendent ability to move audiences and individuals through the power of his cause, his presence, the power of his speaking ability and action."

He got it. No question in my mind Bill Duke got it. I was sure he could get the ball rolling, but he was clear he'd need backing. No knock against him. That was our challenge.

Producer George Jackson was passionate as well. In recent years, he died of a heart attack. We met at a restaurant on Sunset. I was beginning to know my way around L.A., and I was beginning to like it. First of all, nobody seemed to recognize me, or, if they did, they didn't stop or stare or point or have some hustle they wanted to run by me. I liked being anonymous under the azure skies of Southern California. This was agreeing with me big time. I mentioned this to Michelle and to George as we sat down to lunch. George smiled. "That's the way it happens," he said. "You get bit." He seemed to have a passion for the project. He and his partner, Doug McHenry, were involved in a number of films during this period—*Disorderlies*, *Jason's Lyric*, several others. We met Doug later; this first time it was just George Jackson, and he was reverent about Daddy. He said, "It's got to be done. It's a powerful film." He even talked about the importance of telling it right: every detail, from scenery, set design, the works. He spoke in the curious grammar of film, which I must admit mystified me somewhat, but

I had Michelle break it down into English later. George got technical, down to the nuts and bolts of re-creating certain scenes, texture. He was excited about the prospect.

We walked away from Bill, George, and Doug with possibilities. Here were some people who would be interested, but we hadn't met anyone with the ability to green-light a project. Without a script, we didn't have a project. They all said, "We'd have to get a studio behind it."

So we ended up meeting with a couple of people in the studio system as well, among them Ashley Boone at MGM, now deceased. We were trying to get advice on how to pull together a project. Everybody seemed positive from both the studio side and the creative side. They all seemed pumped. We met with HBO Films; as I've mentioned, Michelle was once Director of Business Affairs at HBO, so she knew people there. We were thinking, "Let's not restrict ourselves, talk to everybody," in case HBO was looking at that time to ratchet up their feature film division, and we felt like maybe we could get kind of both angles, cable TV audiences and feature-release quality.

Everybody was interested, intrigued, but the ones who asked the hard questions would say, "What is there really new you can tell us about Dr. King's story? Haven't we heard it all?" That was their feeling. We said, "No, you really haven't." The public has often seen only a very one-dimensional character and not the full three-dimensional person. Particularly in African Americans' stories and lives, we don't portray them as human beings with feelings and emotions and complexities of humor, pathos, conflict. When I read my mother's book *My Life with Martin Luther King, Jr.*, I was in tears when she talked about what she went through in making a decision to come south after they both went to school and met in Boston, to come back to the land of their ancestors' struggle, in a time of segregation, knowing they'd have to struggle, knowing what they'd be giving up, things they shared as a couple. They were well-rounded, talented people who were going to have to come back to a segregated South and give up what could have been a life of comfort, of learning, of travel. To me, there are other stories within the bigger story that need to be revealed. That's where *Gandhi* or *Malcolm X* showed that kind of epic range. My mother and I met with Sir Richard Attenborough, who had directed *Gandhi*. He felt a feature biopic about my father should be done by an African-American director. He was also adamant that though the screenwriter didn't have to be black, the story had to be well-written and original.

We did meet with Denzel Washington and his production company head, an extremely observant and competent woman named Debra Chase. We met at his office, on the Columbia lot. Debra and he thought this was a good idea. He seemed interested. I think what intrigued him was showing another side of the man. A lot of people saw Washington as Malcolm at the time; a juxtaposition of Malcolm and my father was often portrayed as two opposites. However, I felt Malcolm and my father bore the same frustrations, had similar dilemmas, longings, obstacles, and desires for their people to be truly free. But due to the circumstances of their lives, one approached it differently; sometimes you do things not so much because of the emotion of just getting the anguish out, but because you want to be effective, and my father was at root a Gandhian, with nods to Thoreau's *Civil Disobedience* and Reinhold Niebuhr.

Somehow, I must've said something that resonated with Denzel—it could have been merely the challenge of portraying both men, getting lost in both characters. I can still see his face changing, him saying, "Yeah," like he was getting it. People are amazed if they see the story generationally, my father and grandfather's relationship, where my grandfather was personally a forceful man who would tolerate no mistreatment of himself, yet he was a product of his era. Meanwhile, my father was utterly nonviolent, and yet confrontational of the dilemma. He overturned a system with which his father had bargained. The father was converted by his son, based on the proof being in the pudding. My grandfather observed my father's method, saw how it worked. It actually was effective. He had to be convinced; once he was convinced, he tried it and again it worked. It may have saved my grandfather's sanity after nearly everything he loved was killed. He might not have survived the tragedies if he hadn't changed. They would've eaten him up inside; you can't give to others when you're preoccupied. Granddaddy saw the potential for hypocrisy within Christianity, being a minister of the gospel. At some point you've got to be accountable to what you say you believe. The difference between a great person and somebody who appears great is, one lives it and the other talks it. My father talked and lived it.

Denzel said, "Yeah, I hear you." At first I thought he'd be opposed, wouldn't care for the whole idea, because he had just portrayed Malcolm X, so maybe it would have been tough for him to play this different character from the same moment in history. But he wasn't. Maybe he looked at it as a challenge for him as an actor. Michelle seemed to think that was key for interesting him in a role, particularly this one, where the actor says to himself, "I can reinvent a character people think they know, but don't." Actors enjoy that, Michelle said. I think also he was intrigued by the possibility of being on the production side. So I think it was more than just him as an artist/actor on this project. Debra sat and listened. I've no idea if they hashed it out between them later. I could see that the idea resonated with both of them somewhat, but I didn't know how much.

Michelle did most of the talking in the meetings. We were hoping to put together a "package" as Michelle termed it, with a producer, director, writer, and star who could "open the picture." Not just focus on one aspect, but consider the entire "package." Michelle was knowledgeable because of her background in the industry; she had a sense of how you get things "packaged."

We wanted a "studio project" rather than an "independent project," but what we did not want was to go into "development hell."

On the question of whether the director should be African

American, to me, art is art no matter who does it. There are some people who can better relate to certain experiences, but I don't think it's the skin color that enables you to relate so much as your heart and your head—like Maya Angelou says, everybody who's your skin folk ain't necessarily your kin folk.

"Black" is cultural, a state of mind, particularly when you use it in the abstract context, and not about skin color; which led me to believe, then, that it did not have to be a black person who directed, because if it's a state of mind, and cultural, then anybody who subscribes should qualify.

So it followed that if Steven Spielberg got it the way Bill Duke got it then it wouldn't matter. Competence is what matters. Passion. Shared experience. Spielberg proved with *Schindler's List* that he could relate to human suffering. So I was having these kinds of conversations with Michelle, whether or not we should look for the right kind of non-African-American filmmaker, when she interrupted me.

"We may have him already. I've booked us another sit-down. With Oliver Stone."

The first Oliver Stone meeting occurred in the spring of 1992. I was spending enormous amounts of time in L.A., taking meetings. *JFK* was about to come out. We went to Stone's office in Santa Monica, in a building he shared at the time with Arnold Schwarzenegger. It was Michelle, Janet Yang, who ran Oliver's production company, Oliver, and myself.

Right away, he kept looking at my face.

Stone was one of the people we'd heard had been talking about doing a King film, but at that time it was assumed it would be similar to *JFK*—more on the assassination, the controversial aspect. Which, to be honest with you, at that time, we were not necessarily interested in. If Stone wanted to do a controversial assassination film, fine, but let that be kind of in the aftermath; let's get something definitive, get a "biopic" out there. Dealing with the assassination is aftermath.

I wasn't thinking about the assassination at the time. Hadn't dealt with the assassination myself, really, not deep inside. I tried to act as if it was just a business decision, but it was still too painful for me to discuss as film fodder to be callously manipulated. First we need to know who the man was before we start dealing with why he got killed. That was my position.

JFK is a perfect example of what we wanted to avoid. Not that it wasn't a fine movie, with great performances by Tommy Lee Jones and Kevin Costner, just to name two of dozens, really. But in Stone's movie, the president, John Fitzgerald Kennedy, the one who called my mother when she was pregnant with me to offer his sympathies about my father being unjustly jailed—he wasn't even a character in the movie that bore his name.

All we saw was the few seconds of what Abraham Zapruder shot with an 8mm camera.

Then there was the reaction to that movie. It's almost as if people, otherwise intelligent people, became like the three "hear no evil, see no evil, speak no evil" monkeys, refusing to acknowledge there is evil in this world. Judging from the critical reaction to Oliver Stone's *JFK*, you'd have thought it was Stone who'd assassinated Kennedy.

Conspiracy theories bother people. They bother me. They bother most right-thinking people: we don't want to hear it, we don't want to believe it, we just want to live free and safe and pursue happiness, and get by. That's all we want to do, that's all we want to know. As far as my father's murder was concerned, at the time, we thought James Earl Ray was probably the shooter, with help; we had no issue with it otherwise, and we surely weren't looking for any smoking gun. We mostly accepted the verdict and the official story, except we felt they had probably left out some other players. But accepting that James Earl Ray was the trigger-man—no problem with that. So we weren't seeing Stone for any other reason than we heard he was interested in doing a film about my father. We wanted to kind of see what was under his fingernails—find out what he was talking about in that regard.

When we met him the first time, he was sketchy. He said he didn't know what type of film he wanted to do. He seemed vague; he was interested, but he was not ready to commit; he was involved in other projects. *Nixon* was one of the films he was working on, and maybe by then he was finishing *Natural Born Killers*. He had a lot of stuff "in the can" or "on the drawing board" or "in development." He made a comment when I was leaving, something along the lines of "Have you ever considered playing your father? You look so much like him." I just said, "No I haven't; I'm not an actor, but I take it as a compliment." Little did he know that I'd been avoiding playing Daddy all my life. That was the extent of the meeting.

It turned out Oliver Stone really didn't need much of a Martin Luther King character in the movie he had in his head—if he had a vision for it in his head. He wanted to make a point that had little to do with the point we wanted to make. That's the way we left it. Friendly.

Michelle and I began to feel we had exhausted our options at that time. We decided to put the film idea on the shelf for a while and move on.

We sort of forgot the film idea for that time and moved on for a while.

It must have been 1995 when we learned that Oliver Stone was going ahead with a Martin Luther King, Jr., film project, and hiring a writer to create a script. I was immediately concerned because he hadn't contacted us, hadn't invited us to be a part of it. We didn't know what to do, so we requested a meeting. Oliver was not in this meeting; he sent his producing partner at the time, Danny Halstead, who co-produced *Nixon* with Stone. Danny was not a suit. Creative, he seemed as though he'd be a cool guy in the long run; initially he was just following Oliver's orders. They were playing hardball: "We're doing this and we don't need your permission or support." We wanted them to understand it was important for us to be a part of the process. People assume incorrectly that Dr. King is fair use, public domain. No, he isn't. Plus, most important, he was my father.

Danny said, "A biography or a film can be done by anybody about anybody."

"True," I said, "but if you use that person's copyrighted materials, like speeches and the like, then you've got to get permission. That's the law." They were trying to say, "We don't know how much we're using."

I asked, "How are you doing a movie about Martin Luther King and not using his speeches? Unless you do it like *JFK*."

As soon as I said that, I thought, "Of course that's what they're thinking of doing." Like *JFK*. That was not the kind of film we were hoping for, where Martin Luther King would be just the backdrop rather than the main character.

At that time, we were torn. If we were going to do a conspiracy film, Oliver would probably be the best person, yet that's not where our heads were. We were still hoping to attract the director and writer who would agree with our vision of a biopic. It turns out we were in more of a predicament than we knew. Somebody was taking the baby away from us. Do we sit back and just let our baby go? Or do we go with the child to make sure that it's nurtured, cared for? We chose the latter. Better to embrace Oliver Stone and try to cultivate him than to be hands-off and just see what he comes up with. So we developed a relationship with Danny, and started meeting again with Oliver. The last time I met with him was in early 1998.

I asked him straight out, "What type of film are you trying to do?"

He said, "I really want to do a story about the man, not the assassination story."

That surprised me. I'm sure it showed on my face that I was happy to hear it. I'm not a duplicitous character. The way I feel shows on my face. Later I was questioning myself: "Does Oliver really have that in mind, or is he just trying to cool me out? He is a brilliant filmmaker-screenwriter, wrote *Midnight Express*, wrote *Scarface, Born on the Fourth of July, Platoon . . ."*

That's when I thought, "Uh-oh."

It was the Vietnam War thing! That's what had gotten him. That was the recurring theme in his films—working out his own conflict over his and America's participation in the Vietnam War!

Stone's very close to Vietnam. That's his hook. That's what made it powerful for him. Daddy came out against the Vietnam War at Riverside Church on April 4, 1967, in his speech called "A Time to Break Silence," one year to the day before he was murdered. That's what Oliver saw. I don't know if he saw that the media had essentially muffled Daddy after that, which was the only reason he had considered running on a third-party presidential ticket with Dr. Benjamin Spock—so that he would be covered in the media, so that peace and Poor People's campaigns would have to get coverage.

To get started, Oliver had brought in a screenwriter named Kario Salem. We were still kind of skeptical. We didn't know where Salem was coming from. We met with him, we did the interviews, and never really saw a script, so I can't tell you till this day where he was coming from. I know Salem went to Memphis and did research, which made me more uneasy.

My sense was Oliver was going to doctor or rewrite this script—it was going to be his thing in the end. I'd been hearing he was obsessed with depicting Daddy in terms of womanizing. I went to him and said, "What's your position on depicting my father in this light?" Oliver said, "Your dad was really something." I said, "I don't believe it's true. Who are you hearing this from?"

Oliver was saying there was good evidence, in Ralph Abernathy's book and from a woman who'd claimed she was sexually involved with my father the night before he was killed. I said, "I talked to Reverend Hosea Williams, who was there, about the incident; he told me it didn't happen."

This whole thing about the FBI files being sealed for fifty years, these records of my father—if the FBI really had something concrete, it would have leaked out long before now. The tape that my mother received from J. Edgar Hoover was not all that concrete. Mother says you can't tell what is on that tape, or who is on that tape—there were a bunch of people she could not identify—and we were also told that J. Edgar Hoover had his FBI agents fabricate incidents. Mother till this day still claims that was not my father on the tape.

What I was trying to say to Oliver Stone was, "Whatever you do, make sure you're basing it on facts, not innuendo." Stone said, "Maybe I'm too close to it. Let's go talk to the writer, Kario, and Danny." We met with them; now, Stone could have been pulling my chain, but he was saying, "Look, you all make the call. If after you do your research, you come up with something different, I'm open." What I didn't want Stone to do was become obsessed with the perceived flaws both real and imagined of my father; it would be a tragic mistake for him to do a movie focusing solely on the perceived and unproven fallibilities of a great man.

But in the end Oliver couldn't find another figure, a majority figure, within my father's story for the audiences to latch on to. With *JFK*, he'd made a protagonist of Jim Garrison, the district attorney in Louisiana—a public figure who has a revelation, goes after "them," whoever "them" is, that were responsible for the assassination. There isn't that kind of figure in my father's story. One of Ray's attorneys whom I hadn't met then, William Pepper, provided an interesting twist of a character. In my opinion, he became a lot like the Jim Garrison figure in *JFK*, but the reason it's hard to put him in that light is because he had a vested interest as Ray's defense counsel. People have a hard time with his story; they feel he's biased, or slanted toward defending his client, similar to Johnnie Cochran's situation with O. J. Simpson. I believe that any defense counsel is going to be viewed as being biased just for doing his job. Catch-22. I can relate. Stone was drawn to Pepper; Ixtlan, his production company, optioned Pepper's book *Orders to Kill*. It was a mystery, why Oliver was so interested in doing this film. Warner Bros. put it on the back burner. No matter how big you get in Hollywood, you're never bigger than your last film's grosses. *Nixon* didn't do so well commercially.

My sense was that Stone was still grappling with it. He wanted to do the conspiracy/assassination movie, based on Daddy's coming out against the Vietnam War. I was in over my head here.

History says lone assassins rarely use rifles. A list of lone demented assassins is long and quite depressing, and shows the use of pistols, ear-close: Lincoln, Gandhi, Oswald, RFK, Wallace, Reagan, Lennon, Tupac, Biggie, Versace. Medgar Evers was shot in the back with a rifle by Byron De La Beckwith in 1963, but from relatively short range. Vernon Jordan was wounded by long-distance rifle fire; he survived. And one more. JFK. You can see why Oliver Stone would be on this.

My father, at Harlem's Riverside Church, on April 4, 1967, one year to the day before he was assassinated in Memphis, had said, "It is an evil war. We're bombing too many rice fields, running too many peasant humble people out of the villages. It's time for America to come on home from Vietnam." That had to cut into Stone's soul.

Five years later: "Oliver sees the mid-'60s and the transformation [King] was going through," said Steven Rivers, then a Stone publicist. "It's not a whodunit, a birth-to-death biopic, or documentary; it may take years for this movie to come about, if it comes about. But if it does, it's about how toward the end of his life, Dr. King became a leader of the peace movement, how he was perceived by his enemies as an increasing threat."

"Oliver can't afford to do it wrong," Phil Jones said. "Even if he wanted to be capricious, he can't. He has more to lose than we do." Because of this long-term back-and-forth with Oliver Stone, I thought more about the assassination, and James Earl Ray. The working title of Stone's ill-fated production: *Memphis*. I found myself thinking more about Memphis. What had happened there? Not so much in terms of a movie, but for my own life, and the lives of my two sisters and my brother. Maybe we had not been able to move on because we were stuck there.

"It would be a film about Dr. King's life," said Steven Rivers. "It's not a whodunit—though Oliver supports reopening the investigation and a view there's more to learn." Maybe one day Stone's *Memphis*—which would have portrayed our father's emergence as a peace leader dead set against the Vietnam War who was killed by the same interests who killed Stone's JFK—will get made by somebody else. Maybe not. Daddy went to Memphis to help striking sanitation workers and to support efforts to integrate schools and stores, not to protest the Vietnam War. Time passed. A film option we'd given Stone expired in the year 2000. Now my hope is that at some point during my mother's lifetime, a movie on my father will be done.

In the early '90s, I traveled to Memphis, though not for a movie or to investigate my father's murder. It was arranged through Juanita Moore, executive director of the National Civil Rights Museum. The whole movie thing was in stasis—really off the radar screen. Michelle Clark Jenkins was leaving the King Estate soon, but she took this trip with me. While in Memphis, Ms. Moore thought it would be a good idea to meet with her girlfriend who worked at Graceland. So we also met and visited there while in the city.

We toured the National Civil Rights Museum. The museum is housed in the old Lorraine Motel, south of downtown. Michelle and Juanita took the tour with me. There were other people on the tour; among those, a few recognized me; some recoiled; some, after saying hello, let me have space. When I started out on the tour, I was unaware of a wonderful feature that didn't hit me until the end. The way the exhibit was structured, you started out dealing with the history of African Americans, through the Civil Rights Movement. As you move forward in history, the exhibit elevates you: you literally go up as you walk through, you rise step by step; it's almost like you're going to the mountaintop. I didn't have a somber or nervous feeling. Then I got upstairs, second-floor balcony, outside Room 306.

From here, you could see the supposed path of the bullet. It was traced by visible laser-pointer light. At that time, I didn't know what I know now, so I didn't question it; yet the rooming house, window, bullet, pathway, the music they were playing, church music, and the background—it all suddenly seemed morbid. I could feel a cold sweat, and blood rising in my neck—where my father took the fatal shot. I thought of a song, played in the documentary *Montgomery to Memphis*, by Nina Simone, "The King of Love Is Dead." As the documentary ends, during his funeral procession, with the wagon, the mule pulling the casket, that song is playing. It was all jumbled up in my head: What is film, what is real, what is re-creation, when was this music laid in? When I think of my father's death, all of that is what comes to mind; I have mixed emotions—there was always a reluctance for my family to focus on the death. Even the King Center, in Mother's mind, was to be a living memorial. We were approached years before, when the Lorraine Motel was still boarded up, about becoming involved with the National Civil Rights Museum. D'Army Bailey, a judge in Memphis, first chair of the museum foundation, came to Atlanta to entreat us. Mother had problems with it at the time. But it was all so distant. Now I was here. On the very spot.

And then . . . the laser-pointer blue light hit me.

The beam of blue-green light hit me in the chest. I stepped forward. It rode up toward my neck, to my throat. My heart beat faster. My hands clenched into fists.

. . . Unhhhh . . . I almost felt it, I tell you . . . and it changed me. Epiphany is a Christian festival commemorating the showing of Jesus to the Wise Men, celebrated January 6; or it is the appearance of a superhuman or supernatural being. In a strange way, I was feeling an epiphany.

We left the museum without a word. I wanted to leave the city of Memphis. We caught a plane soon thereafter, but it wasn't soon enough. It was like I was in a strange land, and after that tour, it was like I felt unwelcome, foreign, even though everybody was nice enough. I felt now there was something unresolved in me about Memphis. There was this tragedy that had occurred in this city that I didn't quite understand. This was the place where Daddy was killed. It wasn't about a movie, money, or a conspiracy. It was about facing what happened to our lives. I had to know about Memphis— about our father's murder. About me. And about us.

CHAPTER 15

Odd Man In

Many people do not realize that the "I Have a Dream" refrain of my father's most famous speech was spoken extemporaneously. He had prepared his remarks but, moved by the passion of the crowd before him and the tremendous significance of that day in August 1963, his mind soared and led him to those immortal words.

Soon after the speech was delivered, 20th Century Fox Records distributed a recording of the speech without his permission. The recording was important because many people then, as now, had not heard the speech in its entirety. My father sued the record company to stop their distribution of the record on the grounds of copyright infringement and won. Guided by his trusted advisers, he had been copyrighting his writings and speeches since he published his first book in the 1950s as a way of ensuring that the integrity of his message could be vigorously protected. He had also been represented by a New York literary agent since that first book. Daddy understood that the more important and controversial he became, the more vulnerable he would be to exploitation. Later, he in fact gave Berry Gordy and Motown the right to distribute "I Have a Dream" as well as other speeches, believing they would be in safe hands. As evidence that my father's faith was well placed, Mr. Gordy eventually gave these masters back to my family when I was installed as head of the King Center in 1989.

My family and I have repeatedly been attacked in the media and unfairly accused in recent years of trying to profit from my father's legacy. The intentions behind our efforts to protect his intellectual property—his name, image, writings, speeches, and recorded voice—have been mischaracterized and distorted. In fact, as my father did during his lifetime, we have simply been protecting this property in order to maintain, preserve, and protect the integrity of his message. When Daddy died, all of his property—both tangible and intangible—descended to us as his heirs; it happens with every individual. Curiously, these attacks against us did not seem to occur until we had conflicts with the National Park Service, a federal agency, and subsequent to that when questions were raised about the possible involvement of federal agencies in my father's death. Could be a coincidence, could not.

In the early '80s calls and letters started coming into the King Center about a novelty item on the market that was a miniature sculpture of my father sitting upon a base shaped like a coffin. It was disrespectful, tasteless, and tacky and an unauthorized use of his image. We brought suit against the manufacturer, and a Georgia court upheld our right to protect his image and stopped the distribution of the item. But the law requires that in order to maintain a protected image, as well as name and copyrights, you must actively and uniformly police them or risk losing them. Therefore we have been forced to police them in all instances whether that be a tacky image on merchandise or the reprinting of my father's copyrighted words or usage of his spoken words without permission. We issue licenses to those people and entities who have our permission to use my father's name, image, or words that establish the boundaries of that use; again, this is as the law provides.

Yes, the King Estate does in many instances receive fees for these licenses. But when making licensing decisions, we have never put profit over principle; we have always tried to maintain the dignity and the integrity of my father's message. Many nonprofit organizations and schools receive the use of my father's intellectual property for free. However, in many instances where the person or company is using my father's name, image, or words as part of an appropriate commercial use or an endeavor from which they will profit, we do require an industry-standard financial arrangement. Is that unfair?

Even more important, the King Estate may receive monies from licenses, but for the most part these monies are not pure profit. It costs a great deal to maintain and police my father's intellectual property. We have a staff that reviews the thousands of license and permission requests that come in from around the world. Each request requires administrative handling and assessment. And each time we are forced to legally protect and defend our rights we incur major legal expenses. Remember, if we don't actively protect our rights, we lose them, and certainly this is not what my father would have wanted.

Much has been made of the fact that my father gave away a great deal of what he earned during his lifetime, including the $54,000 he received in connection with his Nobel Peace Prize. This generosity is used to argue that he intended to give everything he had freely to the world. Daddy did believe that monies he got specifically for the results of his work in the Civil Rights Movement should go back into the Movement, because it embodied the work and sacrifice of thousands of other dedicated people. However, my father also very clearly made a distinction between income derived from those efforts and income derived from his personal efforts. He believed that his message belonged to everyone spiritually, but his copyrighted words legally belonged to him in life and to his heirs after his death. This is why he put the copyrights for his writings and speeches in his name rather than in the names of the organizations in which he was involved; he knew these copyrights would be passed down to us. My father died with very little money and with few material possessions to be our inheritance. He was a loving husband and father, and he knew that given the nature of his life's work his copyrights were the only way in which he could leave something behind for us. The results of the work of the public man, Dr. Martin Luther King, Jr., unquestionably belong to the world, but the private man, my father, will forever belong to my mother, Yolanda, Martin, Bernice, and me.

There is an old saying that I have learned to believe, "that which does not destroy us only serves to make us stronger." By 1994, I had pretty much gotten myself back on track. I had come to terms with the hurt and indignation I felt from my treatment by some of the board members of the King Center, and my resignation from the King Center and, as a practical matter, a few of these board members who had opposed me during my first term had by this time moved on.

I was happy with the work that Phil and I were doing with the King Estate and my father's intellectual property. We had created effective administration systems and developed many worthwhile projects. Most important, through this work I had developed a new and more intimate understanding of how essential it was to me to protect and perpetuate my father's message. And I believed that in time I could accomplish what I had set out to do four years before.

I came back on board as CEO of the King Center on December 31, 1994. After being voted in during October 1994, I wasn't scheduled to come in until March '95; I was supposed to get a smooth time of transition. I didn't get a honeymoon. Due to a controversy with the National Park Service, an emergency board meeting by phone expedited my coming in three months early. Right away I made this point: "The King Center is the spiritual and institutional guardian of the King legacy. Our main goal is to educate the public about, and to perpetuate and promote, my father's message of nonviolence to people around the world. To achieve this goal, we must protect my father's intellectual property—the images, writings, and speeches that embody his message." For laypeople, I explained that, "Land is the real estate of the past.

Intellectual property is the real estate of now. If you stand back and let others steal his material, then you're affecting every minority writer, every songwriter, every composer, every artist, every story-teller, every creative person—all of that—gone."

Congress, in its wisdom, created the Copyright Act to encourage and protect creative works, including those inspirational in nature. Therefore I have always been baffled by those who attack the fact that my father's works are protected. If Congress had believed that the inspirational speeches and writings of a public figure who is not a public official (as in the case of a U.S. president) belonged freely to the public, it would not have included such works under the legal umbrella of the copyright laws.

One of our biggest copyright battles was with CBS. They own this series called *The 20th Century*, hosted by Mike Wallace. On one evening, I saw a segment of a five-part series aired on the Arts & Entertainment network about the Civil Rights Movement, and there my father was, and there his speeches were, everything from "I Have a Dream" to "I've Been to the Mountaintop" to . . . I lost count. I was sitting there wondering whether to call the lawyers, not really wanting to call anybody, but wanting to go have a tofu steak with onions, maybe call up Good Natured to see what she was doing. The lawyers and I talked. "We can't let this go," I was told. "It's blatant unfair usage of your father's 'I Have a Dream' speech. If you don't say or do anything, you're setting a precedent by your inaction, and it will be more difficult to enforce your copyrights in the future."

I wanted to do the right thing. So first we tried to resolve it without litigation. But CBS would not budge, so we had no choice but to file suit. CBS has a tad more resources than we do, and they had their own legal point—this was their footage. We agreed it was their footage, but it was our father on that footage saying things he had copyrighted. We believed that CBS's usage of the speech exceeded the fair use standard under the copyright laws. The network had included over two-thirds of the speech in a program that it aired and sold on home video. It was making a profit off my father's name, image, and words. So, happy days were here again for the lawyers; we ended up in court.

The federal district court judge ruled at first that the speech was in the public domain; then we won a reversal on appeal, and our rights to the speech were upheld. However, the case was sent back to the lower court to decide some lesser technical issues. Eventually, we settled these remaining issues with CBS. While we felt victorious, we nevertheless incurred close to a million dollars in legal bills for our defense. But again, this was the price of protecting our property as well as an example of putting principle first over profit. We knew going into the litigation that it would be very expensive, and that in the end legal fees would more than likely not be awarded due to the complexity of the issues involved. This principle was especially important to uphold due to the fact that the "I Have a Dream" speech is generally considered to be the most important speech of the twentieth century.

While we faired well in the court of law, we did not fair so well in CBS's court. Less than a year and a half after our settlement was reached, CBS's 60 Minutes ran a biased piece entitled "Selling the Dream," which accused my family, in so many words, of engaging in profiteering in connection with my father's intellectual property. CBS put forth the same argument that had been unsuccessful for them in court, namely that my father's words should belong to everyone. Since they lost this point in the court of law, they attempted to win this point in the court of public opinion. One respected journalist ran an op-ed piece criticizing the motives and ethics behind CBS's airing of this piece in light of the preceding litigation with the King family, and questioned whether it was being done in retaliation. Isn't it ironic that CBS would raise these questions about profiteering when in fact it came out during our trial that the network charges schools and nonprofits $1,000 per minute (with a thirty-second minimum) to use their footage of the "I Have a Dream" speech?

*   *   *

My mother was in the process of semi-retiring from the day-to-day. "With his mother around, he couldn't be a King, only a prince." I'd heard this had been said, and it was repeated to me for effect. "What am I going to tell people I do?" I once asked a colleague before I got the reins. Did I feel I couldn't get respect until Mother retired? It's not my decision, who respects me. The question is better put elsewhere. Some people said, "You're not your father." No, I'm not. Who is? When I went to the Lorraine Motel and the light hit me, it then came back to me that I had to focus and redouble my efforts.

The architects of the Constitution—"Somewhere I read!" my father used to say—had intentions of creating a document and a mechanism to check tyranny. They were trying to create checks and balances, but what they did not address is that, through capitalism, the true government would become global multinational corporations. If you look at it in economic terms, every corporation, technically, is controlled by the wealthiest shareholders. The government is like a corporation. So who controls it? The wealthiest citizens. What is Congress? Congress is like a board of directors. They serve at the pleasure of the shareholders. The president is the CEO, a manager. The people who have the power are the wealthy shareholders. They determine policy. Politicians are the middlemen. Everybody thinks politicians make the decisions. But they don't. The decision makers are insiders. When CNN says before the State of the Union Address, "We're about to hear from the most powerful man in the free world," remember this: the people who pay for the president's campaign are the most powerful, if he happens to win the election. The real issue now, the Cause, is economics and institutional self-empowerment, a concept my father espoused and ultimately gave his life for.

The King Center and King National Park site across the street drew an average of anywhere from 500,000 to 700,000 visitors a year, according to the superintendent of the National Park Service Historic Site. Many of these visitors were young people who were not inspired by the existing static exhibit and wanted a more interactive experience. In response to the numerous correspondence we received on this issue, Phil and I envisioned the nonprofit King Dream Center as a multimedia, emerging experience utilizing all of the latest technology, 3-D technology, animatronics, every kind of mood sensory technology that creates an atmosphere. You walk in, the lights go down and you're instantly transported back to the '60s. You have the March on Washington, where you can hear the applause and feel the energy; an animatronic Dr. King delivering the "I Have a Dream" speech; a re-creation of the jail cell where the letter from the Birmingham jail was written. More tangible than a static exhibit in a traditional museum, it would use interactive technology so people who went through it, particularly children, would feel like they were there and gain a much greater appreciation for the era.

This was put together in a proposal by designers. I didn't know if we could ever get the King Dream Center to the Promised Land of reality due to the fact that our initial funding sources backed away as a result of the controversy surrounding the Park Service's planned visitors center.

In the early '70s, Mother traveled to Boston, reached out to Boston University to try to get my father's papers back. You see, in the '60s, Daddy was trying to decide on a place to house his papers, and at that time Boston University seemed like a logical place because it was in the North and the climate seemed more liberal; there was concern for the safety of the papers if they were kept here in the South. Morehouse didn't have the facilities to do the kind of archival job the papers required. My father put some pages, about half of his papers, at BU with the intention of getting them back at some point; he didn't realize at the time that he was "gifting" them. BU took a position that he was giving the papers to it versus loaning them to a repository.

It was his intention to get them back. He told my mother in the latter part of his life that he wanted to get them back because the

SCLC had been talking about creating an institution to deal with the scholarly aspects of its work, and his papers would've been transferred to that entity. Well, he didn't get around to documenting the SCLC's suggestion in writing. The document BU had received originally for the actual holding of the papers was the one the court addressed.

Mother brought suit to get the papers back. Initially, there was communication between two entities, the King Center and BU. The legal part didn't kick in until the '80s. But, with the appeals process, it was not until the mid '90s that we finally lost for good; the courts in Boston decided BU had clear title to that portion of the King papers. Yet again, we had huge legal bills as a result of this fight. The copyrights were never in question. The author retains copyright, but BU owns the physical documents now, via judicial fiat. They can't publish them without our permission. They can't use them for any purpose other than research. Scholars can come in and read them, but the minute the words are transcribed or in any way published, they need permission from the Estate.

The King Center has the other, greater half of Daddy's papers. Those at BU only go up to his years in school at Boston, his early years to his formative years, so to speak, academically to probably about 1960, maybe through his doctoral dissertation; we have copies of those as well.

Mother's feeling at the time was to just bring everything under one roof, and we felt it made sense for people to come to one place.

Boston University disagreed, in the person of its president, John Silber. I'd never before met anybody so rigid. I'd been told he was that way, that you really couldn't talk to him about this issue. But you couldn't convince me of that until I met him face-to-face. My brother, Martin, and I went up there as a last-ditch effort, before going forward with a trial. What happened was almost offensive. Dr. Silber is a man of average height and medium build, clean-cut, edgy, like flint, and a partial amputee, one arm. He told us how it was not really "our place" to decide what Dr. King's wishes were, and asked who were we to judge; he said the King

Center was no more than temporary housing and he didn't know how long it would be around, but he knew that Boston University would be there throughout time, into perpetuity. Basically, those were his points.

But what right did he have to tell the family that a man's legacy is temporary; that his work, and we, his heirs, my mother, are temporary?

Martin and I moved uncomfortably in our seats. Wood and leather creaked. We'd heard this man was stern. He said things that to our ears sounded self-righteous. He said, "When my father died, he had a very special document that was written in German and he left it, willed it to my brother. You know, that really upset me because my brother didn't even speak German and I spoke German. I was the one proficient in German literature." Dr. Silber talked about how he had to accept that, and live with it, and what right did we have to come in and go against our father's wishes? I was staying with his logic until he brought Daddy and our situation into it. He'd found a way to invent the wishes of my father, to invest them with his own brand of logic and interpretation.

And both Martin and I could see he was intractable. We left the meeting deflated.

Dr. Silber, as we knew he would be on his home court, was effective in rallying support, in effect villainizing the King family and King Center. People who otherwise probably would've been supportive got caught up in the issue being polarized. "Dr. King belonged to everyone." "He was a son of Boston too." Who were we, then, coming to tell them what to do? It got to that level, at which you can't win. At least, I can't. People lose their perspective, and the plainer aspects of right and wrong and ethics and morals, and none of that matters anymore. I've often wondered, since Daddy was held in such high esteem, if there wasn't some inevitable backlash against the next generation, his children. I do know we all learned to walk on eggshells.

What I don't know is if anything could have been done differently to salvage that situation. We were up against it, there in

Boston: the case was so technically driven that even the lawyers, never mind the jury, hardly knew what was going on. The judge gave the jury instructions that, in my opinion, were confusing. It was very technical, and the feeling was that she, the judge, seemed sympathetic to BU and President Silber. I felt there was no way we could have won up there.

So, we lost that portion of the King papers—the physical property but not the copyright. We never physically had them, but the principle of losing something that seemed rightfully ours was disheartening. But we moved on.

We had another incident over intellectual property rights with the late documentary producer Henry Hampton and *Eyes on the Prize*. I met with Henry Hampton and his people up in Boston, and it wasn't so much Henry, but rather his people, who believed that they had a right to exploit my father's intellectual property and not get permission. We were very clear: If it is truly fair use, go about your business, but once you start making Dr. King the focal point, using his copyrighted speeches and selling the video in Blockbuster stores, as you are doing now, we've got an issue. Our policy is simple: If you make money, the Estate should get the industry's standard royalty.

In January 1997, we announced that we had entered into a copublishing agreement with Time Warner Trade Publishing to make available to the public my father's vast body of writings and to republish his out-of-print books. We made this arrangement in hopes of introducing his message of nonviolence to future generations.

With this agreement we really had an obligation to protect our rights. Many decisions hinged on the following question: Now that we are in business with a major multimedia publisher and player, what will that publisher look like paying for rights we in the past haven't been able to protect?

The National Park Service came to us in 1980 at the request of Mother to manage the historic district in which the King Center resides. Initially, once legislation was passed in Congress officially designating this district, the NPS had scant resources to maintain it. The district was the stepchild of the Park Service, because my father still was not seen by many conservative politicians as being worthy of having any national honors. This was before the creation of the King holiday. Consequently, the NPS only had a few of its people operating from one of the row houses across from my father's birth home and it gave tours through that home.

Over the years our locale became a more popular tourist destination, and it attracted more resources; as it attracted more resources, the NPS started acquiring more real estate. Eventually, the National Park Service became the largest landholder in this immediate vicinity. They knew about our interest in building the King Dream Center, but they were interested in building a Park Service Visitors Center that would house exhibits on my father. Two centers would be redundant.

One of the NPS's first big moves was to acquire the old Ebenezer Church through a land-swapping arrangement. In this land swap, the National Park Service got a long-term lease on the original historic church, adjacent to the King Center, in exchange for land that it owned that would go to Ebenezer to build a new church. I think Ebenezer got cash as well. Maybe it was a good move for Ebenezer. I knew as the land-swapping deal was being made that I was blinded by my strong personal ties to the old church and my family. I'd seen my grandfather preach there. I'd listened to the music of my father's sermons there. My grandmother had been shot down there. Now you can't even worship there as part of an ongoing regular church service—which especially affects visitors from around the globe who have never had the opportunity to worship in this historic sanctuary—because of the agreement with the NPS, which is governed by separation of church and state issues.

Because the Olympics were coming to Atlanta in '96, the Park Service wanted to have the best face on the King Historic District, particularly for the foreign visitors. The city of Atlanta wanted its best face forward too. The legacy of Dr. Martin Luther King, Jr., was one reason Atlanta was chosen as the venue for the '96 Olympics in the first place. The NPS sought a $12 million allocation from Congress to make improvements to the King Historic District, including the construction of its proposed visitors center. They solicited my mother's support, saying it was crucial for its success. Mother finally agreed, but she had two requirements for her support. First, the King Center had to be given control over the exhibits at the new visitors center. We wanted to make sure that exhibits were consistent with the Center's message. Second, a portion of the allocation had to be given to the King Center to help with the refurbishment of its infrastructure in preparation for the Olympics. My mother was led to believe that these conditions had been agreed to. But in the end, the NPS got the $12 million allocation and these conditions were not met. However, a few months into the conflict Congressman John Lewis facilitated a meeting between the Park Service and us, where we resolved our differences. As Secretary of the Interior Bruce Babbitt expressed at the dedication of the visitors center, sometimes struggle and conflict in the end serve to strengthen a relationship through better understanding.

Ever since that light hit me outside Room 306 at the former Lorraine Motel (now the National Civil Rights Museum) in the early 1990s, ever since I stood on that balcony where Daddy stood, I knew eventually I'd ask, "Why?" and "How?" I knew when I asked it wouldn't be for revenge or profit. I would seek only to help right the listing ship of my own family.

My cousin Isaac Farris, Jr., was the impetus—he convinced me to look at the assassination. I had busied myself with issues around the King Center, but I hadn't forgotten that light hitting me on the balcony. Isaac was the first from our circle to read William Pepper's *Orders to Kill*. In this book, Pepper details a broad conspiracy involving organized crime, governmental agencies, and individual co-

conspirators behind the assassination of my father. Isaac called me and said, "Dex, I think Pepper's got something. I'm not saying he's right or wrong, but he's got something." As a result, I said I'd read the book. Isaac was aggressive and said, "Why not set up a meeting with Pepper?"

Pepper flew in from London and we met in the living room of Isaac's home. Isaac, Phil, and I were at the meeting. We listened to him intently. After he left, we came up with a plan of action. Isaac looked at me gravely. "The first thing is to confront James Earl Ray," he said. There is a closeness between me and Isaac. Goes back to childhood. He was my first playmate and confidant, outside of my brother and sisters. Also, he's my blood relative. We battled. We played together. We took whippings. Our parents were near-interchangeable. There is a trust, a respect, a knowledge beyond the spoken. "First thing is to confront Ray . . ." Isaac said.

The media proceeded to paint our quest for answers as our getting some type of payoff, where we were puppets and Pepper was puppeteer. We were doing it so a movie would be made, another example of trying to cash in on our name. Of course none of this was true. But, unfortunately, many people tend to rely on what they read in newspapers. I grew up trusting the media because they had been fairly generous to my family and to the Civil Rights Movement; they had, for the most part, kept a spotlight on the injustices of the day. As a child growing up in the eyes of the media, constantly having photojournalists around, I bonded with some of them and felt very comfortable around them. But now that some in the media have turned against my family, I have become wary of a few bad apples that unfortunately can sometimes spoil the whole bunch. I know how often our intentions and views have been cleverly misrepresented. This is not to say that all of our coverage has been bad by any means. For instance, the *Atlanta Journal-Constitution* ran an article entitled "Tasteful Marketing of MLK," which discussed in detail the positive approach we have taken toward the licensing of my father's name, image, and copyrighted words. Now I read the paper and watch television critically. I don't swallow everything. I can't blame people for not knowing the interior motivation of my mother, my siblings, my extended family. But how can it be hard to understand that like any other family in our situation, we wanted to learn the truth behind my father's murder? We needed to confront the issue of the assassination, look at it squarely; we would not shy away from it just because people got upset about it and said, "Don't look any closer at this." If there was nothing to hide, why not?

What kind of man would I be if I went along with that? Who could respect such a man? You can put seeking the truth off to one side, especially within the same generation, or, in our case, my uncles, my aunt, my mother, my grandparents—they put it off to the side. My siblings and I did too, for a long time. But then there comes a time when you just can't keep hiding from it anymore, when it's affecting your life so profoundly, so deeply, it no longer can be ignored except at peril of your own life, health, sanity. Even if people make sour faces, even if the pundits say you're "wrong," even if sanctified folk say it's "part of God's plan." In putting it off to the side, we'd left Daddy on the battlefield. We hadn't gathered his remains, taken them home, honored them properly. I was elected by my family to go over books like *Orders to Kill* to try to make sense of it all.

Most people view my father's assassination as a world event, another moment of collective horror, as it surely was. But as time has passed, they seem to have forgotten that it was equally a very personal event; that it was the defining tragedy in the lives of my mother, my siblings, and me. We needed closure to find real peace.

CHAPTER 16

The Meeting

How did not just the life but also the death of Martin Luther King, Jr., my father, define not just me, my brother, sisters, cousins, and our generation, but also the whole of a generation behind us, the whole of the hip-hop nation? How can that be, when there was no hip-hop nation in 1968?

Oh, but there was a hip-hop nation in 1968. The whole continuum of fashion, music, film, videos, canvas artistry, advertising, and whatever helps define that generation after ours, was already being influenced by the actions of the children of 1968, who would become their parents.

It gleamed in the eyes of the youth of all denominations, combed up and Vaselined down, flirting with their eyes while filing down the rain-slicked street into the fortress of Mason Temple, behind the Fowler Homes housing project, south of downtown Memphis, on a rainy April night of that year. The hip-hop nation, who would be in their twenties and early thirties in the year 2000, were the future children of the children then filing into Mason Temple.

Mason Temple is world headquarters of the Pentecostals—

Church of God in Christ. It all comes out of the church—music, activism, social gospel, culture—all from the influence of the black church. It often takes a form of music. In *Parting the Waters*, author Taylor Branch sensed it: "The spirit of the songs could sweep up the crowd, and the young leaders realized that through song they could induce humble people to say and feel things that were otherwise beyond them." On Wednesday, April 3, 1968, youth of an R&B and gospel world joined the aged, coming by bus, car, and foot to hear my father. And what he gave them was knowledge.

[If] the Almighty said to me, "Martin Luther King, which age would you like to live in?" I would take my mental flight by Egypt ["*Yeah*"], and I would watch God's children in their magnificent trek from the dark dungeons of Egypt through, or rather, across the Red Sea, through the wilderness, on toward the Promised Land. And in spite of its magnificence, I wouldn't stop there. ["*All right*"]

I would move on by Greece, and take my mind to Mount Olympus. And I would see Plato, Aristotle, Socrates, Euripides, and Aristophanes assembled around the Parthenon [*Applause*], and I would watch them around the Parthenon as they discussed the great and eternal issues of reality. But I wouldn't stop there. ["*Oh yeah*"]

. . . I would even go by the way that the man for whom I'm named had his habitat, and I would watch Martin Luther as he tacks his ninety-five theses on the door at the church of Wittenberg. But I wouldn't stop there. ["*All right*"]

I would come on up even to 1863 and watch a vacillating president by the name of Abraham Lincoln finally come to the conclusion that he had to sign the Emancipation Proclamation. But I wouldn't stop there. ["*Yeah.*" *Applause*]

I would even come up to the early thirties and see a

man grappling with the problems of the bankruptcy of his nation, and come with an eloquent cry that "we have nothing to fear but fear itself." But I wouldn't stop there. [*"All right"*]

Strangely enough, I would turn to the Almighty and say, "If you allow me to live just a few years in the second half of the twentieth century, I will be happy." [*Applause*]

. . . Well, I don't know what will happen now; we've got some difficult days ahead. [*"Amen"*] But it really doesn't matter with me now, because I've been to the mountaintop. [*"Yeah." Applause*] And I don't mind. [*Applause continues*] Like anybody, I would like to live a long life—longevity has its place. But I'm not concerned about that now. I just want to do God's will. [*"Yeah"*] And He's allowed me to go up to the mountain. [*"Go ahead"*] And I've looked over [*"Yes sir"*], and I've seen the Promised Land. [*"Go ahead"*] I may not get there with you. [*"Go ahead"*] But I want you to know tonight [*"Yes"*], that we, as a people, will get to the Promised Land. [*Applause, "Go ahead, go ahead"*] And so I'm happy tonight; I'm not worried about anything; I'm not fearing any man. Mine eyes have seen the glory of the coming of the Lord. [*Applause*]

Listen to all of that speech sometime. It covered the entire social fabric of the time. Then it was over. And then . . . pandemonium. Fast-forward past him exiting Room 306 at the Lorraine at approximately 6 P.M. the next afternoon, standing on the balcony, about to go back in the room for his coat, past the report of a single rifle shot; then past infernos, and sirens everywhere; Bobby Kennedy shot in L.A.; Afros blooming, braiding, locking; Ali saying, "I ain't got nothing against them Viet Congs"; Uncle A.D., an expert swimmer, drowning; Jimi Hendrix showing "The Star-Spangled Banner" could be done in amplified electric; *Superfly*, *The Godfather*, and *The Mack* all written, shot, or released within nine months of each other in '72; my blessed grandmother, shot down from the pulpit of my church where I grew up; George Clinton stepping out of a silk and wool double-vented suit and tie in the mid-'60s, cutting the conk off his head, and becoming godfather of a new grooved nation—Puff Daddy's daddy. No one has yet covered Clinton's "(I Wanna) Testify" (1967). James Earl Ray always did say he wanted to hum along to that.

The Staple Singers and Mavis (favorites of Daddy's) came from gospel into secular with a purpose, a cause, with "Respect Yourself," then "I'll Take You There" (1974). Their starchildren became the Winans, Kirk Franklin having church in "His Eye Is on the Sparrow" and "Stomp." "The Sweeter He Is (The Longer the Pain's Gonna Hurt)," cried the Soul Children (1970); they begat BLACKstreet, Jodeci—all out of the church. Louis Armstrong once told a videographer, "It all started in the sanctified church; how you gonna get away from it? That's where the beat started."

Marvin Gaye's "What's Going On." A seminal question coming out of assassinations, like Daddy's, out of conflict like the Civil Rights Movement, like the Vietnam War. Rafael Saddiq of the hip-hop nation could sing "I Been Thinking of You" because Al Green, Reverend Al, sang it from the pulpit of his church in Memphis; Green sang after my father was shot, "How Can You Mend A Broken Heart?" Missy Elliott broke out in '97 with "The Rain (Supa Dupa Fly)," beating a rhythmic raindrop, yodeling the hook. After he was shot, a preacher's child, Ann Peebles, all of four foot ten, kicked the same hook over the same raindrop, over the same yodel, but not as hard a bottom line. Ann sang it hard in Memphis, in '71: "I Can't Stand the Rain." I did my research. I went to Memphis as a man. I saw. The Sound is what you can use. The Sound is what I shared with Memphis. The Sound was in it, and in me. Only the Sound is there. That's all that has to be there. Just the Way. Music is the Way. It holds the message.

I can't stand the ra-in . . . 'gainst my window . . . bringing
back sweet memories . . .

From mountaintop into the valley. The straight-up-don't-give-
a-damn-no-more attitude of mass creativity and material confusion—all the Big Wave of hip-hop, from its saddest to its most
materialistic and nihilistic forms—was born after our father Martin
Luther King, Jr., was shot!

The Sound began when Afrika Bambaataa scratched it up in the
Bronx in the late '70s. I had tried to take it into deejaying. Deejaying had a purpose. The Sound was philosophy, the artists
philosophers. So the Sound, it's always there for me—for us. But
the Sound was not the reason.

The reason, the stimulus, the jump-start that began all the
Noise of Big Wave hip-hop, can be traced back to Memphis, where
a luckless man with no skills named James Earl Ray is said to have
brought down a great man who was my father. James Earl Ray,
who could screw up boiling water; James Earl Ray, who was uncomfortable in the military, not a trained sharpshooter, who had
never drawn down on a person before with a rifle in his life that
we know of or that was ever proved; James Earl Ray, escaped con
doing time in Missouri for a $150 grocery store knockover, who
later said he bought a rifle on orders from a man named Raul, who
supposedly had connections with the Mafia's Memphis branch;
James Earl Ray, who woke up screaming one night at age ten because he thought he'd lost his eyesight (the room was dark),
whose prison warden said he was "fearful," who fellow inmates
called "Trembler." After a lifetime of failure, you mean to tell me
that completely on his own James Earl Ray pulled off a skilled expert sniper's shot—one shot only—that blew off our father's jaw-
bone, severed his spinal column, and broke thirty million hearts
that kept living, giving birth, making music? All that's happened
since is the same thing, over and over again—the best hooks sung,
the good brothers shot, over and over again. Somebody had to try
to interrupt that deadly cycle. Somebody had to say or do some-

thing. Or it would just be the same thing, over and over, until somebody confronted what happened and asked, "Why?" And maybe "How?"

It began with my initial face-to-face contact with Dr. William Pepper, which came in February of '97, with Isaac and Phil. My first encounter via correspondence was probably '95, when he had sent *Orders to Kill* to each one of my family members individually with letters saying, "I would like you to consider what I've written here. I really want an opportunity to bring the truth out, to bring it to life."

At that point, I think nobody could get beyond the fact that though he'd known and worked with our father, he was still Ray's lawyer. He'd written a book about the assassination, in that respect possibly being no different from Ray's first lawyer, Arthur Hanes, who authorized a book called *He Slew the Dreamer*, by William Bradford Huie. Huie and Hanes had a deal. Huie didn't want Ray to even testify in his own defense because it would take away from Ray's comments in the book. This paved the way for the next lawyer, Percy Foreman, who put down Hanes and then cut his own deal with Huie after Ray dumped Hanes and brought him in. Foreman insisted that Ray plead guilty.

Later on, there were several more books about my father's assassination. Dozens of them, actually. Mark Lane, another of Ray's lawyers, Taylor Branch, and even Dick Gregory, wrote about it. Ray also had many lawyers over the years. All along, I don't think we focused on it very much because we were unconsciously not ready to deal with it. Then that blue-green laser light hit me on the balcony of the Lorraine, and I had this feeling that I wanted to know. Why? How? Who?

At first, we hadn't responded to Pepper, feeling we should "just leave it alone."

Fast-forward to December '96; Ray went into the hospital for liver disease and entered a coma. Immediately we started getting calls from the media. Over the years, every time something would happen with Ray, we would get some type of call from the media. Like when he was stabbed in prison and almost killed. Okay, well you're a victim, the victimizer is in prison and something has happened to him, how does that make you feel? In this case, it was "James Earl Ray is in the hospital and there's a chance he may die. Any comment? Do you believe Ray actually killed your father?" This question I remember being asked almost all my life.

I hadn't been there. I was seven years old at the time. So what was I expected to say?

We took the standard approach—"No comment." We really didn't deal with it. Then Ray would recuperate for a time. Three weeks later he'd have a relapse and go back in. Every time that happened, we got a call—not a call, we got bombarded with calls.

I was traveling, on vacation, down to Negril in Jamaica. I happened to call in, and it probably was a mistake to call in and check my messages; I had a number on there. It was a *New York Times* reporter who said, "We're trying to reach you because we have been contacted by the Ray family behind the scenes, off the record." They were making a plea, they wanted to make an appeal to my family; their loved one was about to die; while they know it's awkward that they never bothered in the past, they feel it's now or never, but would we please consider making a statement in support of a new trial for James Earl Ray so that his guilt or his innocence could be fairly determined once and for all?

The Atlanta bureau chief of the *New York Times* had interviewed me in the past, which is how he got my pager number. I had to respond. Now it went beyond just "No comment." I spoke to a woman reporter, following up. The bureau chief was out of the office. I said I'd run it by my family, but to bear with me, because I was traveling overseas. My brother and sisters were traveling; getting everybody on one call would take some doing; be patient, I'll get back.

My brother and sisters and mother and I had a conference call and took a consensus. I went around to everybody and asked, "What do you think?" Bernice was indifferent. She said, "God will judge, brother." But Yolanda said, ". . . I've been wanting to know, Dexter. I feel like we should know what happened. And why." She sounded expectant. Never have I loved her more or felt more powerless to comfort her. Long ago she was exasperated with me for asking why. Now . . .

Ultimately the consensus was, Let's make a statement supporting a new trial. We talked about Marcus Wayne Chenault, Big Mama's murderer, how my grandfather forgave him and made us see the logic of it; how it was Christian; whether Ray did it or not, he deserved a trial. If Daddy was living, he would have forgiven him. He forgave the woman who stabbed him in the chest at a Harlem department store and almost took his life. We didn't know at that point what the outcome would be. We hadn't seen evidence, but we had heard that new evidence had come to light. We said we'd hold a press conference to announce we supported a new trial. That made the *New York Times*.

So when I got back, it was February. That's when I met with Pepper—me, my cousin Isaac, and Phil. Initially I was skeptical. I didn't know Pepper from Adam. But once he told me face-to-face about his relationship with Dad, how he had admired him, how they were friends (authenticated by Mother), and he produced photos of him and my father being friendly and cordial with each other, then told me about why he did it, represented Ray, why you never hear how dedicated Pepper was to Daddy's cause, only that he served as Ray's lawyer in the late '80s; about Pepper and Ralph Abernathy visiting Ray, Uncle Ralph having asked him to meet with Ray, how they concluded he wasn't the triggerman. They weren't sure whether or how he was involved, but they were convinced he didn't act alone.

Pepper made it clear he had this passion to, I don't want to say to avenge Daddy, but he did tell me he felt guilty that he somehow contributed to my father's death by getting him interested in the war, when Pepper wrote for *Ramparts* about Vietnam; he felt this led to Daddy's interest in the war, to his making his antiwar statement on April 4, 1967, at Harlem's Riverside Church in his "A Time to Break Silence" speech, and to Daddy's assassination a year to the day after that.

There is no doubt that Pepper felt like he had to resolve his inner conflict. I could relate to that.

It was 1978 when Pepper first went with Ralph Abernathy to visit Ray. He said he had no intentions of representing Ray, had decided to do so only if he became convinced Ray had been unknowingly involved in the King assassination.

Jerry Ray, James Earl Ray's brother, reached out to Pepper, saying Ray had so many lawyers because he felt he was set up. After conducting a private investigation over a ten-year period, Pepper concluded in 1988 that Ray had indeed gotten a raw deal.

"Don't take my word," Pepper said to me. "You have access to everything I've got. You have that right as family of the victim. Talk to any of the witnesses that I've interviewed. Read the research and the documents. Don't take my word. Meet these people. Meet Ray. Form your own judgment."

With my family's blessing—particularly my mother's and Yolanda's—I decided to get in there and feel it for myself. There's something about looking another person in the eyes and spending time with him and getting to know him as I did with Pepper; there were brief encounters with some of the other particulars. This was no bunch of actors to me. There are things you must intuit, feel. That was my meat, intuiting human actions. I'd done it with figuring out the music. I'd done it when I worked in an environment as a corrections officer for almost two years, where day in and day out I was around people who for a living lied, cheated, stole, robbed; I knew the con vibe.

I got the feeling Pepper was being straight with me.

I then met with Ray. I needed to see—and feel—for myself. I needed to look at it coldly, unemotionally, as a cop would, as a detective would. I tried to assume that role.

*　　*　　*

The convicted assassin of Rev. Martin Luther King, Jr., was running out of time. His liver was quitting, and the Tennessee courts wouldn't give him even a single day of medical furlough from the state pen near Nashville. But before the end, Ray found some comfort. From the King family itself. Oh, it must've been deep for James Earl Ray to shake hands with me, with the mirror image of the man they say Ray last saw inside the crosshairs of a .30-06 caliber rifle. Ray's rifle had been tested by the congressional investigating committee for evidence to spark a new trial. Results were "inconclusive." That Remington rifle may have killed Ray better than it ever killed my father. The last request for testing of the rifle for evidence wound up in Judge Joe Brown's courtroom in Memphis. Pundits would discredit Brown because he starred in one of the TV judge shows; but he was on the bench in Memphis for a long time before that, and was respected. I knew because I asked around among Memphis police. I had to see Ray to confront all of this, so it wouldn't keep being relived, not only in my nightmares, but also in the national nightmare. For my brother and sisters. All of us. Without Ray, there might never be an answer to the question defining the work of even the youngest of the hip-hop nation-inside-a-nation.

The question is: Who shot Martin Luther King, Jr? And why?

Did Ray do it alone? Fine. Just show me how he did it alone, so I can sleep at night. Show me that nobody else had anything to do with it, so I can sleep at night. Show me, and I'll believe.

Is that why I was so polite when I met Ray in a Nashville medical detention ward in March of 1997? No. That's just the way I was raised. No different than my grandfather was with Marcus Wayne Chenault. "Thank you for letting me impose on your time," I said to a desiccated Ray, and yes, some people later said I spoke to James Earl Ray like he was green-lighting movies over at Warner Bros. or something. But I would have said it that way to the Devil himself. "I just want to ask for the record—did you kill my father?" I asked.

Guess what Ray said then. "No," claimed the sixty-nine-year-old convict.

"There's something about looking another person in the eye and asking him a question," I told a small contingent of press right after the meeting. "Spiritually speaking, you yourself can then say, 'Yes . . . I personally feel this now . . . and . . . I think . . . I believe this man is innocent.' "

Then who was responsible, and why? The press asked questions that I usually liked to ask. And there was a reason I said what I did to the press. Most people think I was just humming a script I'd heard from Pepper: "Army Intelligence, CIA, FBI . . ." Could've thrown in the Klan, Memphis police, Ray. Could be any of them. Could be none of them.

When I met with Ray, this was the sense I got: he was a petty criminal who had done stupid things. He didn't have much common sense and said as much. "Look, I ain't gonna tell you I'm totally innocent here. I did mess up and make mistakes. But I did not shoot Dr. King."

A guy who can take somebody out at two hundred feet with one shot is a cold-blooded marksman and killer. I saw evidence that when James Earl Ray was in the military, he couldn't hit a target from a hundred feet with an M1 rifle. So how in the name of God did he hit a moving target in the neck from two hundred feet away in a cramped position with one shot from an uncalibrated .30-06?

When the cameras left, Ray and I spoke privately; I wanted him to know we were trying to get the new trial, get the truth out, whatever it was; we wanted him to have his day in court, and if on that day he was proven guilty or exonerated, so be it, either way. My family deserved to know and needed to know. People needed to know. I asked if he knew of any other people involved, did he have any information he wanted to share with me that was not common knowledge. He kept saying you need to open up the files, sealed FBI files and congressional records. He said he thought we'd find out a lot in them. It was a known fact that the FBI was looking to set up my father and in fact did fabricate things about him and harass him. So I don't know how much the records would reveal the truth, because I think the real nitty-gritty is buried. That's not the kind of stuff you're going to put in writing. He sighed deeply. It was almost like he didn't even care anymore. "Look, I'm tired of defending myself and saying I didn't do it. Go look at the records and then you'll see." It was almost like he didn't want to speak for himself anymore; I got the impression he wasn't going to willingly take the fall. I felt he was telling the truth.

His thing was a liver transplant. He needed to get one done. They weren't letting him out.

He felt if he had a little more time, health-wise, there was a good chance that he could get his trial. Another thing that struck me was that he really just seemed like almost a model prisoner in the sense that if somebody did something wrong to him, it was almost like he would just keep it to himself. I got this sense that he didn't want to cause anybody any problems and he didn't want any problems. I almost felt sorry for him. In a strange sort of way I really felt for the guy; I felt like we were both victims. I told him that. "We're caught in the same web."

If he didn't do it and he's been in jail for almost thirty years for a crime he didn't commit, that's victimhood. The general re-action of people afterward was: "You mean to tell me he went all the way up there and met with this guy and came out convinced he was innocent? What a sucker." This was around the same time of the California mass suicide that coincided with the appearance of the Hale-Bopp comet, where everyone was wearing black clothes and Nike sneakers, out near San Diego. Because of that in-cident, CNN broke away from me and was going back and forth between the reporting on the mass suicide and me; CNN covered it live, then they broke to California; so they caught me meeting with Ray live, but they didn't do the pre–press conference, so what the average person saw was me coming out of this meeting and saying I thought he didn't do it. Commentators, out of context, were giving this impression, "Well, isn't that amazing?" Just go in and meet this guy for lunch and suddenly he's innocent. Snide. But in the press conference after the meeting, I explained I'd already seen evidence I couldn't really discuss in detail, but that I was convinced not just by the encounter. I was convinced before I met him.

I felt the guy got a bum rap. I felt he was a patsy.

My mother and I went to Memphis in February of 1997 to testify before Judge Joe Brown in an attempt to bring a rifle testing procedure into court, in hopes of sparking a new trial for Ray; Ray was hoping to spark his own release from prison so he could get a liver transplant. I did some walking around and thinking in Memphis. I had always hated going there, ever since I was twelve and thirteen and going to the sleep disorder clinic at Baptist Memorial Hospital, all the way until I visited the Lorraine Motel in the early '90s.

Judge Joe Brown was pushing for the rifle test to happen, but there were a lot of appeals, and the DA was fighting it, the state was fighting it, but my mother and I went anyway, and testified why we believed this should happen; essentially, if there was a possibility of finding out the truth, it was worth doing. For a minute it had people on pins and needles because it was looking like those tests might prove something. Then there was a glitch in the system; instructions the judge gave about cleaning the rifle and prepping it were not followed to a tee, therefore they had to request another testing. That's where everything derailed, because the state fought the new test to the point where the higher court overruled Brown and would not allow a second round of testing at a site in Rhode Island. Every time you fire a rifle, a metal residue is left in the barrel. Grooved markings make each bullet like a fingerprint. Each barrel and each bullet has a certain "fingerprint," and leave a certain fingerprint on each other, altered slightly each time the gun is fired, altered to the extent that the next bullet you fire in succession is not getting the same print because residue is getting thicker so grooves are less pronounced. Judge Brown's remedy: a liquid solution you can use that will actually remove residue and allow you to get an accurate reading. With all of that intrigue, Brown, with all his experience, felt that this was not the rifle that killed our father. I don't know all the reasons, but he had informed data that would come out in trial.

To be honest, we felt very awkward this whole time, but that was a snowball effect. I'd gotten letters from people. One began, "I've been a silent supporter for almost thirty years. I've been in silent sympathy with your family and I've been wanting to say these things and get them off my chest." This person happened to be ex-CIA. "I've been there and done that, and I just want you to know you're on the right track. I can tell you for a fact, Ray did not do it."

On and on. Letters. Notes. Phone calls explaining how the process works in terms of setting someone up, how a person can be moved around the country, not know he's being controlled; movements documented, so a person can be framed. When you start getting information like that, what do you do? I'm not an investigator, yet when we talked to the Justice Department, they didn't want to deal with it. What do you do? All we could do was try to get the authorities to give it a hearing. I never heard of a case where the authorities say, "We don't want it because the case is thirty years old and it would open a can of worms." I thought there was no statute of limitations on murder. But the assistant district attorney in Memphis told me, "We don't need to open this; it's messy." But I believe that until you deal with it, it'll stay messy. I was walking around feeling, "We're the victim's family, you're the DA, representing our rights, and you're going against us?"

The assistant DA and I went on *Nightline*. Ted Koppel asked him, "Why don't you just give the man a new trial? If you're so sure that he did it, why are you denying him a trial?" The DA said this much to me, off camera: "If we open this back up, we would have to let Ray walk."

Television hurt as much as it helped. Pepper appeared on the ABC show *Turning Point* and was ambushed by host Forrest Sawyer. In *Orders to Kill*, based on information he received from former Green Berets, Pepper offered a scenario of the involvement of military personnel in the killing of my father. This account concerned a leader of a special unit that was supposedly in Memphis the day of the assassination. Pepper's investigators told him that this guy was dead. In fact, he had been convicted of negligent homicide, served time, and then he relocated to Central America, which is apparently why Pepper's investigators could not find him. But he turned up live on *Turning Point*, and Forrest Sawyer asked Pepper what he had to say to that, and Pepper could only say what he had been told by his investigators. The guy denied all. But of course he would.

In 1968, the Lorraine Motel was a black-owned establishment, operated by Walter and Lorraine Bailey. This was where my father at times took a room for meeting local people in Memphis. He'd already been to town twice that March, but he stayed at the Holiday Inn Rivermont. Though there is some controversy about this, as it appears that he never stayed overnight at the Lorraine before April 13, 1968, on that occasion he was at the Lorraine. Mrs. Bailey bragged about it. A freak snowstorm then rain rescheduled plans. Radio got the word out. Although he was originally scheduled to take Room 202—a protected room on a lower level—his room was changed apparently per an SCLC official's request. He was given Room 306. Daddy had only visited during the day and had reservations at the Peabody Hotel downtown but was diverted to the Rivermont Holiday Inn, where his suite was electronically surveilled. He was on his second trip that March, when he led the march toward City Hall. That march was derailed by rock-wielding youths busting out windows; could have been wild youths, it could have been the Invaders, a "gang" infiltrated by provocateurs, undercover police, and federal agents, including Marrell McCollough, who ended up kneeling over my father's body at the Lorraine. Some people think there were hardly any actual gang members in the Invaders at all, except those recruited by law enforcement infiltrators.

My father had stayed at the Rivermont hotel by the river after the first march had not ended well on March 28. But he stayed at the Lorraine on April 3 and 4. Daddy wanted to put "Negroes" into economic play (as well as focus on where integration really counted), and he knew this was most needed in the cities, where economic and educational segregation was obviously blatant, especially at that time in Atlanta, Birmingham, and Memphis. He had planned the Poor People's March on Washington for the summer of '68. He'd just taken Martin and me with him on a trip through rural Georgia, handshaking, preparing poor people. Higher-ups weren't happy. J. Edgar Hoover called Daddy "the most notorious liar in the country." My father's FBI code name: Zorro. The Vatican hosted him, *TIME* magazine made him Man of the Year in 1963; the Nobel committee awarded him its Peace Prize in 1964. And yet authorities feared violence from him? Guilt transference, is all. In Birmingham, four little girls were bombed out of existence inside the Sixteenth Street Baptist Church in '63. New Orleans? Different world. Miami? That wasn't Miami. That was They-ami. Atlanta was home to the Kings, the Atlanta University Center of five United Negro College Fund schools. Atlanta was the Head. In Memphis, reflection of ancient Egypt atop the Mississippi Delta, most blacks went uneducated. One UNCF school. Yet the people there in Memphis wanted their children educated as much as anybody. More. They were almost uniformly poor. But they were also many. Memphis was the Body. They say kill the Head and the Body will die.

It was for sanitation workers that Daddy went to Memphis. The men had already done the work. They moved 2,500 cubic tons of garbage a week. Hard to find any litter on the tree-lined parkways—as hard as finding up-to-date materials in the segregated schools. It is always the dollars that are most rigidly segregated. Memphis had won an "America's Cleanest City" award ten years running. Retired it. The men had done it, for $1.27 an hour, up to $1.65 if you proved yourself quiet and reliable over a ten-year career. They took it. They took it to educate you, fool. In February 1968, in twenty-two-degree weather, two workers, Echol Cole, thirty-five, and Robert Walker, twenty-nine, were crushed to death inside a garbage packer. The city gave their families a month's salary, and $500 for burial. The union tiptoed in. Wanted $2.35 for laborers, $3.00 for drivers. City wouldn't deal. Laughed, basically. So the Body looked to Atlanta. Most of the Body came up, over and down from the Delta; so they knew well that when somebody slaps a book out of your hand, it's not because you're "acting white"; it's because you're getting ahead. That makes them angry.

Daddy came to Memphis rapping hard. When he finished, 930 of 1,100 garbage men wore signs reading I AM A MAN as they picketed for $2.35 an hour for their children's education.

On March 18, before 13,000 people at Mason Temple, Daddy said, "Y'all know what? We may have to escalate this struggle a little bit." He urged a work stoppage, called for "all Negro public school students to miss class," and suggested a sit-in at the Board of Education.

He came back and gave the "Mountaintop" speech April 3 at Mason Temple before 5,000.

Mayor Henry Loeb, Police Chief J. C. Macdonald, Fire and Police Director Frank Holliman, Public Works commissioners Pete Sisson and Charles Blackburn all realized how much my father knew about how Memphis operated, knew the enterprise of Memphis was based on the poor working for low or no wage, and not being educated enough to do anything about it. Friday, April 5, students were to stay home. Those who could would walk to the Board of Education. Sit on the grass. Adults not in lifesaving jobs were to stay home from work. My father gave the word, Wednesday, April 3. It was to be Friday. The day after tomorrow.

In Memphis, Friday never got there.

Just before 6:00 P.M. on April 4, 1968, Daddy came onto the second-floor balcony of the Lorraine Motel, outside Room 306,

facing the rear of the buildings fronting the east side of South
Main. A sniper was lining up from an angle in a camouflage of
bushes two hundred feet away, straight on. In the parking lot two
aides shadowboxed. Solomon Jones, Daddy's driver, said it was
cool for April; he suggested Daddy bring a topcoat. Looking down,
Daddy asked Ben Branch to play "Precious Lord, Take My Hand"
that night. "Play it real pretty," he asked of Ben Branch.

My father's last request was for music!

Then, just after he answered Jones's request that he get a coat,
a shot resounded. Daddy was down. "I saw a man jump out of the
thicket across the street," Jones said afterward. "He ran. I climbed
up to the balcony. There was a white man there. I don't know who
he was. They say he lived there . . . he covered [Daddy's] face with
a cloth." Earl Caldwell, then of the *New York Times*, also confirmed seeing a figure in the bushes, and Rev. James Orange confirmed seeing smoke rising from the same bushes. Though
Caldwell told the police he saw a man, the police never questioned
him. The bushes were cut down and that area was swept clean the
next morning, only hours later.

A man named Marrell McCollough had infiltrated that "gang"
in Memphis called the Invaders; they'd been held responsible for a
rock-throwing incident that broke up a peaceful demonstration on
my father's last trip to town on March 28. McCollough had been
in military intelligence, had been discharged, and was called back.
He appeared on the scene seconds after the shot, and was the first
person to reach my father. He came running up to the balcony, was
photographed checking my father's vital signs, and attempted to
establish the flophouse as the scene of the shooting. He's disappeared from the scene now. A black cop, E. E. "Ed" Redditt, was
one of a two-man surveillance team on duty in the fire station. He
was pulled off the detail an hour and a half before the shooting—
and escorted home.

Mrs. Bailey, manager of the Lorraine motel, upon learning of
the assassination, ran to her room, locked the door, and collapsed,
having suffered a cerebral hemorrhage. She was rushed to the same

hospital as my father—Saint Joseph's—where she laid in a coma until her death on April 9. My father's autopsy report was filed April 11, 1968, a week after he was killed.

From Autopsy Report #A68-252, county medical examiner, J. T. Francisco:

> Gunshot wound to the chin and neck, fracture of mandible, laceration of vertebral artery, jugular vein and sub-laceration of spinal cord . . . intrapulmonary hematoma, apex, right upper lobe . . . Death was result of a gunshot wound to the chin and neck with a total transection of the lower cervical and upper thoracic spinal cord and other structures . . . direction of the wounding was from front to back, above downward and from right to left . . . The severing of the spinal cord at this level and to this extent was a wound that was fatal very shortly after its occurrence . . . an extensive excavating lesion . . . beginning one inch lateral to the right corner of the mouth and ½ inch inferior to right corner of the mouth; measures approximately 3 inches in length . . . angle of the penetrating wound is approximately 45 degrees from a sagittal plane at an angle right to left.

For a conspiracy all you need is two. One was in the bag with J. Edgar Hoover, who died in 1972 after forty-eight years as FBI director. Hoover, a notorious megalomaniac, was not above pushing a button on a guy. He'd posed smiling with bullet-riddled corpses before, like Machine Gun Kelly, a small-time armed robber also killed in Memphis. Hoover stood by his corpse, smiling. He had my father under surveillance, tried to blackmail him over alleged sex tapes, not for profit but to tempt him to commit suicide. Hoover even sent audiotapes to my mother, but my father said they'd have to come up with something better than that. He wasn't going to respond to blackmail. Then there was the operator of Jim's Grill,

Loyd Jowers. The grill was located beneath the rooming house from where the shot supposedly was fired.

Jim's Grill was behind the bushes from where the shot was most likely to have been fired.

Surveillance of our family wasn't new. My grandfather, even my great-grandfather, were surveilled by the army. "Conspiracy" doesn't mean the Joint Chiefs convened or Aunt Inez in the secretarial pool knew. But, suspiciously, at the last minute Ed Redditt was deemed untrustworthy and was pulled off the surveillance detail. The bushes directly across from the Lorraine and Room 306 were cut down and the area swept and cleared the morning after the assassination, before any search of that area. Loyd Jowers would eventually confirm that Ray wasn't the assassin, that another man, a policeman, had given him a smoking rifle right after the assassination. There was a reported "car chase" on police radio of a white Mustang like Ray's out of north Memphis minutes after the shot, while Ray was in fact going east-southeast out of town, on either Lamar or Summer Avenue. Somebody leaked the fake chase confusion to the local papers—maybe a decent cop. The papers displayed it like news. The police disavowed it, saying there was no chase. There was the rifle left in the doorway of Canipe's Amusements at 424 South Main. If that's the murder weapon, if Ray shot it then left it, he is the all-time idiot.

Then there was the presence of two white Mustangs, less than one hundred feet apart, in front of the boarding house. One being Ray's, with Alabama license plates, which was parked in front of Jim's Grill and in which two eyewitnesses said they saw him driving away some fifteen to twenty minutes before the shooting. The other car had Arkansas plates and sped away after the shooting.

Back in the early '80s, a yokel lounging up on South Main cackled at Jeff Prugh, then a journalist with the *Los Angeles Times*, "A man left it there—only that was before the shootin'."

Who was in the bushes? Who had them cut down? Pepper produced a statement under oath from the deputy public works director, Maynard Stiles, who said that the cleanup was ordered by MPD inspector Sam Evans.

Ray drove to Atlanta on main interstate and state highways. Troopers may have even waved to him. Then he went to London. Portugal. Thought he was off to Africa—Nigeria, Angola, or Mozambique—destinations that would never have entered his mind without suggestion. It was like he was on tour. Yeah, he was financed. By whoever had that end of the job. Probably by whoever gave him up. A combination of somebodies, actively or tacitly. Two months after the assassination, Ray got a surprise at London's Heathrow Airport. He was arrested, coerced into pleading guilty, was convicted, and filed a motion for a new trial three days after the plea. Even if Ray would have done it, did he have the skill to make the shot, a single fatal perfect shot from two hundred feet away from a cramped position with a secondhand rifle? He never was that good. Who actually knew Ray? Harold Swenson was warden of the prison in Jefferson City, Missouri, where Ray spent nearly two years doing time, and from which he escaped by hiding in a breadbox truck a year before Daddy's murder. "Odd," Harold Swenson said two weeks after Ray's arrest in '68. "I won't believe [Ray] did it until it's proved. Didn't seem to be the desperado type, compared to some real bad ones we've got. He couldn't join the team. Not in here."

Judge Joe Brown had the hearing—what was left of it—in Memphis court through August of 1996. Ray's rifle was shot into a barrel in Rhode Island: "Inconclusive," of course. Brown couldn't move forward. Came to Memphis from California years ago on a "Reggie"—a Reginald Huber Fellowship—one of the things my father's death set in motion, things that are slowly being rescinded now. Brown came to serve the underserved. Judge Joe Brown was authentically trying to do justice.

In mid-August of '97, Judge Brown had asked that a special prosecutor be assigned. "The state is not really interested in finding out the truth," he said in frustration. Brown was then lampooned in a scathing editorial cartoon in the *Memphis Commercial Appeal.*

Memphis. I still feel awkward there. Yolanda says the same thing. People in Memphis, black and white, are very warm and hospitable, giving. People genuinely wanted to help us. I felt wrong for disliking Memphis. If I went shopping, if I went out to the drugstore, people were taking pictures. It was just warm, hospitable; people bent over backward. It was almost like they were going out of their way, white and black, to be accommodating; you didn't get the impression it was phony. They were still sensitive to the tragedy, and they were sorry, and they didn't want to carry the burden of it forever. I thought about the fact I had two young black police officers as my security detail, Memphis police officers, and how they seemed honored to have the detail, and the fact that one of them in particular said he was born three months after my father got killed. So here's a thirty-one-year-old entrusted with protecting me in this city; he and his partner were assigned to this tactical unit whose same name had come up in testimony in the court about the involvement of the Memphis police on April 4, 1968. It was weird leaving the courtroom and then getting in this unmarked car; the irony of being embraced by the Establishment on the one hand, but on the other hand, here we were trying to resolve this injustice, even though I knew this detail had nothing to do with it.

My dad—some people called him a communist, a rabble-rouser, an unfaithful husband: all false, but after he's gone they say, "Aw, what a good man he was, how sincere he was, how tragically he died, how sad it is, how noble (now that he's no threat to our comfort)—he deserves a holiday! He's great now because he's no longer a threat. Keep him as a dreamer rather than as a realist and he's great."

But the minute you start dealing with what he was talking about before he died—some people don't want to hear that. They don't want to see that. So I've got to say it the way I find it. I have to say it. A last full measure of devotion. If somebody tells me I can't offer him that, all the more reason I must. The more people try to keep me from it, the more I must do it. Why? Something pulled me back to it. I'm still trying to figure that part out. I still don't have all the answers.

The meetings with Pepper, with Ray, with Memphis, were important.

They weren't the only important meetings I took during that time.

CHAPTER 17

Sampling a Relationship

I interrupt this public quest to talk about a more personal aspect of my life, and to give a view of what it's like to try to have a close personal relationship while trying to be heir to this kind of volatile legacy, after being damaged by the murder of your father when you were a child. It's hard enough connecting with somebody in the first place at the turn of the millennium. So I'm going to let you in. It is a tough thing for me to do, but it has been suggested that I try, so I will.

Mon Ami is a Cuban American. Mon Ami is not her real name, but it describes how I came to feel about her over the four years we were together. We met in February 1996. She was living in Birmingham, Alabama. She worked for a well-known pharmaceutical company. We met in Washington, at a black-tie dinner for the Joint Center for Political and Economic Studies think tank. She was there, even though she was sick. She's a real trooper, and business is business. I was on the dais as a guest. Vice President Al Gore was the evening's featured speaker.

Mon Ami was bored. She'd been a lobbyist at a chemical firm, then director of corporate affairs with this pharmaceutical firm.

Born in Havana, she and her family emigrated to the United States and she grew up in South Florida. She came to America at age two, spoke only Spanish then. Even with a fever, she went to this function; didn't seem to have a lot of time for a lot of B.S.; when you're in corporate America, based in the South, and you're Latina, you've heard it all.

As a young child she knew what money problems were too. Her mom and dad washed dishes, cleaned offices, drove trucks to make money in a new country. They put her through school. She was driven by ambition at her jobs, but when it came to dating, she had no clue. There was little room for an emotional side in her life. She was comfortable as long as she was dealing with a man on a professional level. In Birmingham, she owned a nice house on Baltimore Street. The neighbors thought she was weird because she was the only one in the development not married or with kids. She was hardly ever there, because of traveling. But she said she was having a great time until she realized she was about to be thirty-one. It happens to women. Must be genetic.

Later she said she'd let God know she was ready. Her prayer was, "I know you'll give me what I need; Lord, you sent me here naked and alone, so I know that with you I have everything I need in life, but I'd like to have a partner, be in a relationship if that is your will. If it's my destiny to walk alone, I'm cool with it. Just give me what I need to do it."

So we're at this function. She was in a serious mood, I could see that; she wore her very curly dark hair pinned back; glasses; looking at her watch every two minutes; the only female in her contingent. It wasn't that crowded, as we were in a large hotel ballroom. I was wearing a tuxedo. When she turned her head away, I stared at her across the room. "Hey! Who're you staring at?" asked one of her colleagues, Miles; they were talking. Miles was an African-American gentleman from the West Coast.

She asked him, "Isn't that Dexter King over there?"

"Yeah, you want to go meet him?"

". . . Oh . . . well . . . if he's not . . . not really."

Miles said, "Ah, come on." Well, the next thing I know . . . there I am meeting this woman, and kind of liking it, sort of, maybe . . . I don't know. Miles sits on the King Holiday Committee in Seattle, and had been to the King Center through the nonviolent training program. He told me what a fine lobbyist and fund-raiser she was. I began to think of how she might positively impact the Center—or maybe I was thinking subconsciously how she might impact me. Maybe I thought a few other things, but they were untoward thoughts for the son of Dr. King. She caught my eye.

Too soon for me, a glass was struck by a piece of silverware, calling the room to order.

"Sorry, I've got to go up on the dais. Do you have your business card? Thanks. Well, nice to meet you." I turned around and walked off. Miles asked her in a whisper, "What did you think?" She said, "About your stories, or him?" She told me later she put the episode out of her mind. I didn't.

A couple of weeks went by. I found myself thinking about her. Finally, I paged her. She was in Chicago when her pager went off; she read the number: 404 area code. She was on the phone with a girlfriend at the Ritz-Carlton Hotel on Michigan Avenue, and asked her absently, "Wonder who this is paging me from 404?"

"Hello?"

"Mon? Mon Ami? . . ." I'd never been nervous like this before. My veneer of nonchalance was cracking already. "This is Dexter. Dexter King. I'm pleased you called me back."

"Oh, Mr. King, very nice to hear your voice. How are you?"

"Fine, and you?"

"Fine thanks, I'm returning your page, or trying to—"

"What? Was everything all right with how the phone was answered?"

"Well . . . don't worry about it."

"One reason I'm calling you—is because I'm really interested in finding out more about what you do with your company and its Foundation, and was wondering if you and I could meet so that I can go over some of the plans the King Center has, and . . ."

She'd finished her MBA a few years before; grant-finding, fund-raising, and ally development were part of her skill base. I wanted to know more.

"Okay, that sounds good. When would you like to meet?"

"Next week."

"Let me look at my calendar."

At the time, it was the first week in March.

"I have April 15 available. How does that look for you?"

"Excuse me?"

". . . You know, Mr. King . . ."

"Please . . . call me Dexter."

"All right. Dexter, you know if that's not a good time—judging from your reaction I gather that's not a good time—I have dates available later in April or May, but April 15 is the first time I have available." Hmm. Didn't know how to take it. Seems like you could squeeze somebody in.

We set up a meeting for April 15. A month goes by, I call her and ask, "We still on?" "Yes." She drove over from Birmingham. I'd arranged a tour of the site. Finally, we met. She had her hand out for a handshake; I took it, and kissed her on the cheek; she kissed me on mine, which she said she normally did, because she's Hispanic and that's how they greet, but she also said she'd learned in business that you can't be going around kissing folks; still, she figured, "He's African American, I'm Hispanic, that's what we do in a social setting. He won't read it wrong."

"I want us to have dinner to discuss some things," I said. "Business proposals and possibilities. We need assistance. But I wasn't sure what you'd like to eat. I'm particular."

She said, "So am I, but I can find things to eat everywhere I go."

"But, do you have a preference?"

"My preference is any place I can get vegetarian food."

I looked at her. "You're kidding."

She raised her eyebrows and said, "No. I've been a vegetarian for about twelve years. Why would I kid about that? I know it might be a little weird for some people's taste . . ."

"No, no, no, no, no—it's fine."

I didn't tell her I was a vegetarian just then.

Mon Ami and I sat on the couch and I showed her the architectural blueprints for the King Center. I asked her about the tour, showed her the King Center plans, and right then I was torn because on the one hand there was no doubt in my mind that I was attracted to her, and on the other hand she seemed like a sharpie who could help advise me on directions the King Center was taking. Somehow I'd tamp down the attraction.

That afternoon and early evening Mon Ami and I talked about her career and background. We discussed business over dinner, politics over dessert. We talked about how to help the King Center and if her company could be involved.

It was an interesting, strangely short evening. It was over like that. We were at my car, headed back. She'd left her car in the King Center.

We were laughing and I thought, "Wow, this has been one of the best times I've had since . . . I don't know when." What I didn't know at the time was that she was thinking the same thing. But neither of us had time for that stuff. And we both sort of made it clear without being specific. She had been married before, while in her early twenties, and hadn't been looking for any kind of serious relationship or commitment. Neither was I. I'd taken her to a small café for dessert. We sat at a corner table and my fingers touched hers, and she jumped back a little. We got in my car and drove back to the King Center garage. It was 11 P.M. She had to drive back to Birmingham that night because she had an early-morning flight the next day, had a meeting up in Portland the next afternoon. She would be there all week. We were nearly at the garage. Soon she would be gone. I became pensive. She noticed, and said, "Dexter King, I have a question for you."

". . . Okay."

"Just an innocent question. Out of curiosity."

"Shoot."

"Do you typically play with people's fingers during business dinners?"

". . . No, but, uh, well . . . why do you ask?"

"Well because I'm figuring it might make some of the women uncomfortable . . ."

After I stopped laughing nervously, I had to tell her my interests in her were not limited to business—or so I thought. Some of it was also personal. She said, "Can you please say that again?" I said, "I'm attracted to you. I found you very interesting when I met you and I really wanted to get to know you." She said, "I've got to hand it to you. I'm good, but I didn't see this coming. I spend four hours taking tours, seeing business plans, talking about donations and politics, and this is really personal? Gosh I've really been out of the social scene for a while, then . . ."

I smiled ruefully. "You're getting under my collar," I thought. It was so intense, we spent another hour talking. It was really great. When we finally got out of my car, I said, "It's late and you have a two-hour drive. Maybe you'd like to spend the night here in town. I can . . ."

She looked at me, arched an eyebrow, and said, "No. I have to drive back to Birmingham. I'm going to drive back now."

I said, "I was going to say, I can get you a hotel room. There are a lot of good hotels."

She said, "I have to drive back to Birmingham and I am driving back."

She later told me she didn't think I'd ever heard a woman say no. Little did she know.

I paged Mon Ami while she was in the Pacific Northwest.

"When are you coming back?" I asked.

"Coming back where?"

"I mean, when are you going home?"

"I'm going home tomorrow. I'm flying to Birmingham."

"Do you have a connection in Atlanta?"

"Now, Dexter, surely you must know by now that you can't get anywhere south of Chicago without connecting in Atlanta."

"Really? I mean, do you mind if I pick you up? I'll drive you over to Birmingham."

So we did that. In fact, we saw each other every weekend after that for about six months.

I'd been dating here and there since Good Natured bore the brunt of the funky malaise after I left the King Center in 1989, nearly seven years before. Mon Ami had been dating, off and on, another person located in Birmingham. I met her at the plane. She told me stories, made me laugh; how, her being Cuban, people didn't know what she was outside Florida. Black folks thought she was passing, white folks thought she was black. "When you see life through God's eyes, there is no color," she said. "That's how I was raised."

All I could say was, "Me too."

Going on through the year of 1996, we became closer; eventually she asked where we might be going with this relationship. I felt a chill. I said, "Thought you weren't looking for commitment, that your commitment was to your career? If that's the case, then I'd like to help you advance your career . . . There are many things I have not dealt with in my life on a personal level. I don't want to put you through it." This was toward the end of '96. I knew we were going to meet with Pepper; I knew there was going to be controversy, that there were things coming up like the Ray meeting, the trial. I didn't want her to be hurt by that. But at the same time . . . So what did I do?

I said, "I don't want a heavy, committed relationship."

Mon Ami said, "Oh really? Then what do we call what we have here?"

"You know what I mean."

"No, I don't. Help me. I'm not going to assume. Help me understand."

"I guess what I'm saying is, I'm not in the frame of mind to be committed. There are things I haven't given myself, so I can't give them to somebody else. I suffer depression, anxieties. With what's coming up in my life, I'll be even more distracted. It'll get worse before it gets better."

"I've seen all that," she said. "When you deal with things of your past, some of this will be lifted. Things you suppress have an impact on you physically, mentally, spiritually, and emotionally."

What gave her insight? We started dating in April '96; by June, it was her thirty-first birthday, and I asked her to come to Atlanta. She says it was starting to become clear to her that she was an aberration—I'd had girlfriends, nice ones, but this was something different. It seemed to be so different at the time. Actually, it was similar to what I'd had with Good Natured, only this came when I was older, at a different stage. Maybe. Also, the effect of not having a father in my life to tell me certain things was obvious to her. It might be fair to say we were comfortable with each other. I'd ask, "Is this okay for me to say this, feel that?" There was a profound sadness in her, so she and I had a bond that way; I didn't know how to handle it. It was hard, I couldn't allow myself to feel too deeply about her, or anyone, yet I felt helpless, caught up, as if I couldn't help feeling it. In the end, my conflicted feelings would cost me the relationship. It was like she would take on feelings of sadness and doubt I often fall prey to. She had to learn to manage that. You can't take on other people's stuff. Everybody has to haul their own water. I'd learned from Good Natured not to try and put my baggage on others, but apparently I hadn't learned well enough.

Mon Ami's birthday was coming up. I had a surprise for her. She came to Atlanta. I'd done everything. Made dinner. Didn't let her do anything. I took her out on a boat, on a lake, had made lunch, laid out a blanket, we watched the sunset, I brought out a bottle of nice perfume, big production. I was all over the place, kind of frantic. We got back to my place. I'd forgotten something so now I'd have to run out and get it. She looked at me and said, "Stop, will you?" We were in the kitchen. She said, "Why don't you let me help you? You're boiling pasta. I can do that. Why don't you let me watch the pasta? When it's done I'll take it out. Tell me what you want to do with it, and you go take care of what you need to take care of. I'll do this and you do that. A team."

I leaned back and away from her, on the kitchen counter. I looked at her, and I could feel these waves of emotion welling up inside me—love, fear, but mostly anxiety. She said, "What's wrong? Why are you looking at me like that? You never let me do anything with you, for you—you run around like a wild man . . ." As she spoke, I could feel a volcano erupting from the pit of my stomach up into my throat, choking me and spilling out as hot tears from behind my eyes. I started crying. I knew where it was going. Somehow it made me not secure but very insecure, violently insecure. I knew this was related to the deaths in my youth, yet I could not overcome the impact, the symptoms in my own mind and body. She looked at me and walked across the kitchen, and I put my hands on her shoulders and she put her arms around me. "What's wrong?" she said.

"I don't want to need you! I don't want to need anybody!"

The tears were rolling down my face and I couldn't stop them. "If I start to need you, what happens when you're taken away too?"

I loved her, but that didn't solve my problem. Rather, it revealed it. I thought I was over it. I thought I had gotten over it with Good Natured. I had played out a similar scene with her. But I was older now, at a different stage; this was different, Mon Ami was different, I was different. It turned out that I wasn't so different— I might be at a different stage, but I had the same demons.

Mon Ami had tears rolling down her face and I kept crying, and we couldn't stem the tide. All she could do was comfort me for a little while. She took me by the hand and hugged me and cried and told me, "Go ahead and cry, then. You need to cry. You need to let it go. I'm here." Then she wiped my face and said, "Know what? I can't tell you someone won't take my life. I can't guarantee I'll be here, I can't say I'll live forever or that we'll be together. Nobody has any guarantees. I don't know how long God has destined for me to be on this earth. No one can ever make you that promise. I know what has happened in your life, to your family. But I also know this—you have to let go of that, somehow. You have to find a way to let it go. You have to look at it squarely and deal with it, then move on, because if you don't, it will follow you all your life and never allow you peace. There will be situations in life that will force you to deal with your father's death. God will bring about a situation where you have nowhere to run or hide, but you have to look at it and you have to feel it. All we can live by is faith. You have to be willing to go out on the limb. That's where the fruit is. Out on the limb. You've got to go out there, Dexter."

October 1996. Mon Ami called and said, "You know what? Here's what I've decided. I decided that I really love you and I know you love me and for whatever reason you can't be in a committed relationship with me, so we'll just address it another time. I've already learned a lot from you about myself." I told her, "I've learned a lot about myself from you too."

If someone says, "I love you and I love everything about you," he or she is lying to you. I'm terrible to get along with sometimes. Mon Ami was impatient. We didn't love everything about each other. But to love the other person in spite of those things, that's true love. We had that.

February '97. The first meeting with Pepper is imminent. We are going to look closer at our father's assassination, and maybe after that, my mother, my sisters, my brother, and I will be free. I'm totally distracted. Ami and I are sitting in my living room, eating dinner. By now she's used to the business phone calls at nine at night on the cell phone, on the car phone. The phone rings; it's Phil Jones; I'd already been having conversations about meeting with Pepper. We always pray before we eat, so she was waiting for me to get off the phone. She later said she could feel the tension building, but she didn't know what it was about; I knew what it was about, but I didn't know it was that obvious. I tried not to tell her a whole lot about that. It was my baggage. Subconsciously I felt that would put her in danger.

In December '97, Phil asked her, "We can use some help with the legacy, why don't you come on board?" And after thinking about it, she said okay. I asked her, "Do you think you can do this? I mean, I know you can do the job. But can you handle the job and the personal stuff too?" I knew she had the skills—she was a shrewd MBA.

"Yes," she said, "but can you? Are you committed to it? If you're not committed to changing the face of this, then don't ask me to do this, because people hire me to make real changes that are not easy and often painful. You have your vision; do things your way, in your style; what happened to him is not going to happen to you. Use your other eyes; see what God has before you instead of fighting it."

Many others had said what Mon Ami said to me, but maybe she was anointed in a special way for me to hear her. So she came on board in the summer of '98, and we started shaking things up. By July '98, we placed the day-to-day operations of IPM (Intellectual Properties Management) and the King Center under her authority.

First she was a consultant, then director of external affairs, then managing director. The King Center ran more efficiently. The fact that we were in a relationship gave fodder to office gossip, but that's always going to be there—my father knew that. He was impugned, and his reputation imperiled, by many people within the Civil Rights Movement. But he was patient with it because he had the Cause of that movement—ending segregation. Our Cause now was the next level after that—individual economic empowerment, not nearly so noble a cause. Once, and not so long ago, a simple ride from Atlanta to Birmingham, even on interstate buses, let alone private automobiles, could be fraught with danger. Now, for me and my generation, it was just a ride—we could pop in a CD, make plans to see a beautiful lady, or have her there with us. But we had a Cause too.

Daddy left off with the peace movement and the Poor People's campaign. Our Cause had to be the propagation of nonviolence, the propagation of economic viability and the honoring of our father's legacy and name. One look around at the differences of the living conditions of the bulk of the population—one look at the house at 234 Sunset, and its environs in Vine City, where my mother still lived—made it clear to me. Outdoor advertising for cigarettes, alcohol, and organ donation was very prominent. That's all there was, really. The Cause was now economic.

The office gossip was difficult for Mon Ami at times. But it didn't matter to her what people thought. As long as I was being honest with her. At times, I was honest with her to a fault. She'd ask questions many women ask of men. She'd get straight answers. Sometimes she'd regret it.

A lot of women say, "You better tell me the truth; I can handle the truth," but that's not really true. There were some exgirlfriends of mine around; and she'd run into them at functions, they'd come up to her and kiss her on the cheek and shake her hand and not think she knew that two years ago, five years ago, that person and I were dating; she always knew because I was always honest. We had a bond that way. My mother, my brother, my sisters, from the time she met them, were nice to her. Mother and Mon Ami had their sticking points in business, everybody does, especially since Mon Ami ended up running, as managing director, what Mother built, and Mon Ami was not married to me. Mother respected her acumen. So did I.

Her parents accepted me. I claim no real depth there, though. Her mother is two years younger than mine. Her father came to Atlanta to visit. He and I smoked cigars. Mon Ami and her dad are as close as Mother and I. He's her best friend. So we're smoking cigars. He says something in Spanish.

"He said you're not holding the cigar right. How can he not be holding a cigar right?" Mon Ami translated for me, smiling. "So I said to him, 'Dad, his father wasn't around to teach him. Why don't you?' "

Damned if Mon Ami's father didn't show me how to approach smoking a Cuban cigar, right then and there, right down to the attitude with which you smoke a Cuban cigar. Mr. Ami had a laid-back, quiet persona, which Mon Ami always said reminded her of me.

I'd never before been romantically involved with anyone I worked with professionally; it was awkward for me. We became involved first, then it turned out she had so many qualities in terms of her training, skills, and was in the right place at the right time. She was loyal, dedicated, efficient. I saw her as my "significant other." One of the things she helped me to see is I have big problems committing on a personal emotional level. I can commit to a cause, an idea—but a living being of the opposite gender? People I love, who touch my heart, I keep them at a distance. All four of us, the children of Dr. King, are like this. None of us is married, none of us has ever been married. None of us has children. So there are issues there.

If I've still got insecurities or problems about how to express myself, and about how to make it all okay, well, I wish I didn't, okay? I'm impressionable. I take in data and send it back out like a refracting lens sometimes. Mon Ami not being African American, for instance. Once we were out and a sister as light-skinned as Mon Ami came up to me yelling, "Sellout! You sold out!" I said, "Why do you say that to me?" I was trying to be rational; she was totally emotional. The fact that she could just come up to me, a stranger, and tell me that, and more: "We look up to you! You're supposed to be our black prince. Look at you with this snowbunny!" I said, "Not that it matters, but she's not white, whatever that is, she's Cuban. Like everyone, she has African ancestry too. Not that it matters, but you've missed my father's message if that's what you think."

I can't deny it affected me.

*   *   *

Mon Ami and I went out for four years and also advanced the business of the King Center. The truth is, in my heart, I felt strongly for Mon Ami, but I also was not ready to make an ultimate commitment. She was the closest woman to me apart from my mother. Then she wanted more and I didn't know if I was able to give her more. Part of her wished I'd step to her on faith.

Once, she was ill with walking pneumonia. I went to Birmingham to nurse her back to health. She talked about how I was so loving. And I did often show her the sensitive part of me, but it was under glass; maybe she was able to see it, access it for a minute; there was a small window of time. Then that window closed; it was frustrating for her. Because she saw this relationship as having potential, and then, it wasn't happening . . . all relationships come to a point where you either take it to the next logical point or level, or you accept it for what it is, or it just kind of peters out. We were coming to that turning point. She said she never considered going out with a man who wouldn't be committed to her. She said she couldn't be proud enough to pretend she didn't love me, or that we didn't have a bond. There was something between us I'd never experienced.

It bothered me.

Right before I was going to meet James Earl Ray, I said to her, "It's too chaotic right now." I saw a relationship like ours as something you had to maintain and nurture. Not something that just happens. My whole point of view then was that I needed to break away so I could focus on James Earl Ray.

She said, "All right. I understand."

So when I went to meet Ray, Mon Ami and I were apart. She had friends who ran one of the largest government relations lobbying groups, a minority lobbying firm in Florida that wanted to expand into Georgia. They asked her to come on board as vice president, set up the office in Atlanta. She did that in June '97, and didn't tell me. No reason for her to, really. We weren't seeing each other. Still, when I found out, it bothered me. It did. I can't deny it. I didn't want to lose her, period. It was very difficult for her, very tough. How could she find her place in this relationship where she was committed to a person who was not committed to her? It seemed I was moving further away, not just from her but from everyone. More bogged down. More lost in my own thoughts. Getting ready. Add that to my whole commitment phobia. Mon Ami brought back to me the awareness that faith doesn't mean terrible things aren't necessarily going to happen, but that if they do—and they probably will—you can overcome any adversity with faith.

In business, she was very effective, good at what she did, with a sense of how to get things done; she was pragmatic, intelligent, able to separate business from personal. I had given her a hard time on the other levels because of my personal frustrations, phobias, inadequacies, stresses, and pressures; you tend to take things out on the people closest to you. While I know it's not fair, the reality is— who else are you going to share them with? Who else? If you live with a cop, where does he take all of that stuff after work? And my situation has been similar in terms of mental rigors and, as I said, the transformation I went through during that period. It took a major toll on us.

The James Earl Ray meeting in March 1997, what followed in Memphis during the Joe Brown hearing, my investigation of the assassination in Memphis, and the decision to file the civil suit against Loyd Jowers, operator of Jim's Grill on South Main Street in Memphis, in 1999—all of this was a turning point in the relationship between Mon Ami and me. I was stressed out. I'd never dealt with anything like it; once I saw what was going on, what we as a family had to do before we could put this to rest, it was constantly in my head. I was thinking about it all the time, about ramifications of looking into it, about being torpedoed in the mass media, about fearing for the personal safety of loved ones. All of this meant I never fully relaxed or let my guard down. I was afraid. I questioned everything and everyone; you start saying, "If that can happen over there, who's to say people might not hurt my loved ones?" Attacks in the media, evidence of things unseen—it all helped distance me from Mon Ami.

I told myself this distancing was for her own good and for her protection. I'd received death threats and become very cautious as a result of reopening the investigation surrounding my father's death.

The minute I shut Mon Ami out, she could not deal with it. She felt I was unable to believe in her, I wasn't able to engage, compounded by that part of me that had never dealt with my dad's death. By the spring of 2000, the process of shutting Mon Ami out had taken a year. It was true that for the first time I was dealing with Daddy's death in a serious way. Mon Ami had completed her work at the Center for the most part and it was time to move on. Or stay. We agreed that one way or another a move would have to take place once the civil trial was over.

CHAPTER 18

Home Front

When in doubt, go home. Go see Mom or Dad. If you can. If you're that lucky.

When I go home, I go to 234 Sunset. She'll be there. She's always been there. And thank God she was, or else the four of us might be totally disconnected from living. She sacrificed for us.

For the longest time, there was always a thought in her of growing old and dying there. But during the late '90s, I became concerned about her safety. Vine City, never fully tranquil, had changed, as a reflection, as part of the echo of the rifle report, so to speak—a sign of the times.

Crime is worse than when we were growing up; the crimes are more violent because of the nature of this drug epidemic of crack cocaine, which did not exist when we were growing up. It is a drug that seems to cause not just addiction but also a sordid, soulless madness, without conscience. I've watched things worsen in Vine City. For years, I lived in Midtown, in a townhouse, behind a gate. Mother needed to be in a place where she wouldn't have a lot of maintenance issues, and where she could live her life in peace. She wants to entertain, have a place where she's not so public; 234 Sunset is on the tour guides' route, like in Hollywood, when they take out-of-towners around to see the "homes of the stars." Except that Vine City isn't Hollywood. Mother doesn't have privacy. Not at 234 Sunset. Never did.

Growing up, we'd have to be our own sentries. When the tour buses were coming, we'd have somebody posted, up on the hill as lookout; if we were outside we'd run into the house, or back through the alleyway, or we'd hide behind the bushes and trees. Tourists would get off the tour buses sometimes and come right to the door, and knock, and if anyone answered they would actually ask if they could "come in and look around." They were dead serious. At times, tourists would pull up into the driveway in buses, or in wood-paneled station wagons, vans, RVs with out-of-state plates, and say, "We're from Lawrence County, Alabama!" or "Just pulled in from Hopkinsville, Kentucky!" or "Wichita, Kansas!" or wherever it might be. "We just want to have a look around . . . wonder if we could get a tour of the house?" Or "Can we look around?" This was frequent enough to be looked out for, especially in the summer. We really had little or no privacy at home after my father's death; even to this day my mother is exposed in this regard.

I began thinking, for practical reasons, that it would be a good thing for her to move from the ancestral home. The question would be, to where? It's a hard thing to even think about, let alone do; and you can relate, I'm sure, if you have a family ancestral home where you were raised, and where you lived, and where some of the closest people to you lived and died. Because of so many memories, so much emotion, so much life being accomplished and lived out there, you feel like you're abandoning part of your life, maybe even abandoning the people who lived with you, who helped you, and who are no longer living—it's like as long as you're still there, they still live.

Nobody can walk away from that cavalierly—well, some people can. Some people can't or don't walk away from it at all. It's not easy to move from an ancestral home. She's dealt with it all these years. She wouldn't leave on her own. She's just that type. In her golden years, she has a right to live the way she'd like to live. She's done all the living for others. Now let it be for her.

I've been concerned for her well-being there; it's like she's trying to preserve something, she's always tried to preserve what Daddy wanted done. He wanted to live there in the first place, to the disagreement of our grandfather, partly to appease the people who tried to damn him by calling him bourgeois. But I believe he would've changed with the times. The fact that this is not the same neighborhood it was once, even though it was the 'hood, society then was not in as bad a shape at the bottom as it is today. You didn't have the same kind and strength of drugs in Atlanta in the '60s and '70s. It's a whole different vibe, a wholly different reality today.

Most people we grew up with didn't come from a lot of money; neither did we. People were of more meager, humble means, but still had values, and they would generally be good people. They just didn't have much, didn't have a lot of education. But today, no telling what's going on. Could be a college graduate who fell victim to the crack pipe or meth or Sherm, angel dust, or heroin, but especially crack cocaine, and is killing or robbing not to have something but because crack will make you do anything to get more of it. It's been as epidemic as AIDS in many ways. None of this was true or even thought of when I was growing up in Vine City.

I've always been concerned about Mother. Living alone there doesn't bother her so much, or so she lets on, but I want more for her than she wants for herself. I feel like we as a people marched and were beaten and jailed and died and we did all these things so we could move a person like her into a position of dignity and reasonable comfort and convenience in life. Not that she's chafing to go. But something as simple as being able to go outdoors on the patio or being in her backyard is important at her age. The way the house is set up, there's not enough space, she's exposed, and if she wants to do some entertaining, she doesn't have the facilities. Even though she's done it over the years, now it's just not conducive. Things have changed.

*   *   *

When I was growing up, no one would think of breaking into our house. But in 1996 there was a burglary at 234 Sunset. A man broke in while Mother was asleep. For some reason the alarm didn't go off even though the thief broke a window. The alarm's sensor was not working; it didn't go off. This thief, after ransacking the living room and study, came into the bedroom where Mother was sleeping. There, he stood over her—deciding what, God only knows. "Do I kill her? Do I rob her? Rape her? Who is she?" Did he know? She didn't know he was there at first. The only reason she knew later is because he'd taken things out of the bedroom before he escaped. She heard him as he left; that's what woke her up. By God's will, she got the chance to wake up.

The police found this burglar eventually, he had taken a King Center two-way radio from the house; she'd had it placed in the battery charger. The cops found him because he was talking on the two-way radio, believe it or not. King Center security heard him, and asked for his location. The police were able to locate and apprehend him, interrogate him, do an investigation; they found he'd stood over my mother for a long time considering whether to kill her. Then he saw a picture of my father. He was also responsible for three rapes and the murder of an elderly woman in the neighborhood. We were left with the fact that he didn't touch my mother. We figured either he must have recognized some King family possession in the living room, or he recognized Mother, or maybe he saw a picture of my dad in the bedroom. That's what he claimed. Something scared him off. We don't know what, but thank God, he didn't harm her.

After that happened, I was more concerned for her safety, even though she doesn't worry about it. I would have moved her out of there then. She said no. But I think she was ready by the end of the '90s. The issue became, could she afford to do it? We began to have conversations with the National Park Service about them buying the house and turning it into a National Historic

Site—it was one already anyway, unofficially, and had been since our father was killed. It would make more sense if the Park Service bought the house from her. She can't buy much house today, not for what she paid for that one. At her age, the question becomes, does it make sense for her to buy a house? Maybe a condo? I only knew it made sense for me to help her do whatever she wanted to do.

I had long talks with Mother about what would be the right thing to do with my father's legacy as it relates to her care and comfort. What would he have done in this situation?

We knew he was very self-effacing about monies, as they dribbled in to support the struggle against segregation, as they came to the SCLC or Ebenezer Baptist Church. But he won that struggle, posthumously. Would he have put a price tag on things like his own papers, or his ancestral home, or his own intellectual property, or his image, as far as commercial use of it went? Would he want us to benefit from it if we could? I'm sure he would, mother said, because he licensed his intellectual property and writings to support his family while he was alive. He put a value on himself. What struggle would he support now? Would he want his widow imperiled? I had to guess in the end. I made an educated guess. To help his wife seemed to be a good guess, or a guess I could live with, even if nobody else could.

I asked my mother about this—could a man risk alienating his family from the rest of society by trying to do the right thing by his family? She said it was a dilemma, all right, but that life is full of them. She thought it made more sense to think—or know in your heart—that he would do whatever he could, not for himself, necessarily, but certainly for his family.

People have compared my family with the Kennedys. But the Kennedys had wealth. My father's generation of Kennedys, JFK and RFK, and their siblings and cousins—they were born into wealth. In fact, I don't know too many folks who have made it on their own. Wealth begets wealth. Auctioning Jackie Kennedy

Onassis's belongings—that's okay. The Kennedys have had the privilege and luxury of being seen and even at times portrayed as do-gooders, humanitarians, public servants. But they also have had the luxury of many resources already accumulated when they got here.

Often academics and historians come to do research with us among all Daddy's documents at the King Center, then later they complain that "Most people donate their papers," but most of the people who "donate" things, the Carnegies, Rockefellers, DuPonts, Fords, have means, fixed asset accounts, stock investments; they sit on boards, have corporate equity, other assets, things of material value that made them able to afford their admirable philanthropy; and I'm sure they get a tax benefit from giving away something of value. But nobody talks about that. It seems the heirs of Martin Luther King are held to a higher standard—a higher standard of poverty.

I had a conversation with an editorial writer who has been consistently critical of my family. She said, "I didn't know your mother was still living in Vine City. There was a rumor she lived in Buckhead. In a mansion." That's my point. There are myths out there because people don't ask questions. Frankly, a lot of them don't want to know answers. They'd rather keep the mythology going; if they were to find out it's false, then they'd have to ask themselves—why would this woman be living in Vine City if she can afford to move someplace else? She has to be out there earning her keep like everybody else. What would make her so unique that she could just exist without having an income? Her husband was prematurely taken away, so she was the primary breadwinner for the family for so long, until we all grew up. Her youngest child was five years old when her husband was killed.

What would you do?

Because of who she is and because of the expectation the public has put on her, she has to have an infrastructure around her just to move. We can't have it both ways. If we want her to be this myth, if we want the legacy to belong to the ages, be fair with the woman; if not, it would be a disservice to the man.

But for some reason, with some people of my father's generation, there's this expectation that if you're not struggling or suffering, then you're not correct; you're supposed to stay in poverty. We're the only ethnic group that includes some who actually fight being affluent. Some of us actually apologize for overcoming economically. No other ethnic group does that. People who come from so-called Third World countries, they come to this country and see it as the land of opportunity. They're trying to distance themselves from their impoverished past. They want to get ahead; in America, the land of opportunity, you can.

As a family, we are different from the Kennedys or the Bushes not only because of ethnicity and our lack of inherited wealth. We are different because their celebrity has a tie to officialdom: Senator Kennedy, Attorney General Kennedy, President Kennedy, Vice President Bush, President Bush—the list seems endless. Meanwhile it was almost like Daddy was an unofficial President, of black people, of progressive people, of peaceful people. His title was never officially bestowed. This was what I could do, for him—maybe and probably it was all someone like me could do for him. I could do this best by staying quiet and observing and letting others figure it out. To put him in the record properly. Our struggle was born out of tragedy. To overcome this legacy and get to the Promised Land was the new cause. Whereas, with the Kennedys, it was kind of reversed; patriarch Joe had made a fortune. Our family legacy was working to bring the least of people into the mainstream, to be economically empowered, ultimately. Would that not include us? Or would it preclude us?

JFK was popular and had a mystique, Camelot. My father's mystique was as this ascetic, pious, supermoral holy man—it was taboo to bring him up in certain ways. Poverty makes it harder to uphold this mystique. With resources, you have the luxury of helping people, giving back. That's not taking anything away from the

Kennedys or anybody else, but they had choices. We had to take what was given, make the best of it, as the downtrodden always do; the least of these always must be more prepared, twice as good, ahead of the game, because you have less to work with, and no margin for error. You must be more resourceful, even if extraordinary resourcefulness is not in your nature. Or was blasted out of you, early on.

CHAPTER 19

A Way Out
of No Way

The Library of Congress had first approached my father two years before his death about acquiring his papers. My mother remembers it clearly. In 1997, at the time of contention between Stanford and Emory universities over where the researchers' copies of Daddy's papers and other civil rights collections housed at the King Center should end up, we heard from the Library of Congress again. Here's what happened.

Both Stanford and Emory are fine universities. It was a win-win. We wanted the papers in the best repository. Then the Librarian of Congress, Dr. James Billington, wrote a letter to Mother expressing an interest in acquiring my father's original papers held at the King Center, saying why the Library of Congress is the best repository for this important part of history. The conversation had been initiated with Daddy thirty-odd years ago. We went with that sense of propriety.

The Library of Congress has many historical papers from prominent African Americans—Frederick Douglass, Thurgood Marshall, Booker T. Washington, most recently Jackie Robinson, and some others. It was thought to be the logical place to make papers accessible to future scholars. The way we left it at that time was, we'd let things cool off between Stanford and Emory, because the print media in Atlanta were killing us, as usual. A few local scholars made a big deal about the papers leaving the South and going to Stanford, where historian Dr. Clayborne Carson was already in the process of collating them, and among other things was using them to cobble together *The Autobiography of Martin Luther King, Jr.*, as well as other works, like *The Papers of Martin Luther King, Jr.*

An antagonistic professor at Emory University was one of those voices saying it was problematic if the papers left the South. The professor may have spoken up because Stanford seemed on the verge of having one-upsmanship over Emory. Emory came to the table and tried to scare Stanford off; then Emory came to us and said they were interested, sent some people in to look at the papers. We wanted some African-American involvement; Emory put together a consortium of Atlanta University Center's Woodruff Library, Emory's library, the Atlanta History Center, and the Auburn Avenue African American Research Library. This consortium came and met, through the good graces of Dr. Chase, president of Emory. They then decided they needed to come in and look at the papers. The professor from Emory said, Don't let the papers out of the South. But then, after the Library of Congress came in, that didn't seem right either. When it comes to Daddy's legacy, some people are too hard to please.

The truth may be that people don't want us, as the heirs, the estate, to benefit. We've tried to avoid looking at it that way, but that seems to be the bottom line. This would confirm their remembrances of the generosity of spirit that they saw in my father, which our critics falsely assert is not us, though they do not really seem to harbor it in themselves.

Bringing in Sotheby's was Phil Jones's idea, and it was a good one; it would be our way of authenticating the value of the King papers. We knew they were valuable. For years we had said Daddy's papers and his estate had value. One of the residual effects of slavery is that anything African American is judged to be valueless, especially intellectual property. You have to prove twice that it has worth. It's not a question of your word. It's a question of a collective psychological scarring. We brought Sotheby's to the table. We knew they'd auctioned valuables from some of the most prominent institutions and families in the world, including the Kennedys.

We needed an independent appraiser, a reputable professional firm that had expertise in appraising documents and manuscripts. Sotheby's came in and appraised, and valued the King papers collection at $30 million.

Later the Library of Congress got an independent appraiser to come in. He appraised the papers at $30 million-plus. These appraisals were done independently. We set no price. Afterward, the professor at Emory began saying the papers were overvalued, and not worth what these two independent appraisals said they were. His low estimation of the papers' value was ironic, given that his access in researching his book had helped win him a Pulitzer Prize.

We met with the personification of the Library of Congress in August of 1999. Mother, myself, and Philip met with Dr. Billington, the Librarian of Congress, his deputy, General Donald Scott, an African American, Congresswoman Cynthia McKinney (D–Ga.), and Jim Clyburn (D–S.C.), chair of the Congressional Black Caucus. The latter two came to us and said they thought it was a good time to secure this collection in the Library of Congress archive. They thought the climate was right, and most important it should be done to further place Dr. King in his rightful position in national history. They said, "We want to do this, but we want to keep it very close to the vest, because we don't want it to get bogged down in political posturing."

We expressed how we did not want to be put in an awkward position of having to justify the move of the King papers to the Library of Congress. Dr. Billington reached out. Representative Clyburn felt he had the support to get this done in the House, and he wanted to champion it. He wanted the Black Caucus to make this a priority. Clyburn is a passionate man. He popped into the meeting.

Billington spoke the most. He's a man of precise bearing, erudite, scholarly, probably in his early sixties, but in no need of glasses. He is clean-cut, fairly tall, not given to overstatement, or to suffer fools. He spoke of the two hundredth anniversary of the Library, how the King papers would be a great gift to the nation from the Library of Congress, about how Dad was misunderstood, how people thought of him as "just a minister," which was admirable enough, but that he was much more. Dr. Billington talked about Dad's scholarly side, how he was versed not only in philosophy and religious texts, but also in anthropology, sociology, and Gandhian techniques—that Daddy was a learned man of deep spiritual thought, what old folks in the church would call "God-troubled."

I could tell Dr. Billington had read about my father's works, and understood that this was more than an African-American preacher who led a few marches. Dr. Billington put him in the context of a new American revolutionary along with George Washington, Thomas Jefferson, James Madison, Ben Franklin; when you think of the Civil Rights Movement, you think of a new era of leadership, taking the country on a leap forward in its independence and freedom of mind, of heart, of spirit.

The papers take many forms: book manuscripts, typewritten; an amazing amount of handwritten material, such as the Nobel Peace Prize handwritten speech; a lot of his working papers from when he was preparing speeches, and hundreds of sermons; his letters that he sent and received, amazing letters, from and to Eleanor Roosevelt, Malcolm X, Muhammad Ali, JFK, Josephine Baker, Jimmy Hoffa—more letters from more historical figures than I should even try to list here. And many of his annotated books. He had a library of books that he read and reread; he would write in the margins, so it's actually a dialogue between him and great authors.

Fascinating stuff.

You can go in among my father's papers and stand a real chance of going blind, there's so much dazzling material. You can see his thinking in these papers, you can see what form it took, where his thinking was shaped, how it evolved, developed over time, how it changed. You can see the development of an entire important period in American history. How anyone could say it was not worth any certain dollar figure is beyond me. You can see some of his earliest notes from school; when he would prepare for a sermon or speech in the seminary, he would write on little three-by-five index cards. On every subject, he would have an index card or cards that described his thoughts on it. The volume of his collection in terms of the actual number of pages, I'm not exactly sure of; I've seen different numbers and estimations, but from culling through the papers and studying estimates I'd say at minimum several thousand pages or pieces of text-bearing documents. There was a question of whether the document count should include annotated books, so the actual estimate varies. It is a most comprehensive collection.

It's wrong.

I believe that the knowledge of the suffering black Americans have done holds back some white Americans, causes them to fear black Americans, to fear retribution. But African Americans are a forgiving people.

My father represented the closest that African Americans came to having a singular sense of oneness. His mission was sanctioned and even sanctified by God. You can't go into a home with occupants of a certain age without seeing a photo of our father—particularly that old photo of him, JFK, and RFK. Langston Hughes said it: somebody's got to tell my story—"I think it will be me." The key is controlling your destiny. Putting yourself in the picture.

Yes, my siblings and I are the sons and daughters of Martin Luther King, Jr., products of our environment, but we're also our own individual men and women, and we have our own views about politics, love, relationships, life. We don't want to be relegated to running from who we are; we want people to know us presently and in the future rather than from the past; the past is history and not very pretty, and we have to know what happened so we can make it over. That's what we're grappling with—to understand the past, yet somehow get beyond it, as the children of Martin Luther King. And we are in some ways emblematic of the whole. There's a reactionary posture with some in black leadership, having a reverse effect in terms of moving forward because what we've done in an effort to promote ourselves as people has isolated us to a point of having to renegotiate what we've already achieved.

Racism today is not as overt. But a posture is taken by some in black leadership in which everybody who has a different opinion than it holds is wrong. The majority will not respect and embrace you if you don't allow room for diversity. The very thing they are saying they want, they don't include. Black leadership has to be able to pass muster. We still have the problems, we still have crime, we still have poverty, we still have lack of education and resources. I made a commitment when I had that epiphany on the balcony of the Lorraine Motel, in terms of coming back to the King Center, picking up the mantle to try and help Daddy's legacy somehow; I never saw myself as a traditional leader. Rather, I saw myself as a behind-the-scenes institution builder who was not just going to give speeches and try to inspire people. I do believe in at least trying to create or preserve lasting things, human diamonds, like my sisters Bernice and Yolanda, my brother, Martin III. Don't focus only on the symptom, focus on the cause as well.

What tends to happen with leadership (not just black or white leadership) is that the ceremony happens first, the announcement comes, then leaders backtrack to capture the sacrament, people's hearts. Lincoln did the ceremony by freeing the slaves legislatively with the Emancipation Proclamation, but the sacrament was men and women dying in the Civil War, at Gettysburg, at Antietam. Victim/victimizer, slave/slavemaster having sacrament in their hearts, that was even more difficult to achieve, as seen by the failures of Reconstruction, the subsequent rise of the murdering Ku Klux Klan, White Citizens Councils, then denial of suffrage, then, after the turn of the century, the rise in lynchings, the *Birth of a Nation* film, then the Red Summer of 1919, the torching of the economically successful Greenwood section of Tulsa, Oklahoma, in 1921 and the killing of three hundred innocent black people. That whole process of post–Civil War subjugation is what causes there to still be racism lingering 140 years after Lincoln signed the Emancipation Proclamation. After growing up in an environment of ceremony and sacrament, I saw more ceremony after my father's death; but people still felt left out, particularly black people, who felt downtrodden, needing validation. Other people felt threatened, like whites who railed against processes like affirmative action. We have all found out together that the ceremony alone doesn't do it, no matter how much money you put into people's pockets, no matter how much wealth a community generates; if the people themselves within their hearts aren't right, if they don't feel good about themselves, don't feel or get treated equal, things won't change.

Leadership, whatever and whoever that is, has to do its part, black and white. Both races need to understand that it's not just African-American psyche that needs support; white America needs to realize that its psyche also needs reparations and support—forgiveness, education, and a feeling of security that's obviously lacking there as well.

The history of America has left us all insecure, I'm afraid. Saying "I'm sorry" or giving out comparatively meager handouts isn't the only solution.

Everybody talks about what Dr. King would have done and what the Civil Rights Movement accomplished or didn't accomplish. Did it hurt more or help more, in terms of integration? There is validity to the statement that integration opened up doors and avenues that left indigenous home businesses in the lurch. A lot of this has to do with the fact that some black businesses were not operating competitively. Free enterprise means competition. You have to be competitive. My father knew integration meant competition; part of competition is knowing and charging fair market value and delivering goods in a timely and effective manner. That did not happen many times. Often there were reasons why, often it was kept from happening by outside forces. Distribution channels were often closed for minority-produced goods and services. In many cases resources weren't there, loans were not forthcoming; red-lining for business and private housing was no myth—it happened. It may in fact still happen.

The problem—or solution—was, and is, what's in people's heart of hearts. One who addresses this is Magic Johnson. With his multitude of businesses, from cineplexes to restaurants, he's saying to black consumers, "We can have nice things, should demand them, be able to go into a nice theater, shouldn't have to go to a di-lapidated, run-down theater not being maintained, not showing a first-run feature. We can have a multiplex." He has one of his chain of Magic Johnson Theatres multiplexes in Atlanta; it's one of the most successful. He also put a Magic Johnson's T.G.I. Friday's restaurant next to it, and is doing well. This stems from mentality, commitment, and investment—a way of being. It requires stew-ardship, maintenance. The people who were fighting for integra-tion didn't always understand the technical sides of expanding an economy. Look at the 2000 trade agreement with China: 1.3 billion Chinese can't be wrong—not as consumers, at least. Any business-man will tell you that as long as the customer buys, the customer is always right, no matter his politics.

People can talk about the negatives of integration, but look at the positives. The South in particular. Its market share increased a hundredfold because what was traditionally a segregated, backdoor dollar now came in the front door, en masse, and from there mo-mentum took over. We all know by now who often sets the con-sumer trends in the United States. That black dollar and black aesthetic built up the economy of the South and created opportu-nities for everybody—just as it had done in the Greenwood section of Tulsa in the early 1900s. But what we have failed to do post-integration is create opportunities in our community; we've been so busy gaining access and maybe acceptance that we did not build a more permanent infrastructure. In cases we may have had it, but it was destroyed in the wake of the assassination of my father in 1968, and it was never rebuilt, in some cases not even now, thirty-five years later. We strive for recognition, so much that we have almost told people we don't want to be part of the mainstream. You can't have it both ways.

I'm just saying that we need to understand—as my father understood so clearly—that we are a minority and the only way you are going to transform the majority is to assimilate with it to effect change.

Are we colored, Negro, African American, Afro-American? This question is hard because, when you look at the African continent, it's made up of many regions, countries, tribes, peoples—it's a world unto itself; a continent, not a country. It's impossible to go back and recapture that which was lost. What can happen is acknowledgment that this is the case.

There has to be a realization and acceptance of where we stand. I was watching Tavis Smiley on *BET Tonight* before Bob Johnson and Tavis came to their parting of the ways. Karl Kani and other fashion designers were on. A woman called in and said, "When are you ever going to do a cheaper line?" Why is it that black folk or artists are always expected to drop their prices and give things away, then those same people who ask you to do it will go out and spend top dollar for Tommy Hilfiger? We've got to balance the practical side of it and move on. Right on Auburn Avenue, that area could be a major economic engine, an additional economic engine for the city of Atlanta. It already has critical mass in terms of visitors and potential customers. You have people coming here to the King Center, but then they leave. They park, come in, look around, ruminate, then they're gone. Why not create a destination where people come down and stay a while—eat and sit and spend time? You've got the beginnings of the infrastructure. All you need is to put the right things there to interest people, so that when they come, they stay longer than twenty minutes, they stay and spend more money that fuels the local economy.

*   *   *

We have since made up in terms of the issues at hand with the National Park Service, but there is still the inevitable coexistence. They're interested in purchasing our real estate and our buildings. The King Center edifice is a depreciable asset. This is not land that's going to be used to build condos twenty years from now. This is historic land. Maintenance is a liability. Maintaining a fixed asset is only going to get more troublesome. Who will be responsible for it after Mother and us are gone? It'll fall into disrepair over time. With the mandate of preserving the buildings and grounds, and doing facility management, the Park Service makes sense.

And so it happened that our friends and confidants were subject to human nature, human frailty, just as we Kings were; if we ourselves are subject to all that, then we can all probably rest assured we shall meet resistance until the end—until the legacy is out of our hands, until we're in our graves, unmourned, possibly misunderstood. The more I learned, the more betrayed I felt we were by some of the big names within the Civil Rights Movement. Perhaps they felt betrayed by us. Sadder still would be not standing up for what you believe. Worse still would be laboring in the wrong, and if proven wrong, refusing to admit it and go on together to the next problem.

The resistance was from people who, in their hearts, didn't want to place value or be seen approving placing value on something African American. Because it's associated with a black individual, it's not supposed to command the same respect. We heard, "Most people donate their papers to the Library." Those people were presidents still on the public payroll. The government paid the family of Richard Nixon $18 million for papers, tape recordings, and other materials seized after Watergate. The Zapruder film, a few seconds of 8mm film of the Kennedy assassination in Dallas in 1963? In 1999, the government agreed to pay Abraham Zapruder's family some $15 million for those mere seconds—not the rights to the film, mind you, but the film itself. The rights are retained by the Zapruder family. I don't know what it's all worth. I go by the standards set, appraisals of the professionals like Sotheby's and the Library of Congress, and comparative rates paid for the Nixon papers, the Zapruder film.

There's been a lot of political posturing about blocking the Library of Congress purchase of the King papers. Whether that will translate into blocking it into perpetuity, I don't know.

The journey will be difficult, but in the end we'll get where we're going. That's in my gut—Daddy's real, spoken legacy will survive and flourish. In many ways, it is fitting and proper for the lion's share of his papers to be going to the Library of Congress. I don't know why people would object, unless they are objecting to what he stood for. They say, "Dr. King wouldn't have wanted this," or "The papers aren't that valuable." Prove that by his five blood heirs. As long as you respect my mother and siblings, then you can discount me. No need to discount the whole family. Just me. As long as Mother's angle of repose is comfortable, and her mind clear, and my sisters and brother are free to pursue their own level of love, peace, and happiness, then I'm fine. One last move to safeguard Daddy's legacy and know the truth about his assassination might assure Mother a final comfort and clarity. This move would be the civil trial of one Loyd Jowers.

CHAPTER 20

The Reckoning

It had never been confronted in open court. Not for us, by us, the family of the victim.

We were in collective shock in 1968 when James Earl Ray was shot through the legal system as if greased, with first Arthur Hanes then Percy Foreman as his lawyer. For us, it was hard enough just to accept Daddy's being dead, to accept what people said and did in the aftermath, to accept the different reactions from others, to accept what the authorities said about who killed him. "Try to move on," I remember people saying. As if. As time went on, deep down inside, all the adults in my family—Mother, Uncle A.D., Granddaddy, Big Mama, cousin Alveda—felt there was more to it. I, me, Dexter, the last one, ended up as point man for all those years of muffled questions and suppressed doubts. My family looked to me now. Right or wrong, they looked to me. For my family. For my father. You tell me—what was I supposed to do?

Robert F. Kennedy's assassination was quick on the heels of Daddy's, not to mention heightened tensions in the country, riots, burning in nearly every city, major and minor, after Daddy was killed; a dissolving hope, a swelling of the ranks of groups like the

Black Panther Party for Self-Defense in Oakland, or the Nation of Islam, the Blackstone Rangers, or Black P-Stone Nation in Chicago, Crips and Bloods in L.A. George Clinton and Parliament singing "(I Wanna) Testify" could not lift the mood for long. The feeling was, no matter who is involved, what can you do? What recourse do you have? You felt helpless to do anything else but think about it, roll it over in your mind, try and figure it out. Suffer in silence.

Even if Ray did it, did he do it alone? The force of will behind this murder—did he possess that? Was he that brave, that resourceful, to escape under the noses of law enforcement without any help? Was he competent enough to make that shot? Anyone behind him, or with him, we'd never be able to find out. Even if we did . . . how do you fight a feeling? How can you change what's in people's hearts? That took a man like Daddy. And he was dead. That's what the world and we lost. I felt hollowed out inside about it, but I didn't know it at first. If asked, I said and I believed I was fine. But it also became for my own soul's sake that I tried to find out all I could about why and how Daddy was killed. My sisters and our mother had looked into my eyes and asked me to try. So I did.

Somehow, my logic must have escaped scholars. They can interpret Shaw, Nietzsche, or Churchill, somehow, but they can't understand me. I find it all hard to believe, that looking into one's own father's murder seems somehow illogical.

Leading up to the civil trial, in the late fall of the year 1999, people asked me, "Why look into it?" The most innocent and well-intentioned people said this, as well as editorial columnists and scholar-authors with books and their own interests to protect and, maybe, I don't know, axes to grind, although I don't know why anyone would grind an ax on my family's backs. Many people said I was wrong for looking into the death of my father. Was that going to stop me? Are those the people I saw when I looked in the mirror? Or did I see Mother, Daddy, Yoki, Marty, Bunny?

That's who I answered to in the end. It was as simple as our mental health.

Before he died in 1984, my grandfather Martin Luther King, Sr., patriarch of our clan, said, "In my heart, I never believed Ray was alone in his plan." And then he wept. And then he died. So that's part of my legacy too. I'd disappointed him. I'd never heard the Call. This seemed like the least I could do. For years, for many reasons, I had averted my eyes. I could stand to do that no longer.

Shortly before the Jowers trial began, the verdict from our appeal in the CBS case came in; we had won a reversal in federal appeals court. The attorneys called Mon Ami. She came over and knocked on the door. She said, "We won. You will not be the sibling or heir that lost your father's copyrights. You did what he would have wanted." I hoped that this legal victory would bode well for the new legal journey we were about to embark on.

With William F. Pepper serving as trial counsel, we, the family of Martin Luther King, Jr., as heirs of the victim, filed a wrongful death suit, a civil suit against Loyd Jowers, the Memphis owner/operator of a place called Jim's Grill on South Main Street, one block due west and upland from the Lorraine Motel, adjacent to Canipe's Amusements. Jim's Grill and Canipe's were first-floor establishments. Over them was the flophouse and back window from which Ray is said to have taken a single shot on April 4, 1968, that changed the landscape of America and five lives in particular, those of Coretta, Yolanda, Martin III, and Bernice. Me too.

Our main purpose in filing this suit was to get to the truth by hearing testimony under oath and having evidence submitted into court records to create an official permanent record of what had occurred around this tragedy. We were concerned that with the passage of over thirty years since my father's death, many relevant individuals would die without having their knowledge officially recorded. In other words, we believed it was now or never. We only sought a ceremonial $100 damage amount in the trial because we were more interested in getting the truth than in getting money.

By this time, Loyd Jowers was an aging, frail, seventy-three-year-old. He bore a resemblance to Byron De La Beckwith, who, thirty-five years after the fact, was convicted of killing Medgar

Evers in Mississippi in 1963. Jowers was not accused of shooting anyone. But in his dotage he claimed to ABC TV reporter Sam Donaldson that he'd helped carry out the King assassination, and admitted it to William F. Pepper and to Andy Young, both times in my presence. Jowers contended that his place, Jim's Grill, was used as a staging area of sorts. The .30-06 rifle, supposedly the weapon Ray used, was found in the foyer of Canipe's Amusements on South Main, close to Jowers's grill and a few hundred yards from the muddy chop of the Mississippi River.

In the 1993 interview with Sam Donaldson, Jowers claimed to have been in on it, and said the murderer who handed him the still-smoking murder weapon was not James Earl Ray. Pepper himself had received information from army informants that two teams of army snipers were in the area, perhaps as backups to a contract killer. All this confusion could have been avoided, maybe, if the congressional committee hadn't, in 1979, sealed all its documents regarding the case for fifty years. Fifty years. That would be 2029. By then, Bernice, the youngest, will be over sixty.

We approached President Clinton about creating a truth and reconciliation commission, similar to the one created in South Africa to investigate crimes by the government against its people. The commission would have subpoena power and the ability to grant immunity from prosecution in exchange for the truth. Since our government had been implicated, we felt it was very important to have an independent, nongovernmental body established. But President Clinton turned it over to the Department of Justice. We wanted the truth, not retributive justice. We had lost in the criminal proceeding in Memphis, where we tried to get the rifle tested when Ray was seeking a trial. We could no longer pursue a criminal trial since Ray had died in 1998. Therefore a civil suit was the only other legal remedy we could employ to get at the truth. So starting Monday, November 15, 1999, there was a proceeding in Shelby County (Memphis), Tennessee, and some seventy witnesses would testify, including Andy Young and Rev. James Lawson, one of Daddy's friends and the leader of the Memphis protest back in

1968. All this testimony went into the record so that historians who want to research it will have an official record of these versions of what happened.

We were not seeking monetary damages. We were not in it to try and bankrupt anybody or gain publicity. We were only seeking truth. To have Jowers offer to put into the record his information pertinent to this case. Jowers never had been officially interviewed by the authorities. He was written off as not credible. He said that if he got immunity from prosecution, he'd tell all he knew. He was never offered immunity. The Department of Justice would have to investigate, follow up, which we believed it didn't want to do. People were getting old, like Jowers. In a way he was a more important witness even than Ray. Ray didn't have to know anything. Jowers was in his seventies, not in good health. His memory was good, but physically he had deteriorated, as had others who were close to the—what to call it?—the . . . event? This was the time to get every scrap of firsthand knowledge down.

At the beginning, Mother, Martin, and myself rotated in and out of the courtroom. We all wanted to be at the opening, but Bernice and Yolanda couldn't be there. So we took turns. My mother stayed through Tuesday, Martin came in Wednesday; I was there until Thanksgiving—they had a short week. The following week, Yolanda was there. I can still see her, dressed in dark clothing, huddled against the wet chill in a spitting rain outside the Memphis courthouse, being interviewed by Ricki Kleiman on Court TV, looking so very vulnerable to me. Seeing her there steeled me against all the doubters who questioned this course. If only to make my sister feel whole . . .

Judge James E. Swearingen handled the proceeding. It was a circuit court trial. He felt it should be over by Christmas. The jury was sworn in; it couldn't have been more racially balanced—six blacks and six whites. Ordinary people. Lewis Garrison represented Jowers. Swearingen was an African American and well-respected among black Memphians, although I wondered if he would be affected by what had happened to Judge Joe Brown when he had the rifle ballistics hearing in his court. Judge Brown took it on the chin for even trying to hear evidence then. Much would be made of what Judge Swearingen allowed testimony-wise in this trial, and there was the somehow built-in skepticism by some in the media, about our credibility as plaintiffs largely because we had retained Pepper. But I thought Judge Swearingen wanted to let the witnesses speak.

I would be among the last to testify. Mother was among the first on the stand. You could see the respect and empathy in the eyes of the jurors. She has maintained her dignity a long time. I felt protective toward her.

Within three days, the courtroom was nearly empty. Court TV pulled its gavel-to-gavel coverage. This was no O. J. Simpson trial. The media did not seem to want the public to hear the evidence, so there was no live TV coverage when Andy Young took the stand. Uncle Andy was questioned by Pepper, then cross-examined by Garrison, who, by the way, said he agreed with "80 percent of [the Kings'] case." Andy Young, without wavering, testified that he met with Jowers for four hours a year earlier. "This was a man who was very sick, and who wanted to go to confession to get his soul right," Uncle Andy said to the jury. He said Jowers told him some Memphis police officers and federal agents met at Jim's Grill several days before the assassination, and the group included Marrell McCollough, who had been hired by the CIA later, in 1974. Uncle Andy also said that Jowers told him "a Mafia figure" gave him money to hand over to a man who delivered a rifle to Jim's Grill before the assassination. Jowers told Uncle Andy that he was in the back of the grill when my father was shot by a man hidden in the bushes (the area cleared and cut down the night after the assassination) and this man, a Memphis police lieutenant, handed the smoking rifle to Jowers through a back door. Jowers told me the same story. He said his place was used as a staging area.

Jowers was not present for Andy Young's testimony. He had been in the court for the first couple of days, but his health was declining and the long days took a toll. I watched him sitting in his threadbare suit and droopy white socks and tried to imagine him young and hateful. Now he was preparing to meet his Maker. Trying to get right. After Uncle Andy stepped down, Pepper promised the jury he'd play a two-hour tape documenting Uncle Andy's meeting with Jowers that next Monday.

I listened to Judge Joe Brown testify that next Monday, November 23, 1999. As noted, Judge Brown was a criminal court judge in Memphis; Pepper called him as an expert witness in firearms. Brown told the jury he believed "The rifle [that prosecutors used to implicate Ray in the assassination] was not the rifle used to kill Dr. King. In my opinion, that is not the murder weapon." He looked levelly at the jury. Whether people liked it or not, it was happening. We were now taking Daddy back. As Judge Brown spoke, he held the Remington GameMaster .30-06 hunting rifle. "This weapon, literally, could not have hit the broad side of a barn," he said. An FBI report showed that the rifle had never been sighted in (never calibrated and aligned).

Judge Brown is a recreational hunter. Guns are a hobby of his, and as a criminal court judge, of course, he has had a lot of experience with forensics experts and weapons, and knows the law. But when asked on cross-examination by Garrison if he had any formal ballistics training, he cited none. After his testimony, the press sought the opinion of the prosecutor in the criminal trial, John Campbell. He said Judge Brown's testimony raised more questions about Judge Brown than it did about the so-called murder weapon, or Ray's guilt. That's how it's often done: if you have a "black" expert witness, then his credibility is subtly undermined, not for a particular reason, but because of—well, touch the skin on your arm.

Garrison could've objected to Joe Brown being called, but didn't, and the county prosecutor took Garrison to task publicly. "The problem is, if no one is objecting, it makes no difference," Campbell said. "He could've gotten up there and said he was an expert in nuclear physics." Garrison's position consistently was that his client was a small cog in a massive conspiracy. Pepper's evidence was amply demonstrating that that was the case.

Joe Brown is a righteous man who tried. He tried when he had the rifle in his court to get a new trial for Ray. But he met staunch resistance every step of the way. He could only do so much, and then he was summarily removed from presiding over the criminal trial by the Court of Appeals without a hearing.

For the first time, I started to identify with my own feelings. Then I saw the brutality of the autopsy photos . . . my God . . . how horrible . . . I had never seen the photos. I'd had no desire to see any of them. I was caught off guard. An autopsy photograph was submitted into evidence and shown in court. I was upset with Pepper. We didn't talk about it beforehand. I felt very awkward sitting there, even though it wasn't one of the most gruesome ones. It showed a shot of my father's back where the bullet lodged; you couldn't see a face, who it was. When photographs were first sent to me by Pepper, I'd put them away. No desire to see them. Now they stared at me even in my sleep.

Pepper had sent all his archives to the King Center in Atlanta, and said, "I'm giving these to you separately; they are sensitive and I'm pretty sure you don't want them mixed in with all the other stuff."

We got a copy of the autopsy report and the x-rays as well. Understand that all of this for me was still working out my private hurt, the pain . . . the death itself. The morbid side of it. The tragedy. Everybody dealt with it intellectually, but very few people had to deal with it emotionally.

At least I was able to admit in my heart of hearts that I hadn't dealt with it emotionally.

It felt like I was in a foreign city—another planet—anytime I went to Memphis. As a child I had no real awareness of the things surrounding the assassination. But from the very first time I visited there as a child, the city felt alien. The Monday after Daddy's death, on the eighth of April 1968, was my first time there, for the march to City Hall that Dad never got to complete. I remember the wrecked faces and wracking sobs and images of smoke, black clothing, shrieking. I went to the sleep clinic at Baptist Hospital when I was twelve with these images in my head. Then I returned as an adult, finally, to the Lorraine Motel.

I wanted to hear Betty Spates testify, but it turned out she did not testify in Memphis due to her own long-held fears for her safety, though we did have the pivotal official deposition from her put into the record during the trial. Who was she? As a seventeen-year-old girl, she'd worked at Jim's Grill; she was there on the fateful day, April 4, 1968. Pepper first interviewed her in Memphis in 1989. She told him, "There's no doubt [Ray] did not kill Dr. King. I know that for a fact."

After five years of investigating and developing a measure of trust, Pepper met with Mrs. Spates again. She revealed much, not only about that April 4, 1968, day at Jim's Grill on South Main, but also about relationships you don't hear about in the wells of Congress, when senators are fulminating in denial about issues pertaining to their African-American citizenry. Betty was numbered among this citizenry. The pretty seventeen-year-old had not only been a waitress at Jim's Grill, she'd also been the young black concubine of the married Jowers. Jowers had a cot set up in back of the ground floor of Jim's Grill for their assignations. She went to the grill around noon that day, went back toward the kitchen, calling Jowers. He came through the back door carrying a rifle. He did not appear to be under stress. She asked, "Loyd, what you doin' with that gun?" He replied, "Gonna use it on you, if I catch you with a nigger." She was black herself. That's how sick it was, and is. To placate him, she told Jowers she would never do that. He told her he was kidding anyway. She told Pepper that Jowers broke the rifle down and took it into the grill. She did not follow him to see where.

Jowers had always discouraged her from coming around on Thursday, a day when his wife often stopped by. But she was there that day. Mrs. Jowers called her "whore" and told her to "Get out!" He came between them and told Mrs. Jowers to "Get out yourself," then told Betty Spates to get behind the counter and go to work. Mrs. Jowers stalked out. This was around 4 P.M. Shortly thereafter Betty Spates went across the street to see some friends at another establishment. She came back around six. The three grill regulars weren't around.

She noticed that the door between the eating area and the kitchen was tightly closed. Thinking this unusual, she opened the door and noticed that the door leading from the kitchen outside to the back was ajar. Just then, she heard what sounded like a loud firecracker. Seconds later, she saw Jowers rushing from the brush area through the door, carrying another rifle. She was convinced it was a different gun from the first one. She told Pepper that Jowers was "out of breath" and "as white as a ghost." His hair was in disarray, the knees of his pants were muddy. When he caught his breath, he noticed her. He didn't look angry, but frightened. He asked her, "You wouldn't ever do anything to hurt me, would you, Betty?" He went to a counter inside, put the rifle on a shelf beneath the counter. Betty remembered the rifle—dark brown stock, a scope, a short barrel.

Betty Spates had gone on to say that a few months after the assassination, she was visited by three men in suits who offered her and her sisters new identities, relocation, money, for their own protection. She refused. Two of the men returned five years later, repeating the offer, which was again refused. Pepper had filed Betty Spates's primary affidavit with the court; the *Nashville Tennessean* had published its contents. And now her statement was on the record.

After all seventy witnesses testified—providing evidence, among other things, of details of the Mafia contract, the army backup presence, army photographers on the roof of the fire station, the suppression of evidence, the failure of the Memphis Police Department to form the usual four-man security team (all consisting of black police officers) for my father, and the identity of Ray's contact, Raul, which was confirmed by documents produced by former FBI agent Don Wilson—Judge Swearingen gave the case to the jury.

"Guilty," I said in the phone call to Mother. "They came back guilty. Loyd Jowers was found guilty of conspiracy involving federal, state, and local government agencies."

It was Wednesday, December 8, 1999. I also called Ami. "You must be relieved," she said.

"I am. I really am . . ."

At the courthouse after the verdict, I was emotional; it was cathartic. There were things I wanted to say and I got them off my chest. At the press conference after the verdict, I said, "I'm appalled anybody would think we're doing this for money. We've lost money doing this. We've had to spend money. This is being said . . . to distract people, get them off the issue. Anyone who sat through four weeks of testimony from seventy credible witnesses would know the truth's here. The question is: What will be done with it? What will be learned?" I spoke what I felt—not good politics. Nobody to blame. Just tired of hearing we'd been "duped."

I thought the verdict in the Jowers civil trial was historic, but the establishment pundits said I was wrong. By their decree it wasn't history. Many experts kept repeating this: "It doesn't mean anything. It doesn't mean anything. It doesn't mean anything at all."

If I kept repeating it, one day I might believe it, and one day after that, it might become fact. That's the way it works, isn't it? I started out saying, "I think that this is history being created," as I left the courthouse. "This is the highest form of democracy, independent jurors rendering a verdict. So we're very happy." I believed it was history, a few scholars did not. The Emory professor told *Memphis Commercial Appeal*, "It certainly has made the Tennessee state judiciary look like a laughingstock." He said the verdict would have "zero" impact on history. My eyes burned as I read this. Lewis

Garrison, Jowers's attorney, bemoaned how Ray's current and former prosecutors convinced appellate judges to stop subpoenas that would've forced them to testify. "Why didn't they come help me in this case?" he asked. Congressman John Lewis said, "Who participated in the conspiracy and why? Did law enforcement agencies? Did individuals at the state level in Tennessee? Did members of U.S. intelligence?"

"I think history is being created," I said. "The history books aren't going to be rewritten," said Gilbert T. Sewall, director of the American Textbook Council, based at Columbia University. One of several "single gunman" theory authors wrote an editorial in the *Washington Post:* "To those unfamiliar with the case, the verdict seemed a culmination of a long effort by the King family to determine who was behind the assassination. To others who have followed the case, the Memphis trial was not about seeking the truth but a ploy to obtain judicial sanction for a convoluted conspiracy theory embraced by the King family."

I couldn't help but wonder if the professor at Emory and the "single gunman" theorist were protecting their life's work, their credibility as historians and scholars, their own sanity, in a way. That is only natural. I understand that. I was protecting my family, also only natural. I hoped people might understand. After all, these "experts" had already written one version of history, with Ray as lone assassin of Martin Luther King, Jr., and they'd been feted and awarded for it. Maybe I'm slow to catch on, but it seems they had a vested interest in history remaining the way they said it was. "It's not history. It doesn't mean anything." I'd have to keep repeating that. Maybe one day it would become true.

Nobody in our family agreed with these scholars' assessments. How is that we, my family and me, were disqualified from having a valid thought about a matter that impacted us and our lives and futures to a far greater degree than it impacted anyone else? We were said to be dupes of Pepper. I guess we are dupes all right, but of whom—well, that depends.

It was not history, they kept telling us. It meant nothing. It meant zero. Except neither Martin, nor Bernice, nor Yolanda, nor Mother, nor Isaac, nor my cousins agreed with those statements. Rather, they thanked me.

At any rate, the trial accomplished what we needed, closure. It would be nice if there was official acknowledgment, but we never thought this would happen. We did what we could do. We did something. If it isn't history, if it means nothing, keep on repeating it; maybe it will come true. The truth, crushed to earth, will rise again. For now, a flawed man like myself, a son who lost his father, can sleep at night, look in the mirror, maybe move on. That's all. That's enough.

The Justice Department's report on the new evidence we brought to them from Jowers and Donald Wilson, a former FBI agent who had found documents in Ray's car that had phone numbers for Ray's handler, Raul, and for the Atlanta office of the FBI, came in after the trial. My hope was they wouldn't whitewash and attempt to discredit the whole trial, but I thought that was probably what would happen, and it did. In William Pepper's new book, *An Act of State: The Execution of Martin Luther King, Jr.*, he addresses the Justice Department's report and gives a full account of the Jowers trial. (The full and complete trial transcript is available on the King Center's Web site at www.thekingcenter.org.)

So we can say, "It's not history, it's not important, it means zero," all we want, if it makes it easier for us to get by in the day-to-day. However, that negation won't stop legitimate, credible future researchers. As authoritative as some of the King experts think they are, they are not the last word, or even the last King experts. More of them will come along. As the writer and poet Sterling Brown once said, "Strong men keep on coming." History has a way of being relived by future generations who will address it in a new way; you get new perspectives, new people looking into things, frankly, people with less of a personal agenda. That's the great thing about our Constitution, the First Amendment: you can't stop people from looking at public records; you can seal them for fifty

years, as Congress did, but sooner or later the time will pass, somebody will get curious. Can't sweep it under the rug forever. While
the public may not get the benefit of official sanction, the records
will bear it out. Do the majority of Americans believe the official
story? Well, it's not like people are walking around asking, "Oh
gosh, could this actually happen?" I believe whoever killed Daddy
was aided and abetted. It was not a one-man deal. If that's unim-
portant to the minutes of history, if that means nothing, then so be
it. Then neither do we. We never have meant anything at all, except as the footstools for those who would make good names and
a good living off of our misery. We didn't pursue it for any other
reason than to get the truth on the permanent record, so we could
feel like we'd done everything we could've done. We owed Daddy
that.

Some months after the trial was over, in March of 2000, we as
a family got a good public thrashing in the pages of *TIME* magazine.
A columnist who did not attend the trial wrote an opinion piece
called "They Have a Scheme: Can Martin Luther King's Heirs
Handle the Truth?" In this article, he stated that the Justice Department was completing its review of new evidence coming out of
the Jowers trial, and was about to conclude that my family's "alle-
gations" were not "credible" and provided no basis for criminal
charges. "In other words, they are hogwash," he said. He described
it as "a wild-goose chase to satisfy a tragically deluded family." He
called the civil trial in Memphis "a fiasco," said Jowers changed his
story so many times "it ought to come with a version number, like
computer software." He then for some reason also impugned the
character of Judge Joe Brown: "Ballistics testimony was provided
by Judge Joe Brown, the TV judge, who has no expertise in the
field." As for the jury verdict ordering Jowers to pay $100 in dam-
ages to the King family, he continued, "King's younger son Dexter
exulted that the verdict was 'the period at the end of the sentence'
as far as the King family is concerned, it's their story and they're
sticking to it no matter what DOJ says . . . The real mystery is why

King's heirs, who more than anyone should want the truth, prefer to believe a lie."

Did this columnist believe that Ray was the gunman? Why was his tone bitter toward us? Were we making it harder for him, somehow? Why did those who'd only written about the Civil Rights Movement believe one thing, while Rev. Lawson, Uncle Andy, and so many others who actually lived the Civil Rights Movement believe otherwise? And, last but not least, if it had been the columnist's father who had been murdered, would he be so utterly dismissive, so protective of the status quo?

After the trial I was on a high. Mon Ami felt like she might get the man back she originally fell in love with, not the baggage of the past three and a half years. Don't know how it ended up going toward questions of commitment again, but I guess, after all, that's where it always goes. After the trial we went on retreat to the Four Seasons Resort in Scottsdale, Arizona. I went through a lot of emotional changes, but the thing that made me open up to her was also the thing that made me withdraw. I'd created a wall around me and my emotions. I suppose that it's been a real sob saga for me.

Finally she said, "This is it." I looked at her and said, "Fine."

After the trial I started to smile, to be more carefree. That's when she started talking about whether it was a good idea to be committed. I knew Ami wanted more. She said, "I'm not going back to the same thing. Been there, done that, read the book, saw the movie, heard the CD." It would be four years we'd been seeing each other in April 2000—four years, off and on.

I told her I wanted and needed to move out to L.A., to be alone to clear my head and heal, live out there for a while, to see if I wanted to live there permanently. Six months. Then I could make a move. I'd been drawn to the West Coast when I'd stayed with Michelle Jenkins in Pacific Palisades, back in 1992.

Mon Ami looked at me and said, "Oh? Is that right?"

I was moving to L.A. to start the new millennium. She said she'd help me find a place. "If that's what you want to do, go on with your bad self," she said. There was something about the way she said it. This is where she got off my merry-go-round. "We've come this far, but if you don't feel we can commit yet, that's cool," she said. "I support you, when you've got an issue I'll listen, if you ever feel you're ready, you call me and if I'm available, I'm available. But I would doubt it . . ."

There had been periods of time when we broke up before—when the Ray meeting was coming up, where I didn't want her along for that. I said I'd call her afterward. Four months later she still hadn't heard from me. One time we were going off on vacation to an island. I was telling her to play it by ear two days before the plane took off, because I was all tied up with Pepper and all these other things. I asked her to call one day at five, and she did. I was going through something and barked at her, "I can't deal with this and you right now," and hung up. Yet we always hooked back up. Those days were gone. Frankly, after the trial, and the resort at the Four Seasons in Arizona, things threatened to get more serious between us. I talked to Mother and my siblings about it—about what would they think if I ended up asking her to marry me. She tried on engagement rings. The whole bit. But I kept saying to her, "I need the time away—in L.A."

"After what I've been through with you, I guess I do too."

Every couple of days early in January 2000, Mon Ami would prod me, even though she knew I was thinking of going away. "So are we still committed?"

"Um. Yes. We're committed to each other's well-being, for sure."

"How does that feel?"

No answer.

"You doing okay?"

"Yeah, I'm doing okay with it . . . feels . . . good."

"Okay, then."

In a few weeks, as my deadline for moving out to L.A. approached, at the end of January 2000, I said, "Ami, I've been thinking hard about this. I still have issues within myself I need to resolve. I don't want to put you through any more hurt or pain; but I think I just need to make my move and follow this other thing and—"

"Where are you going right now?" she asked.

"Right now? Home."

"Home? What home?" she asked.

That stung. I came over to her place the next day. Had a basket of flowers, this big bottle of wine, good intentions, standing at her front door. "What are you doing here?" she asked.

"People are staring. Please let me in," I said.

She let me in and said, "You can sit over there." She sat across the room.

"Dexter, do you think that what we have is not normal?"

". . . I don't know."

"The very thing you think you can't have—you have it now, you're living it, and when you're not thinking about it, you're doing good at it. Dexter . . . I love you."

". . . I don't see why you would."

"Because for some reason God has given me the ability to see not what other people want me to see, not what other people have told me, not what you want me to think about you. I see who you are and I'm hoping somehow I can help you let that out. I don't know if anybody knows what they deserve. People know what they want. If L.A.'s what you want, so be it. Uncover the ghosts within yourself. You need to be okay with yourself in order to be okay with being with anybody else, or you will never see what you have in me, because you don't truly see all of who you are.

"I don't know what the future holds," she said. "But I think what this has done is help you find a key to unlock a door that was closed a long time ago that can never be closed again. You can never go back. At the King Center, there is a centralized system now, things move quicker, easier. More corporations are involved. If the properties are sold, that's only land. What the Center does can never be sold, because what you do is preserve the legacy. You have put together a structure to bring the state holiday commissions under your leadership. There are King Centers around the world that should be tied here. The future is good if you communicate the message. You have to be the one telling the story, if you want it told right. So, that's it."

"Ami, I'm going out to L.A. to live. Give me six months . . ."

Mon Ami looked at me levelly. "I ain't gonna give you six seconds. Oh, I'll go out there with you, help you find a place, help you set it up, always be your friend, but as far as waiting here for you—the hell with that. You ain't getting six seconds after that, let alone six months. Let me tell you something else. You have gotten all that you are going to get, because I have given all I have to give to this particular type of relationship. I love you, I'll always be there for you, as a friend, but I ain't giving you six seconds if you move to L.A. You want me to wait another six months while you . . . what? Are you out your mind? No. No. No. It will not happen. No."

"Well, then . . . Ami . . . I . . . no . . . It's a shame you can't be more understanding."

"Now you're really trying to get my goat, Dexter King," she said. "You can't sell I'm not understanding to anybody that knows our situation. You can't give that away. If you move to L.A., Dexter, then you ain't getting six more seconds from me, let alone six months. But know what? It's okay. Because you will have lost the best thing that happened to you. Proverbs are full of stories about that, you fool. You would have lost the best thing that has happened to you, but that's okay, because you know what? We'll still be friends the rest of our lives."

CHAPTER 21

Free at Last

Free at last, free at last . . . but free to do what? Go where? And with whom? I get off the plane and enter into a brilliant blue day in L.A. I find my place easily. It's a place on the beach. I sit in the sand with my pants legs rolled up. I listen to the roar of the waves breaking in off the Pacific. They'll always be there. They'll never stop. As long as there's an earth, a sun, a moon, and the tides. I walk along the beach at the ocean's edge, getting my feet wet, thinking, "On Christ the solid rock I stand, all other ground is sinking sand." I know what sinking sand feels like. Feels like—this. I see a boy of six or seven. We resemble each other, I think, as though we might be related, although I don't see how this could be. But he looks at me expectantly, as if he knows me, or wants to ask me something. I try to ignore him. But I find I really can't . . .

Later I meet with the Man from CBS. His name is Leslie Moonves, head of the network. We are meeting about the CBS case. The estate lawyers won a reversal before a federal judge. "We could keep paying lawyers," I said. CBS has deep, deep pockets; we do not. They could take it all the way to the Supreme Court, I remember what one once said. Copyright and intellectual property are the real estate of the future. I am about to repeat this to Mr. Moonves. But I wait. He is smiling.

I say nothing. We will agree to agree today. He is a nice and pragmatic man. He is in a good mood. He has authorized a show called *Survivor.* And it has done very well for CBS, soundly beating *Who Wants to Be a Millionaire.* At the time, *Who Wants to Be a Millionaire* on the ABC network, was not only the number-one-rated show—it was four of the top five shows. ABC was riding high, and heads hung low over at CBS. Ratings are important because they dictate the rates the networks can charge advertisers. Leslie Moonves decided to green-light *Survivor* on May 31, 2000, after two previous denials. It beat the pants off *Millionaire.* *Survivor* had been getting 25 million viewers—1.3 million more viewers than all other broadcast networks combined. Leslie Moonves was therefore happy. And I was getting there.

A few months later the CBS case is settled. Mr. Moonves and I have dinner. His *Survivor* is still going strong, outdrawing everything but Super Bowls. He's ecstatic. We discuss prospects. He turns reflective; the first *Survivor* ends in September. I wanted to tell him I wish his version of *Survivor* could go on forever. I don't tell him that I've waited all my life for my version of *Survivor* to end.

I go to Los Angeles Lakers NBA basketball games. They are the playoff games, conducted with a great intensity. The games are held near downtown L.A., at the Staples Center. The Philips Arena in Atlanta has better sightlines. But here at Staples Center, I feel I am in a better seat.

The Lakers, with young stars Shaquille O'Neal and Kobe Bryant, are going for the NBA title. I've been invited to the game by producer and television personality Byron Allen. We've hit it off. He is smart and savvy. He owns the TV shows he is involved with as a personable host. He has innumerable contacts. He hears buzz. All the buzz. He's been talking to this hot African-

American female screenwriter about Mother's book, *My Life with Martin Luther King, Jr.* Byron says he loves it. I love it too. Hollywood people are good at agreeing. It is a fairly new experience for me.

We sit near Paul Allen as the Lakers play the Portland Trail Blazers. Paul Allen, he of Microsoft wealth, owns the Portland Trail Blazers. Steven Spielberg sits near him. Spielberg nods knowingly, spreads his mouth in a smile, and cocks his head in artistic appreciation when one of the Trail Blazers makes a play, even though he is a Lakers fan. Paul Allen is one of the primary investors in the DreamWorks studio run by Mr. Spielberg, Mr. Geffen, and Jeffrey Katzenberg, who is also present. Mr. Katzenberg says something wry about "knowing who to cheer for." I shake hands with Mr. Spielberg. He seems a nice man, and, on balance, a good man. He was given an NAACP Image Award, came to get it, spoke well. Maybe things will be all right in America. Maybe . . .

Many stars are at the Lakers playoff games, stars so big the world knows them by first names only—Dustin, Denzel, Arnold, Jack. I get lost in the crowd. No one pays me much attention. The anonymity is like a warm blanket. I go back home. Out here I can do what I want, maybe even be whoever I am. Why not? Michael Ovitz was also at the Lakers game. He once ran the Creative Artists Agency, and served as the president of Disney for a short stint. In the early '90s, Michelle Clark Jenkins and I talked with him about prospects for a movie about my father. He told me he was recently on a podium with my brother, Martin, said Martin spoke before he did, wowed the room, left a tough act to follow. I smile . . .

Funny how it broke down—Yoki and me, child No. 1 and child No. 3, in California, in "La-La Land," trying to make our way, Yoki as an actress; Martin and Bernice, No. 2 and No. 4, in Atlanta, in Washington, D.C., on Saturday, August 26, 2000, at the "Redeem the Dream" rally, on the Mall, in front of the Lincoln Memorial, almost thirty-seven years to the day from the March on Washington, where Daddy gave the "I Have a Dream" speech. He wanted his children and all people judged by the "content of their character," not the color of their skin. Thirty-seven years later, Martin III, gray-bearded now, told the gathered crowd, estimated at 100,000, that the dream hadn't been fulfilled—not when an unarmed black man named Amadou Diallo could be shot forty-seven times by a group of five New York policemen who emptied the clips of their automatic pistols into him for holding up his wallet in the foyer of a Bronx apartment building.

The "Redeem the Dream" rally was organized to protest police brutality and "racial profiling," the bad habit of many law enforcement jurisdictions of stopping and harassing motorists because of skin color. The March was co-organized by the SCLC, of which Martin had been installed as president—it is the activist arm of what could gently be called our father's legacy.

Earlier in August, Martin had written a letter, as president and chief executive officer of the SCLC, to Cedric Dempsey, president of the NCAA, National Collegiate Athletic Association, requesting that the NCAA move three of its basketball championship game sites from Atlanta, because Georgia uses the Confederate battle flag as part of its state flag. The current governor of Georgia, Roy Barnes, said, "It's a difficult issue, about which discussions are ongoing," and then I thought back to past Georgia governors, from Lester Maddox to Ernest Vandiver to Jimmy Carter. They all had to react one way or another to three men who had been named Martin Luther King. "The right one got the name," I thought. I'm proud of my brother Martin Luther King III.

On the Friday before the rally, Martin and Rev. Al Sharpton had met with Attorney General Janet Reno at the White House to both ask and demand that the federal government withhold funds from any police department or state highway patrol agency that practices abysmal and often deadly "racial profiling" or shows a pattern of brutality. For example, the Prince George's County Police Department, in the year leading up to the rally, had shot twelve people, killing five of them, and two other black men had died of injuries incurred while in police custody. A black motorist was five times more likely than a white motorist to be stopped "on suspicion," or general principles, on the New Jersey Turnpike, and on a stretch of I-95 in Maryland, African Americans, who constituted 17 percent of the motorists, were 56 percent of those stopped and searched. My older brother, Martin, said that we were all "still awaiting the day when we can raise our children to respect police first and fear them last."

The loudest reaction at the rally was reserved for two women named King on the podium. Bernice, her face a study of burning concentration, got the loudest ovation when she spoke. She has the Way, a knack, the voice, power, the deep spiritual conviction my father had. She was the one who got that best. She introduced our mother to the crowd: "She helped etch my father's name in the consciousness of the nation. While raising four children, she helped raise a nation."

Words on a page do not do Bernice's oratorical power justice. I hope you get a chance to hear her sometime. Somehow, I think maybe you will. Hearing her brought tears to my eyes as I watched these serious activities from three thousand miles away; I called up Yoki, for comfort.

Yoki not only comforted me. She also steered me into acting. It was something I had always been interested in but never felt free to try, being a "son of King." I was approached by the producers of *The Rosa Parks Story*, about an acting job, portraying my dad. It was a CBS TV movie, with Angela Bassett in the lead role. The whole experience of it was a real treat.

When I first got out to L.A. I met with one of the producers, Howard Braunstein, and the writer, Paris Qualles. At the time they told me they were developing the story and the script was being written, was almost completed, and would I be interested? Would I consider playing my dad? The person with the expertise was Yoki. I asked her, and she said, "Well, why wouldn't you?" Before she said that, I was ambivalent about it, torn. They came back to me later and said they had gotten the green light and they really wanted me to consider it. They wanted me to portray him. Nothing big. Mostly it was a speech scene, and a couple of other scenes. But I would have to act. Yoki said it was a good opportunity to test the waters, see if it was something I wanted to do. She didn't say "to see if it was something I *could* do." She assumed that if I wanted to do it, I could. Good kind of sister to have. Initially I had reservations because I never wanted it to appear that I was seeking to portray my dad, didn't want to seem like I was putting myself on some kind of pedestal, having critics saying and thinking I was being self-serving in some kind of way, just still very sensitive to some of the negative criticisms of the past. Finally I gave myself permission to do it, to explore my options in life like other people do.

I was nervous, but gave it a go. I was to be in about six scenes, and the most moving part of it, I guess, was actually doing one of my dad's speeches in the church. The film was shot on location in Montgomery in May of 2001, and the big speech scene reenacts one of the first Montgomery Improvement Association mass meetings. It just so happens that that speech is in a recently released Warner book *Call to Conscience*, and we also have the audio on CD, so I kept listening to that speech my dad gave, over and over and over again. Yoki worked with me on my overall character development, my acting persona, getting into character.

Once I got down there, I didn't have Yolanda to lean on anymore. I saw Johnnie Carr, one of Rosa Parks's best friends and the person who became president of the MIA after my dad left, and she was happy to see me. She is elderly now, but she was on the set every day and actually was one of the extras. The woman who was portraying her in the movie, Tonea Stewart, is head of the theater department at Alabama State, and had a recurring role with the late actors Carroll O'Connor and Howard Rollins on the CBS TV series *In the Heat of the Night*. She also portrayed Samuel L. Jackson's character's wife in the movie *A Time to Kill*. She was very helpful to me as well. She worked with me between scenes, going over the scripts, lines, coaching me.

I really morphed into my father. I felt like I was in his spirit and in his soul, thinking, being in Montgomery in the mid-'50s. What it must have been like for a twenty-six-year-old black man in that space and time, to be thrust into a defining moment of leadership, then to be subjected to the atrocities of the day, with his young wife and a newborn (Yolanda!). All these emotions were at play in me. When I came on the set to deliver the speech, everyone was so supportive, a collective emotional embrace, and you could feel the spirit of community from the crew, the extras, the cast; there were a lot of talented people there and I drew from them all and I imagine I felt the way my dad must have felt at times. I felt uplifted.

Julie Dash (*Daughters of the Dust*) was the director. And she got it out of me. When I gave the speech, she and then everybody else came up to me afterward and said, "Great job, Dexter!" "Uncanny!" And it was a powerful moment . . . *My friends, there comes a time when people get tired of being trampled over . . . and we're not wrong . . . If we're wrong, the Supreme Court of this nation is wrong . . . if we're wrong, God Almighty is wrong . . .*

It was uncanny. It was powerful. The timbre and tremor of his voice—it just came naturally. That's what I was saying about being in his spirit. That was the easiest part, giving his speech, believe it or not. The hardest parts were the dialogue scenes, when I had to try and mediate a disagreement among the members. But I got through it, with the help of Julie Dash and Tonea Stewart. Angela Bassett would come over from time to time and whisper in my ear, tell me what to focus on, how to focus, giving me tips to try this or that. It was a great experience.

I have to give credit to Yolanda. She was always obviously the actress. When we were young, she inspired us to pursue it. We used to go with her on a regular basis to an acting workshop in Atlanta run by the parents of Eric and Julia Roberts. Yolanda was part of their controversial production *The Owl and the Pussy Cat*. She played a prostitute. Very controversial, for Yolanda. Dr. King's daughter, playing a prostitute? I remember so well. There was an uproar at Ebenezer. Granddaddy was still alive then, and preaching, that's how long ago this was, and he wasn't going to the performance because the church members were ganging up on him about it. But Mother said, "You know, she really would be hurt if you don't come." He showed up at the last minute and Yoki was surprised, and pleased, and gave a good performance, and afterward he came over to her and said, "You know, it wasn't that bad. You did really good, girl!"

As for me, the experience was very pleasant. I think acting has possibilities.

There is also a CBS miniseries about my mother's life being written by Tina Andrews, and another HBO movie is being developed after the success HBO had with *Boycott*, the film starring Jeffrey Wright as Dad. I've developed a good relationship with Colin Callendar, head of HBO Films. He feels he has found a way to tell some of these stories in a manner more contemporary, so they aren't considered so much of a history lesson, and therefore boring to young folks. Julie Dash raved about *Boycott*. She loved it. So I think more and more people in the film industry are seeing the dramatic value in these stories from the era of the Civil Rights Movement. There's a lot there.

The King Center facilities, along with 234 Sunset, Mother's home, our home, are also in stasis, much like the papers. The National Park Service would at some point like to turn 234 Sunset into a National Historic Site.

I sit on the beach on the Pacific and wonder if I'll ever understand the ironies of life, or if I'm supposed to. Here comes that little boy again. He is quiet this time. "Maybe you're just supposed to live—let the chips, double standards, mistakes, and bad guys doing good things and vice versa just . . . fall where they may," I say to him.

There are still forces out there that do not want what's best for Dad's legacy, or for my family to be in any way comfortable; they want to take everything away. They believe they're entitled to their viewpoints of our father, yet we can't have a viewpoint about our own father.

What would you have done? For me it's been a burden, because . . .

I don't know what to do.

I wasn't so wedded to any one course of action. If my father's wishes were to turn his bequest over to the people and the jackals, so be it, let them fight it out, even though I have a feeling I know who would win a battle for the meat of his heritage and legacy. Jackals win scavenging contests. If I knew he wanted that—so be it. But he didn't say that, and his conduct in documenting, copyrighting, and licensing his work and litigating to protect it said the opposite. He didn't get to the Promised Land with us on a physical plane, but we can still hear him: "I'm telling you tonight that we as a people will get to the Promised Land!" I can never know for certain what he would have wished. If he'd been allowed to remain in my life longer, maybe I'd be more sure.

It has always been a difficult emotional and psychological issue, and I find that people will always bring it up for us to ponder. I talk to Yoki about this all the time. She's why I might be alone sometimes but never lonely. Sometimes I wish my parents had raised the kind of children who wouldn't care what people said. I want to do the right thing. He's not here to consult with me. But my sisters and brother are. I feel I have an obligation to uphold them, what he upheld. So I try. In the end, that's all we did, as his children. We tried.

My siblings and I are still waiting for the moving of documents, the King papers, his documentation, in his own hand, to an appropriate custodian. The Library of Congress has approached us about acquiring the papers. It was always contingent on Congress's approvals. Basically the deal got tabled. The Senate approved it, authorized the Library to enter into negotiations, but the House did not. The bill never made it to the floor. There was a lot of debate and filibuster over the papers—whether they were worth it, if the price was too high. A political football. In the end, raising of the funds was not approved, so discussions broke down. The pending legislation is really nonsubstantive. There are two parts to the bill, legislative and appropriation. Without funds, it's de facto, a nonissue. The Senate voted unanimously to support the legislation. But the House . . . it got bogged down.

This is an era of transference—transferring the legacy that should be a part of the American landscape into the American landscape. Some may see irony in this as well, that a jury in Shelby County found that a onetime café owner and "the government at several levels" conspired to assassinate Dad. Some may see it as justice.

All of this represents my father's ascension into the mainstream of American history, into the pantheon of honored American lives, and therefore into American society and life. As an African American, I am proud that my father has been receiving accolades and recognition traditionally reserved for a more "elite" class of non–African Americans.

We give Mother all the credit. She did all of the things that people acknowledge or attach to greatness: lobbying to get a King holiday, lobbying to build a nonprofit living memorial, striving to create a permanent place where people could embrace, appreciate, and learn from my father's achievements. If she had not been a goodwill ambassador, a steward, a torchbearer, my father's work might have largely died with him. Without her popularizing his legacy the whole thing would have faded into memory. No matter what J. Edgar Hoover's opinions of my father were back in the '60s, no matter whose hands were behind his assassination, my father has been recognized as a great American by the American institutions, by the federal government itself, which is, ideally, only an extension of the people. All the people. Even the flawed people. The shining eyes of Mother mean the people have some of their validation. My father will be etched in the history books and in people's minds forever.

He may not have gotten there with us physically—but he did get there with us in spirit.

Atlanta, Georgia.

"If I can have your attention. At this time I want to introduce to you my cousin; I grew up with Dexter Scott King, who is the president of the Martin Luther King Center; he has taken the time to come out to personally greet us; so let's give him a hand, Dexter King . . ."

"I want to first thank Reverend Vernon King, my first cousin, somebody I hold near and dear to my heart. We grew up together. I won't tell you about any of those stories. Because if I told you, you might ask him to step down . . . But we're all a step down from Dr. King, aren't we? And we can't help that, can we? But look at it this way. He does give us a goal, something to aspire to.

"I want to first thank you, then welcome you here to the King Center and the King Historic Preservation District on behalf of the Park Service, which operates this facility in a fine fashion; what you'll be seeing as you go through this historic site is American history; you'll see the tomb of Dr. King, my father; historic Ebenezer Baptist Church; the birth home, where my father grew up. I want to say I think it's important we as a community take the time out to really understand what the King legacy represents. Particularly for the youth, you who may not have been around, or aren't old enough to appreciate what the Civil Rights Movement was about, what evolution of history brought us to, in pointing us to where we are today, where we might be tomorrow.

"There's still a lot of work that has to be done. This memorial, this institution, is actually a living and breathing institution. You are the institution, and so am I. As long as you and I are living and breathing, then we might become better, help each other become better, help America become a better place. We might not think so now, but you, even you, as young as you are, one day you won't be so young, and you'll have children of your own. And they might not be perfect children, they might be flawed children, they may end

up being children who had to deal with tragic, flawed circumstances, but they will be your children, ours, and you and we will
want the best for them. So there's still work to do, programs to
enact to make sure that people understand and the future public is
educated about the life, work, and philosophy of Martin Luther
King, Jr.

"Now, we're not trying to give him all the credit. Many others
contributed and gave their time and talents and lives to the cause
to make sure that all people would be seen as having an equal opportunity in this society. So in many ways, my father is symbolic of
many other names and people. In honoring him, you honor them
all. So on behalf of the board of directors of the King Center, me,
and my mother, who could not be here, but who some of you have
seen or met before, I welcome you, welcome you wholeheartedly,
thank you for your interest and time; to Reverend King, thank you
for your leadership. We hope you all will enjoy your stay here.
While it may be that shortly you leave here, walk away with a sense
of purpose and fulfillment; continue to encourage others, who may
not have the time or may not have the ability to be here, to make
the trek, to make the journey to learn more about our history. Remember this great legacy that we all are a part of. I apologize for
not being able to spend more time with you, but if you can feel the
spirit of my father here, then me not being around will be no great
loss to anybody.

"My job was to see to it that you got to him. As you go through
you'll see that there are a lot of people from throughout America
and the world, and the future world, that are here with you, and
will be spending time with you, in this and the world we share, so
I again thank you and I hope you enjoy the rest of your stay. May
God continue to bless each and every one of you.

"During my tenure over the last eight years as the King Center
president, I have been fortunate to have had innumerable inspirational moments. However, I will take this opportunity only to mention a couple of them. Two of them involved former president Bill
Clinton. The first in 1994 when President Clinton asked my

brother and I, along with Ted and Ethel Kennedy, to fly aboard Air Force One to Indianapolis, Indiana, to break ground for a Peace Memorial dedicated to the memories of Robert F. Kennedy and my father. This memorial is located on the spot where Robert Kennedy spoke on the night my father was killed. He was campaigning in the African-American community and calmed the crowd with his now famous remarks. These remarks were credited with preventing rioting in Indianapolis while other cities burned.

"The second incident was accompanying my mother to the White House for a State dinner honoring former South African president Nelson Mandela. This historic event inspired me because of what it represented in terms of paying tribute to the liberation of a man and his people.

"On another occasion I had the privilege of meeting His Holiness the Dalai Lama on his visit to the King Center. I remember my sister Yolanda commenting on how his spirit reminded her of my father's.

"I also met with Israeli former prime minister and Nobel laureate Shimon Peres on his visit to our Center, where he presented me with a silver plate with the dove of peace etched upon it. We discussed the importance of using my father's principles of nonviolence to bring about peace in the Middle East. I truly hope and pray that someday there will be peace in that region, and both Jews and Palestinians can live together as sisters and brothers."

The Kings, flawed like everybody else, are good people.

I gladly face that now, in addition to the rest of what I inherited, as part of my obligation and birthright. Now I have to at least try to identify and find and attend to my own little dreams, because the legacy, obligation, birthright, inheritance, responsibility is not my only allotment, not all that I am, does not solely define who or what I can be. I finally figured out why I had always asked, "Why?" I never finished the question—why was this happening to me? I had always waited for things to happen to me, instead of doing things myself. I realize how much has to be done in terms of bringing this legacy—and myself—full circle. What is still missing today is the spiritual element that really causes his message to live, in terms of breaking down barriers in the mind, believing you can overcome obstacles, believing we can get along, not have to solve our conflicts with violence.

It's funny, every year we have our King celebration, we get letters and hear speeches from politicians; you hear speeches from senators, congressmen, talking about how great Dr. King was to this nation, how he led the nation out of racial strife, used nonviolence, how he should be applauded, but the same people will turn around and vote to start a war without diplomacy or other means first. So it's almost like people recognized it in him, in my father, but still don't want to apply it for themselves. Have I sorted out the role of spirituality—faith—in my own life?

I have decided to seek a deeper level of life. Faith has really been a key ingredient in my sustenance. I've done a lot of work. I mean internally. The process has been very therapeutic for me out here. Being on the ocean. Being alone. Being at peace with that. Recovery. Recovery is the word I'm looking for. The recovery is almost complete.

I could not have endured all of the ups and downs, the tragedies, controversies, conflicts, trials and tribulations, if it were not for my faith in God, believing in a higher power that ultimately the things we cannot see shape us; faith being defined as the evidence of things unseen, and uncontrollable even, when you truly surrender yourself to it. There's really a point of submission where you say, "I've done everything humanly possible, and it's out of my hands. It's bigger than me." That's when you submit, and know everything's going to be all right. "Let go and let God." That's what I embrace now. It's not my nature; I am controlling in terms of wanting to know reasons why. I'm skeptical, but I don't let it drive me; I'm cautious by nature, a lot has to do with the experiences that shaped me. But I've thrown caution to the winds about spirituality.

My father once said, "Unearned suffering is redemptive." If

that is true—and life has taught me it is—then he earned his historical place a thousand times over. Not only did he die a violent death diametrically opposed to his ideals, not only did he die martyred to a great cause, but also his widow suffered, his children were at times considered pariahs . . . but that's all gone now.

What I see for Atlanta, the home of my youth, is that it continues growing on a steady path. Daddy's legacy is one of the city's biggest claims to fame now, the thing that undergirds it. Andy Young says that's why the Olympics came there, the African delegates delivered it to Atlanta. We didn't win all European nations. We got a few votes, but it was that bloc of the African continent saying, "I haven't been to Atlanta, but isn't that where Dr. King is from?" Yet his surviving family continues to be attacked, for no reason except none of us, his children, turned out to be him. All of us together are him—the part that's left on this earth. The King Center's original purpose was to be a nonprofit programming organization educating the public, serving as a clearinghouse of information and training in nonviolent techniques. It was also intended as—and has become—a repository of artifacts, a learning place. It serves as a blueprint provider, a kind of resource manager, focusing more on the software, the message. It can help take you there.

After I spent a few months in California, Mother came to visit me. When she looked out over the ocean from my heightened vantage point, all she could say was a word I'd never heard her say before: "Wow!" Then she said, "It's . . . so beautiful . . . only God could create such as this."

Mother hasn't left Atlanta—not yet. I'd like to see her spend her later years in a comfortable place, giving out her yearly children's book award, being representative. At peace. She deserves it. Where Mother will go from 234 Sunset, Vine City, only time will tell. One reason L.A. appealed to me is that I know Yolanda—my not-so-terrible big sister Yoki—is very happy out here in Los Angeles, living, working. She had a guest shot on an episode of the TV series *JAG*. She played a judge, of all things. Played it well too. She always did have that knack.

My father's legacy is universal. It's not limited to Atlanta, Georgia, or the South. It tends to follow one around. He changed a social landscape in Atlanta, and places like Montgomery, Selma, Birmingham, Chicago, Cleveland, Harlem, Memphis, and L.A. His base was always Atlanta. He was a not-so-simple country preacher—not so simple at all.

For me, it all comes back to communication. We all want to find the right vehicle to communicate. I plan to try to do it by venturing out here on the West Coast, in L.A. I feel liberated by the anonymity of it, the new, open spaces, the creative environment, the feeling of a frontier, and of being more free, the fluid, constant yet eternal change of the waves coming in off the Pacific. There is power in their sound and in their eternal force, the feel of the spray, the ions in the air. A reinvention of self. I feel free to do it now. For a long time I never felt comfortable being thought of—as honorable as it is—as the son of Martin Luther King, Jr. I'll be at peace when I have something on my own. Self-expression is subjective; people don't care who you are. They care what you can produce, how you make them feel. I hope and I fear at the same time. I hope people will accept us, the children of Martin Luther King, Jr. I hope people will accept me. I know now I'll live, whether they do or not. So I start again. Fresh.

The terrorist attacks and subsequent events on and after September 11, 2001, have profoundly rocked and changed America forever. Once again, my father's message of nonviolent social change seems relevant. As one who has lost loved ones through violence and tragedy, I continue to pray for the victims and their families as they endure a long, difficult recovery. My brother and sisters are okay. Martin's heart is in the right place. Bernice—you may hear from her one day, in a spiritual way. She will always be a special messenger. Don't take my word for it. Just listen to her. You haven't heard the last from her, as a spiritual guide, as an orator.

Yoki—she's so creative, expressive, so honest and unafraid. She's like our Daddy too. Like one of my father's sermons. I love her very much. Maybe one day she can come up with another new role for me. Prince Charming always was a stretch.

As for me, I've left Atlanta, but it will never leave me. Vine City, Collier Heights, West End, Cascade, Ebenezer, Galloway, Douglass, Peachtree, Morehouse, Spelman, the AU Center, Sweet Auburn, the King Center, Midtown, Buckhead; Uncle Andy, Isaac, my cousins, aunts and uncles, my friends, even my foes, and some people who were both friend and foe—none of them will ever leave me.

I think of this and all of them while overlooking the Pacific Ocean, listening to the roar of breakers rolling in. I am reminded of my father's voice, how it comforted me, and does still.

Freedom never comes easy. Neither does life; maybe that's part of my contribution. Maybe to show how easy it isn't, is my contribution. I don't know. I've learned that not knowing is permissible—it carries no shame. Part of a journey is struggle, failure. You still must give yourself permission to live. Would he approve? Would he disapprove? I let it go. I didn't follow tradition, but it wasn't because I didn't want to be about my father's business. It was part of a greater plan. God's plan. Any scholar who wants to dispute that—feel free. No more about me now. I'm unworthy. I know it. I feel glad to have this opportunity to remember.

I sit on the beach. I feel stronger with each passing minute, each bracing inhalation of sea air. I stay near the water. I see the little boy. He looks like . . . Daddy. The boy finally asks me:

"Can you show me how to walk on water?"

". . . I don't think I can," I say.

"I know," he replies.

"But it's all right," I say.

"I know."

I hear my father's voice inside the waters. He walks with me and he talks with me and he tells me I am his own, and the joy we share as we fade into memory, none other has ever known. We plot a course in the Promised Land. It's up to Yolanda, Martin, Bernice, me, and you. I pray for health, understanding, character, progress. I hope God is not finished with us yet. So our story really ends at the beginning. This is our story, this is our song. So was it Written, in a minor key.

It's not sad. It's life.

INDEX